Military En

Tactical and Peacekeeping Operations

Intermediate | B1 | STANAG 2

Coursebook

Robert Buckmaster

The English Ideas Project

Military English:Tactical and Peacekeeping Operations: Coursebook

Copyright © Robert A. Buckmaster 2019

Cover Photograph by Sean Clee, Press Officer, Photographer, US Army; Public Domain

First published in 2019

Printed by Amazon Create Space

Published by

SIA Buckmaster Consulting: www.rbuckmaster.com

and The English Ideas Project: www.englishideas.org

Contents

Phase 2 Units 57 to 175 — 109

Welcome to the Course

This is an Intermediate/B1/STANAG 2 course in Military English for **tactical** and **peace-keeping operations** for enlisted soldiers, and officers up to the rank of Major.

The course is useful as a pre-deployment course or a pre-training course if you are being sent for training in an English speaking country, or will be trained by English-speaking instructors.

There are three components to the Course:

1. This **Coursebook**: with lesson materials.

2. The **Workbook**: with grammar and vocabulary tasks, peacekeeping reading tasks, writing tasks, consolidation tasks and reference material and more.

3. The **Downloadable Resources** to use on a computer, tablet or smartphone: these are photographs and pictures, maps, audio files, audio transcripts, and briefing slides for you to use in the lessons.

> Go to **www.englishideas.org/MilitaryEnglish** for links to the downloadable resources.

This Coursebook has three phases:

Phase 1 is a mix of general English, general military English and some specialised military English.

Phase 2 concentrates on specialised military English.

Phase 3 is mainly about practising your English while solving tactical and peacekeeping problems.

The course should take you about 200 hours to complete; more if you do all the consolidation tasks in the Workbook.

Good luck with your learning!

Robert Buckmaster

Course Aims and Outcomes

This course is designed to teach you how to **operate effectively** in multinational tactical and peacekeeping operations. By the end of the course you **should be able to do** the following in English.

Interpersonal Skills

- Talk about your family
- Talk about your career
- Talk about your home
- Talk about your leisure interests e.g. hobbies, sports, films and music
- Socialise e.g. make arrangements to meet
- Ask and answer questions
- Give personal opinions on topics like personal equipment

Professional Skills

- Understand common acronyms and abbreviations (see Workbook)
- Use the NATO/Phonetic Alphabet
- Tell the time
- Talk about the weather
- Talk about your army and unit structure and purpose
- Talk about your training
- Make radio calls including MEDEVAC/CASEVAC
- Understand Tactical Combat Casualty Care
- Understand land navigation
- Describe rural and urban terrain
- Describe people and clothing
- Give a short professional briefing supported by visuals
- Understand ROE
- Understand and describe base security
- Understand and describe convoy operations
- Understand and describe checkpoint operations
- Understand and describe the use of observation posts
- Understand and describe patrol operations
- Understand [and give] orders
- Understand the differences between tactical and peacekeeping missions, patrols, ROE, OPs, checkpoints, and convoys
- Understand common survival situations
- Understand and solve common tactical and peacekeeping problems
- Write a short report (see Workbook)

The following main military topics are covered:

- Acronyms and abbreviations (see Workbook)
- Army and Unit Structure/Organisation/Purpose
- Bases
- Checkpoints
- Convoys
- Force Structure And Formation Purpose
- Forces e.g. Paratroopers, Infantry, Armour etc.
- Land Navigation
- Military Careers
- Military Hardware e.g IFV, MBT etc.
- Military Training
- Movement
- Observation Posts
- Orders
- Overwatch
- Patrols
- Peacekeeping Missions
- Personal Equipment
- Radio Communication
- Security
- Survival Situations
- Tactical Combat Casualty Care
- Tactical and Peacekeeping Problems
- Terrain
- Time
- Training
- Using Interpreters
- Weapons
- Weather

Grammar (see Workbook): The main **functional grammar** areas covered are:

- describing scenes, terrain, people and clothing
- suggesting/explaining/justifying/reporting
- agreeing /disagreeing and giving opinions
- past narration and evaluating past events
- asking and answering questions
- making comparisons
- discussing hypotheticals
- talking about future plans

The other **main grammar** areas covered are: noun and verb phrases | word order | prepositions | collocations | and text grammar.

Briefings

You will need to make briefings during the course.

There are four kinds of briefings.

1. Group Briefings

You will work as a team and prepare a presentation using the prepared slides. One of you will present. The others will be the preparation team helping the briefer to prepare. The whole group has the responsibility for the quality of the presentation.

2. One-Slide and Two Slide Briefings

Here you will work alone and prepare a briefing using the prepared slides and speaking notes. You will have one or two slides to present on your own.

3. Simulation Briefings

You will work in a group and present on a scenario. This will include demonstrating radio calls. PowerPoint slides are not necessary for these presentations.

4. Tactical and Peacekeeping Problem Briefings

You will work as a group and solve the problems and then present your solutions to the class. PowerPoint slides are not necessary for these presentations.

Options for Briefings

What technology you have will determine how you present briefings with slides.

There are a number of options:

- Use a computer/tablet and projector and present the slides on a screen.
- Use smartphones: everyone views the briefing slides on their smartphone while the briefer talks.
- The speaker puts the information from the prepared slides onto large sheets of paper or the black/whiteboard and uses these instead of the slides.
- Use a print out the PDF of the briefing slides.

Feedback

You should get two kinds of feedback on your presentation.

1. Your colleagues will give you **public positive feedback** on the **good aspects** of your presentation, and explain what they did not understand.
2. Your teacher will give you **private feedback** based on the form on the next page and will decide if the you need to do the briefing again.

Briefing Feedback From The Teacher

Provide feedback on the following areas:

Briefer Confidence:

Was the briefer confident?

Eye-contact:

Did the briefer make eye contact with the audience?
Did the briefer scan the whole audience using the lighthouse technique?

Body Language:

What was the briefer's body language like? Confident? Defensive? Aggressive?

Audience engagement/focus:

Was the audience engaged/paying attention/interested/bored?

Briefing Structure:

Was the briefing well-structured?
Was the information well-sequenced?
Were transitions signalled?
Were the key points emphasised?

Use of Briefing Visuals:

Did the briefer make effective use of the visuals?

Voice:

Was the briefer's voice loud and clear enough to be heard and understood throughout the room?
Or was the briefer's voice too quiet/loud?

Pronunciation:

Think about: word individual sounds | word stress | chunking | pausing | intonation

Language used:

Think about range and accuracy in:
verb forms | noun phrases | word order | appropriate terminology

Errors made:

What language errors were made?
Which of these errors impeded communication?
Which were just slips?

Improvements to be made:

What are the main areas to focus on?

Decide on the key improvements to be made and tell the student.

Mix good feedback with constructive feedback: good point / weak point / good point

Phase 1

Units 1 to 56	General English
	General Military English
Workbook	Grammar
	Consolidation Tasks
	Military Abbreviations
	Report Writing
	Peacekeeping Missions

Unit 1 Introductions and Questions

Question Forms | Tenses | Word Order

T1 | Speaking: Briefly introduce yourself to the class

My name is _____

I'm a _____

I work in/for/at _____

T2 | Grammar: Questions

What questions would you need to ask to get the information in T1?

Language Reminder: Questions

Question word order is very important. The first word(s) in a question tell you what kind of question it is and if it is a present, past, future or hypothetical question. See page 252 in your Workbook

What	*do*	*you*	*want?*
question word	question verb: present fact	person	verb: information needed

Do	*you*	*like*	*ice-cream?*
question verb: present fact	person	information verb	noun: information needed

---

T3 | Grammar: Question Time

Study the examples.

Which questions are about facts now? Which are about facts in the past?

1. Are you happy?
2. Were you at the party?
3. Where did you go to school?
4. What do you do?
5. When did you join the army?
6. Do you have any children?
7. Do you like ice-cream?
8. Where were you born?
9. Where do you live?
10. How old are you?

T4 | Listening: Listen to check

Which words are stressed most? Does the intonation rise ↗ or fall ↘ at the end of the questions? Practise the questions.

T5 | Grammar: State or Activity?

Study the examples.

Which questions are about a state? Which about an activity in progress?

1. Where do you live?

2. What are you doing?

3. What's your job?

4. Where are you going?

5. What were you doing last night at 8 pm?

Which verb forms do we use to talk about states?

Which verb forms do we use to talk about activities and on-going processes?

T6 | Grammar: Reorder the words to make questions

1. or married you single are?

2. any you sports do do?

3. do what you hope to do in the future?

4. in doing what time you like do free your?

5. did army you why the join?

6. you children do have any?

7. birthday did do on you your what last?

Practise asking the questions with your partner.

Make sure you stress the right words and use a rising intonation.

Listen to your partner – is the question pronounced correctly?

T7 | Speaking: Ask and Answer

Everyone stand up and mingle and ask questions from T3, T5 and T6.

Write down the answers.

Tell the class about the most interesting thing you found out.

Language Reminder: I play | he/she/it plays etc.

Your partner says: "I play football."

You tell the class: "He/John plays football."

Remember:

  I **do** | he/she/it **does**   I **have** | he/she/it **has**

Unit 2 The NATO Phonetic Alphabet

Learn the NATO Alphabet

A	ALFA	AL FA
B	BRAVO	BRA VO
C	CHARLIE	CHAR LEE
D	DELTA	DELL TAH
E	ECHO	EK OH
F	FOXTROT	FOKS TROT
G	GOLF	GOLF
H	HOTEL	HOH TELL
I	INDIA	IN DEE AH
J	JULIET	JEW LEE ETT
K	KILO	KEY LO
L	LIMA	LEE MA
M	MIKE	MIKE
N	NOVEMBER	NO VEM BER
O	OSCAR	OSS KA
P	PAPA	PAH PAH
Q	QUEBEC	KWA BECK
R	ROMEO	ROW ME OH
S	SIERRA	SEE AIR RAH
T	TANGO	TANG GO
U	UNIFORM	YOU NEE FORM
V	VICTOR	VIK TAH
W	WHISKEY	WISS KEY
X	X-RAY	EKS RAY
Y	YANKEE	YAN KEY
Z	ZULU	ZOO LOO

T1 | Say the alphabet after your teacher

T2 | Say the alphabet very quickly

T3 | Say the alphabet alternating with another student

> A: Alfa
>
> B: Bravo
>
> A: Charlie
>
> B: Delta

T4 | Say it backwards quickly

T5 | Dictate your full name

T6 | Dictate your address

T7 | Dictate your car number plate

T8 | Write down five capital cities

> e.g. Washington
>
> Dictate these to your partner.

T9 | Dictation

> Dictate five pieces of equipment for your favourite sport to your partner. They should guess the sport.

T10 | Write out a sentence

> Choose one word from the sentence to spell. Dictate the sentence to a person across the room: *The moon rises in the east I spell East Echo-Al-fa-Sierra-Tango.* Everyone talks at once.

Unit 3 Describing Photographs 1

T1 | Vocabulary: Study the diagrams below

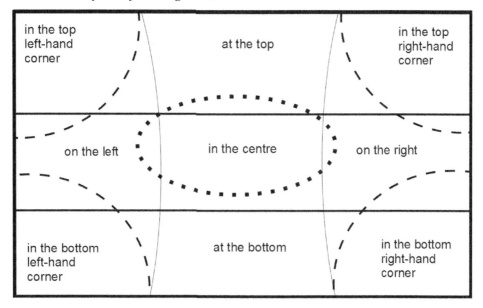

This diagram shows the position of things in a photograph.

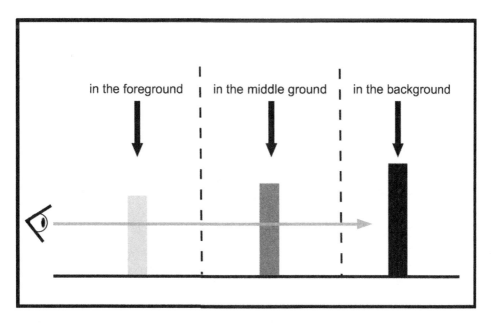

This diagram shows the idea of foreground, middle ground and background.

Look at P3.1

T2 | Vocabulary: Read to Check

Look at P3.2 and read this description. Is it correct?

> The picture shows a river running through a town. In the foreground there is a grey surface of some kind. On the left there is a blue sculpture – of a map, two buildings and a cyclist. In the centre there is a grassy embankment and a single tree. In the background there are some buildings, a bridge over the river and a tower. On the right you can see cars parked in front of a three-storey building.

T3 | Vocabulary: Complete this description of P3.3

> The picture shows houses in the mountains. [1] _____ of the picture there is a garden with washing hanging on the line. [2] _____ there is a white two-storey house with a balcony and a red roof. [3] _____ is a wooded hill. [4] _____ of the picture there are some trees and another white house with a grey roof; and some more house roofs. [5] _____ there are tree covered mountains. [6] _____ there is a grassy slope and some trees. [7] _____ there is a ditch, an earth embankment and a wire fence. The sky is blue with some white clouds.

T4 | Writing: Write about P3.4 and P3.5. Check your partner's descriptions

T5 | Speaking: Describing Pictures

Look at P3.6 and P3.7. Describe them to your partner but make mistakes.

Listen to your partner's description. Correct their mistakes.

Language Reminder

There is _____.

There are _____.

Questioning: Are you sure that's right?

Correcting: It isn't on the left. It's on the right.

Unit 4 Describing Photographs 2

This unit practises the internal relationship view of descriptions of photographs (and scenes). You should be able to accurately describe where things are in relationship to other things which you can see.

T1 | Vocabulary: Study the two diagrams below

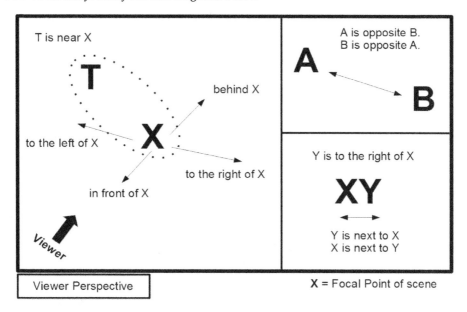

T2 | Vocabulary: Read to Check

Look at P4.1 and read this description. Is it correct?

> The photo shows a scene in a Serbian café. In the foreground, there is a table with a beige and a red tablecloth. On the table, there is a tea glass, and an ashtray. On the left, there are two men sitting at a table in front of the counter. The man on the left is dressed in a black top, and blue jeans, and is wearing sports shoes. The man sitting opposite him is wearing a striped top, and is sitting with his chin on his hand. There are two glasses on the table. Behind the striped-top man, there are two men in orange jackets standing at the counter. The man on the right has a beard, and the man next to him is clean-shaven. There is one more person in the photo. He is on the right, sitting by the wall, at a table by the window, under the TV, smoking, and looking out of the window. He is wearing a blue and grey jacket, a red t-shirt, and a grey baseball cap.

T3 | Vocabulary: Complete this description of P4.2

behind	behind	behind	centre	front
front	left	left	left	right

> The photo shows a winter scene in a forest. There is a group of people gathered around an open fire in front of some trees. The ground is covered in snow. In the [1] _____ of the group there is a blonde woman in a black jacket, blue jeans and a multi-coloured hat. To her [2] _____ there is a tall girl in a black coat and blue hat with a fur pompom. To her [3] _____ there is a group of three people. There is a woman in [4] _____ in a red jacket and black hat holding a sausage in the fire. [5] _____ her is a woman in a grey coat and grey hat. [6] _____ her is a woman with long brown hair, in a beige coat, hat and scarf. [7] _____ them you can see a grey car parked on the road. To the [8] _____ of the fire are two more people. In the [9] _____, a man in a black coat and orange hat is squatting down by the fire. To his [10] _____ is a girl in a purple coat and multi-coloured trousers, with a red scarf and grey hat.

T4 | Writing: Write about P4.3 and P4.4

Check your partner's descriptions.

T5 | Speaking: Describing Pictures

Look at P4.5 and P4.6. Describe them to your partner but make mistakes.

Listen to your partner's description. Correct their mistakes.

Unit 5 Training

Present Simple | Active | Passive | First Conditional

T1 | Speaking: Talk and Report 1

Look at P5.1 - 3. What can you see?

T2 | Speaking: Talk and Report 2

1. How long is basic training in your army?
2. Where does it take place?
3. What do soldiers have to do in basic training?

T3 | Reading: Read and Answer 1

Answer these questions about the US Army's **Basic Combat Training** (next page).

1. How long is the training?
2. What do the recruits do in each phase?
3. How is it different from your army's basic training?
   Agree on the differences with your colleagues.

T4 | Reading: Read and Answer 2

Answer these questions about the US Army's **Advanced Individual Training.**

1. What further training does an infantry soldier do?
2. How is it different from your army's specialised training?
   Agree on the differences with your colleagues.

T5 | Reading: Read and Answer 3

Answer these questions about US Army **Special Forces Training** on the next page.

1. How long does it take to become a SF soldier?
2. How is it different from your army's special forces training?
   Agree on the differences with your colleagues.

T6 | Language Analysis: Analyse the Text

T7 | Listen and Read: Listen to a reading of the texts

Which words do you need to practice saying? Which words do you need to learn?

T8 | Writing: Write texts about three types of training in your army

T9 | Speaking: Briefing

Prepare a briefing for your teacher about the training which you have received.
Practice, then deliver your briefing. Be ready to answer questions.

T10 | Consolidation Tasks

Basic Combat Training (BCT) in the US Army lasts for ten weeks. The first three weeks [Phase I (Red)] concentrate on developing physical fitness, team thinking and behaving and thinking like a soldier. Drill & Ceremony training begins in Week 1 and classroom instruction focuses on the seven "Army Core Values". During Week 2, recruits start learning unarmed combat, map reading and land navigation in two-man groups, Tactical Combat Casualty Care, and do training on obstacle courses, both individually and as part of a team. In Week 3, trainees learn about Nuclear Biological and Chemical Defense, Landmines, and their standard-issue weapons, and do a one night Field Training Exercise (FTX) called Hammer. In each Phase, the recruits have to do the Army Physical Fitness Test (APFT) to higher standards, and at the end of each Phase pass tests on what they have learned. In the four weeks of Phase II (White) recruits go through Basic Rifle Marksmanship and combat training. They do obstacle course tasks, Tactical Foot Marches, and more PT and drilling. The trainees must pass marksmanship tests with their weapons and optical sights in full kit. The Anvil FTX in Week 6 tests them on squad tactics , TC3 and NBC attacks. In the last part of training [Phase III (Blue)], recruits do more training on weapons, and learn about subjects like convoy operations. They have to complete the 10 km and 15 km Tactical Foot Marches, and a Final APFT test, which they must pass before moving on to FTXs and Military Operations in Urban Terrain (MOUT) training. Week 2 of Phase III finishes with a special 96 hour FTX: the Forge, which tests everything done on the course, and which recruits must pass. In the final week of training they practice for graduation which takes place at the end of the week.

Advanced Individual Training: Advanced individual training (AIT) depends on the soldier's Military Occupational Speciality (MOS). Infantry soldiers have a combined BCT and AIT at one school called One Station Unit Training (OSUT), generally held at Fort Benning, Georgia. At Infantry School AIT a soldier learns how to maintain and use small arms, anti-armour and indirect fire weapons systems; learns to operate and maintain vehicles; conduct land reconnaissance; learns about minefield safety; learns how to operate communications equipment; and how to prepare fighting positions and construct barriers.

Special Forces Training: Army Special Forces 'Green Beret' candidates complete BCT, and AIT for Infantry. Then they train for three weeks at the Army Airborne School. After this school there is a special four week preparation course at Ft Bragg, North Carolina. This concentrates on physical fitness and land navigation to prepare the soldier for the Special Forces selection course, the first real phase of SF training. If you pass the selection process you can join the Special Forces Qualification Course (SFQC), which has five phases and can last up to 62 weeks. If you complete this course you qualify as a Special Forces soldier. Then you will have Live Environment Training (LET), which is Immersion Training in foreign countries, and this varies in length.

Unit 6 Questions 2

T1 | Grammar: What do you remember?

What questions do you remember from **Unit 1**?

Write five questions down. Check them with your partner. Is the word order correct?

Ask and answer the questions with your partner.

T2 | Grammar: Past, Present or Future?

Study the example questions below. Which questions are about the past?

Which are about now? Which are about the future?

1. Will you be at the party on Friday?
2. Where do you live?
3. What did you do last night?
4. Do you have any plans for the weekend?
5. Are you happy?
6. What are you doing?
7. Where were you born?
8. Are you going anywhere in the summer?

Ask and answer the questions. Report what you find out.

T3 | Grammar: Specific Past or Before Now?

Study the example questions below. Which questions are about a specific past time?

Which is about sometime before now? Which is about before now/up to now?

1. Have you been to Paris?
2. What did you do last weekend?
3. How long have you lived here?
4. Did you see the CO yesterday?

Ask and answer the questions. Report what you find out.

T4 | Grammar: Reorder the words in 1 – 8 to make questions

1. long how you lived have here?
2. you been a lot have abroad?
3. hobby you a do have?
4. in long how army you been have the?
5. John later you be will seeing?
6. birthday your you having a party for are?
7. going are next you shopping when?
8. you to meeting be go to will the able?

T5 | Listening: Listen to Check

Which words are stressed most?

Does the intonation rise ↑ or fall ↓ at the end of the questions?

T6 | Speaking: Ask and Answer

Everyone stand up and mingle and ask questions from T4.

Write down the answers.

Tell the class about the most interesting thing you found out.

Language Reminder: I play | he/she/it plays etc.

Your partner says: "I play football."

You tell the class: "He/John plays football."

Remember:

| I **do** | he/she/it **does** | I **have** | he/she/it **has** |

Language Revision Tasks

Reorder the words in the sentences.

1. doing 8 pm you last What night were at?
2. birthday did do on you your what last?
3. in doing what time you like do free your?
4. through picture The a town river running shows a
5. and grassy the single centre there is a embankment In a tree
6. left the counter front table there On are men at a in of sitting two the.
7. the US Basic in weeks Combat for Army lasts (BCT) ten Training.
8. need progress Soldiers with to allowed demonstrate two their final weapons before being proficiency to to the weeks.
9. Infantry a maintain arms use soldier learns how At to School and small
10. Qualification Course pass join Forces Selection you you can the Special If

Check in Units 1- 5.

Unit 7 Ranks

T1 | Speaking: Find out what rank your fellow students are

Who has the highest/lowest rank in the class?

If you have the same rank, who is senior?

T2 | Grammar: Passive Forms

Study these examples. Underline the verb forms. #1 has been done for you.

1. He <u>was accepted</u> into the army in 2005.
2. He was shipped out (sent) to Iraq with his unit in 2007.
3. He was promoted to corporal in 2008.
4. He was made a platoon sergeant in 2009.
5. He was awarded a battlefield commission to second lieutenant in 2010.

Language Reminder: Passive Verb Forms

Passive verb forms tell us something about the **subject** of the sentence.

Example: George was accepted into the army.

George [subject] *was accepted* [passive form] into the army.

This means: George applied to join the army and the army accepted him.

Agree on a translation of sentences 1 – 5 with your class and teacher.

T3 | Reading 1

Read through **Text 1** on the next page and add ranks to the table of ranks.

T4 | Reading 2

Read through **Text 2** on the next page and add more ranks to the table of ranks.

T5 | Language Analysis: Analyse the Text

T6 | Listen and Read: Listen to a reading of the texts

Which words do you need to practice saying? Which words do you need to learn?

T7 | Speaking: Talk and Report 1

Are the ranks in your army the same or different?
What are the differences?

Complete the comparison table of the equivalent ranks in your army in your Workbook.

Text 1

Audie Murphy was accepted by the U.S. Army on the 30th June 1942. After basic and advanced infantry training he was shipped out as a private to Casablanca in French Morocco on the 20th February 1943. He was promoted to private first class on the 7th May, and, after the Sicily landings, to corporal on the 15th July. Murphy was then promoted to sergeant in Italy on the 13th December 1943. In January 1944, Murphy was promoted to staff sergeant and he was made a platoon sergeant in B Company following the battle of Cisterna in February 1944. He was awarded a battlefield commission to second lieutenant on the 14th October 1944 and made platoon leader. In Germany, on the 16th February 1945, Murphy was promoted to first lieutenant and he was made a liaison officer at Regimental Headquarters.

Text 2

Jack Spivey joined the U.S. Army in 1974 as a second lieutenant. He was promoted to first lieutenant while serving at Fort Hood with the First Cavalry Division. In 1979 he made captain and took over C Company of the 2nd Battalion. Spivey was promoted to Major in 1987 and served at West Point. On his promotion to Lieutenant Colonel in 1989 he commanded the 2nd Battalion of the First Cavalry Division back at Fort Hood and in the first Gulf War. He retired in 1994 after 30 years service.

Table of Ranks	
9.	18. General
8. Sergeant Major	17. Lieutenant General
7. First Sergeant	16. Major General
6. Master Sergeant	15. Brigadier General
5.	14. Colonel
4.	13.
3.	12.
2.	11.
1. Private	10.

T8 | Writing: Write out ten sentences like the examples below

A 4 star general **outranks** a 3 star general.

A colonel is **a higher rank** than a major.

A 3 star general is **subordinate to** a 4 star general.

> You can also use:
> *'is outranked by'*
> and *'a lower rank than'*.

T9 | Speaking: Talk and Report 2

Talk with a partner.

Agree on the roles and responsibility for some ranks in your army.

Use the language below.

...is responsible for...	...commands....	...leads....	....runs.....
...is in charge of.....	...makes sure that...	..helps X to do..	...has to..

'A platoon sergeant is responsible for......'

T10 | Writing

Choose two ranks and write a paragraph about their roles and responsibilities in **your** army. Use this frame to help you.

Title

A _____ is responsible for _____.

He (or she) has to _____.

He (or she) should _____.

A _____ needs to _____.

The most important thing a _____ must remember is to _____.

A _____ must never _____.

T11 | Consolidation Tasks

Unit 8 Family

Present and Past Verbs | Active and Passive Forms

T1 | Vocabulary: Check you know the words

mother	father	son	daughter	sister-in-law
husband	wife	uncle	grandson/daughter	mother-in-law
brother	sister	cousin	godfather	father-in-law
niece	nephew	aunt	godmother	brother-in-law

T2 | Reading: Read the text about this soldier's family. What do you learn?

I don't have a large family. There's just me and my wife and my wife's parents. My parents are both dead. I was orphaned when I was quite young. I get on with my mother and father-in-law though. I was brought up by my uncle and aunt. My uncle, my father's brother, took me in when my parents died. Their son, my cousin, is like a brother to me. As I was an only child I don't have any real brothers or sisters. My wife has a sister and she's married with two kids – a boy and a girl, so I'm an uncle. My nephew and niece are still at school but the boy wants to join the army like me. I got married two years ago and my wife is pregnant and we're expecting the baby in June. I hope its a boy.

Draw a family tree for this soldier. (Check with P8.1)

T3 | Language Analysis: Analyse the Text

T4 | Listening: Listen to this soldier talking about his family

What do you learn about the soldier's family?
Work together to draw a family tree for his family.
Then listen again to check. (Check with P8.2)

T5 | Speaking: Prepare a talk about your family

Tell your partner about your family. Listen to your partner talking about their family and then tell the class what you found out. Draw a family tree to help you.

T6 | Speaking: Summarising

Work together as a class and decide:

1. Who has the largest immediate family [spouse and children]?
2. Who has the smallest immediate family?
3. Who has the largest extended family?

Unit 9 My Role and Responsibilities

Present Simple | Modal Verbs

T1 | Speaking: Talk and Report

Write down 5 things you are responsible for.

Tell your partner. Tell the class what your partner is responsible for.

T2 | Listening 1: Listen and Make Notes

Listen to these five soldiers talking about their responsibilities.

Write down each soldier's rank, and what he is responsible for.

T3 | Listening 2: Choose one speaker. Listen again

Write down exactly what he says in the first two sentences.

[Check T9.1 – T9.5]

T4 | Listening 3: Listen again

Use your transcript from T3: underline the words he says with most <u>stress</u>.

Why are these words stressed? Mark where he /pauses/. Why does he pause where he pauses? Check with your partner.

T5 | Speaking: Prepare a talk about your role and responsibilities

Use this frame to help you.

Language Reminder
I am a/an X.
I am responsible for Y.
My main duty is to make sure that _____.
I manage the _____.
I have to _____.
I help the A to do B.
I also should _____.
Every day I have to _____.
During operations I am in charge of _ [making sure that] __.
The best/worst thing about my job is _____.
If I could change one thing in my job, I would change _____.

Mark which words to **stress** and where you will pause /.

Tell your partner about your role and responsibilities. Listen to them. Give them feedback on their speech. Do they stress the right words and pause in the right places? Then tell the class about your role and responsibilities. Be ready to answer questions. Listen to your colleagues talking about their roles and responsibilities. Give them feedback. Did you understand everything? Did they stress the right words and pause in the right places?

Unit 10 My Home

T1 | Speaking: Talk and Report

Look at P10.1 with a partner. What can you see?

Check with P10.2.

T2 | Vocabulary: Check you know the meaning of these words 1

flat/apartment	semi-detached house	detached house	terraced house

T3 | Vocabulary: Check you know the meaning of these words and phrases 2

chair	kitchen	bathroom	drawers	coffee-maker
garage	balcony	terrace	garden	washing machine
hall	cupboard	bookcase	shelves	en-suite bathroom
rug	wardrobe	coat rack	carpet	pre-fabricated
roof	faces south	radiator	ceiling	music centre/hi-fi
table	window	sofa/settee	armchair	timber-framed
shed	bedroom	spacious	storage space	basement/cellar
study	computer	light and airy	utility room	microwave oven
stairs	cramped	pots and pans	roomy	greenhouse
TV	floor	dining room	sofa bed	guest bedroom
brick	shower	wooden	open plan	running water
bath	living room	attic	dishwasher	central heating
tiles	asbestos	metal	thatch	swimming pool
mirror	bed	stool	toilet/WC/lavatory	

T4 | Vocabulary: Sort the words

Rooms	Furniture and fittings	Building material	Household goods and equipment	Description	Amenities	Parts of building
					Running water	

T5 | Vocabulary: Complete this description if you live in a house

Delete the unnecessary words and add words in the gaps.

> I live in a **terraced/semi-detached/detached** house. The house is made of **bricks/wood/metal/pre-fabricated concrete**. It **has/doesn't have** a big/ small garden. The house is **one-storey/two-storeys/three-storeys** high. The roof is made of **tiles/metal/thatch/asbestos**. In the garden there **is/isn't** a greenhouse **and/or** a shed. There **is/isn't** a garage for our **car/cars**. In the house there are a **kitchen, living room, bathroom, dining room, study, utility room, toilet, basement, cellar, attic** and **one/two/three** bedrooms. The **kitchen/ living room/main bedroom** is the biggest room in the house. **As it is a bungalow all the rooms are on the ground floor. On the first floor there is a kitchen, living room, bathroom, dining room, study, utility room and toilet. On the second floor there is a kitchen, living room, bathroom, dining room, study, utility room and toilet.** In the kitchen there is _____. In the living room there is _____. My favourite room is _____ because _____ .

Tell the class about your home. Who lives in similar homes?

T6 | Vocabulary: Complete this description if you live in a flat/apartment/barracks

Delete the unnecessary words and add words in the gaps.

> I live in a **flat/apartment/barracks**. The building is made of **bricks/wood/metal/pre-fabricated concrete**. It is a _____ **storey** building. The roof is made of **tiles/metal/thatch/asbestos**. There **is/isn't** a garage for our **car/cars**. There **are some/aren't any** parking spaces for cars outside the building. In the **flat/apartment/barracks** there is a **kitchen, living room, bathroom, dining room, study, utility room, toilet** and **one/two/three** bedrooms. The **kitchen/ living room/main bedroom** is the biggest room in the **flat/apartment/barracks**. In the kitchen there is _____. In the living room there is _____. My favourite room is _____ because _____ .

Tell the class about your home. Who lives in similar homes?

T7 | Speaking: Briefing

Prepare and give an oral briefing to the class about your **dream home**. Be ready to given reasons for your dream home's requirements. Remember this is your **dream** home – it does not exist. Use '*would*'. Like this:

I would have a big swimming pool in my house because....It would have three bedrooms.....

Unit 11 Promotion

T1 | Vocabulary: Study The Examples

Are the words in **bold** verbs, nouns, or preposition + (adjective) + noun?

Underline the verb phrases.

Are the verb forms active or passive?

Which sentences are about the past?

Agree on a translation of the sentences with your class.

1. He was **promoted** to the rank of sergeant.

2. He was **demoted** from sergeant to corporal.

3. He was **reduced** in rank to lieutenant.

4. The court martial **demoted** him to private.

5. He was **busted down** to private.

6. He **reverted** to being a two star general after commanding CENTCOM as a four star general.

7. He applied for a **transfer** to the artillery.

8. He was **transferred** to Minden army base in Germany to serve with the British Army of the Rhine.

9. I was **posted** to Aden in 1978.

10. I have been **posted** to Gibraltar – I leave next month.

11. My **posting** lasted 3 years.

12. It's a hardship **posting** – you get extra pay.

13. He spent six months **on secondment** with another regiment before returning to his regular unit.

14. He was **seconded** to the infantry to serve as FAC.

15. He was sent to the Embassy in Amman for six months **on detached duty** from the Task Force.

16. He has been **assigned** to teach a course at the Military Academy.

17. My best **assignment** was leading jungle warfare training in Borneo.

18. He is **on assignment** in Sri Lanka.

T2 | Reading: A Soldier's Career

Read about a soldier's career on the next page.

1. How many times was he promoted?

2. Was he ever demoted?

3. Was there anything unusual about his career?

A Soldier's Career

Joe Ronnie Hooper served in the United States Navy from December 1956 to 1959, reaching the rank of Petty Officer 3rd Class. He then enlisted in the United States Army as a Private First Class in May 1960. He volunteered for Airborne School at Fort Benning, Georgia and was then assigned to the 82nd Airborne Division at Fort Bragg, North Carolina. He was promoted to corporal during this assignment. He served in Korea with the 20th Infantry in October 1961 and he was promoted to sergeant there. He was assigned to the 2nd Armored Division at Fort Hood, Texas for a year as a Squad Leader and then as a Squad Leader with 101st Airborne Division at Fort Campbell, Kentucky. He was promoted to staff sergeant in September 1966 and assigned as Platoon Sergeant to the 508th Infantry in Panama. He was reduced in rank to Corporal in July 1967 as an Article 15 non-judicial punishment. He was promoted to Sergeant in October 1967 and assigned to 101st Airborne Division and deployed to Vietnam in December as a Squad Leader. He was discharged in June 1968 but he re-enlisted in the Army in September 1968. He served as a Platoon Sergeant with the 5th Infantry in Panama until August 1970. From April to December 1970 he served as a Pathfinder and as a Platoon Sergeant with 101st Airborne Division (Airmobile) in Vietnam. In December 1970 he was commissioned as a Second Lieutenant and served as a Platoon Leader until April 1971. He retired in February 1974 as a First Lieutenant.

T3 | Language Analysis: Analyse the Text

T4 | Listening: A Soldier's Career

Listen to a soldier talking about his career.

Write down his ranks and where he served and his duties.

Rank	Where based	Duties

T5 | Transcript: Review Transcript T11.1

Which words/phrases can you use to describe your career?

T6 | Speaking: Talk and Report

Talk to your partner about your career.

Report to the class about your partner's career.

T7 | Consolidation Tasks

Unit 12 Describing People

T1 | Speaking: Talk and Report

Look at P12.1 with a partner. What can you see?

T2 | Vocabulary: Check you know the meaning of these words and phrases

tall	dark brown	slim	well-built	average weight
adult	handsome	thin	old	good-looking
fat	thickset	green	short	20-something
brown	late fifties	child	blonde	strong-looking
blue	twenty-ish	skinny	attractive	overweight
curly	middle-aged	wavy	ugly	mid-thirties
beautiful	teenager	long	sexy	early-twenties
pre-teen	light brown	pretty	straight	average height

T3 | Vocabulary: Sort the words from T2

Age	Height	Hair	Body build	Attractiveness	Eyes

T4 | Vocabulary: Answer the questions about the words in T2

1. Which words are negative?
2. Which words are synonyms? What is the difference between them?
3. Which words would you **not** use on an official form?

T5 | Vocabulary: Check you know the meaning of these words and phrases

beard	scarred	bald	receding hairline	tattooed	stubble	moustache

Which words are (generally) only used for men?

T6 | Grammar: is or has?

Choose the correct verb form.

1. He is/has very handsome.
2. She is/has very beautiful.
3. He is/has bald
4. He is/has a moustache.
5. He is/has a beard.
6. She is/has slim.

7.   He is/has a receding hairline.

8.   He is/has a tattoo on his arm.

9.   He is/has tattooed.

10.   He is/has scarred.

11.   He is/has a scar on his face.

12.   She is/has overweight.

13.   She is/has blonde.

14.   She is/has blonde hair.

15.   He is/has middle-aged.

16.   He is/has in his mid-thirties.

17.   She is/has twenty-something.

18.   He is /has twenty-ish.

19.   He is/has well built.

20.   He is/has strong-looking

Now translate the sentences into your language

T7 | Grammar: Questions

Write questions based on the words in **T2** and **T5**.

e.g. Is he very handsome?   Does he/she have a moustache?

Then work with a partner.

Take it in turns to ask and answer the questions about students in the class.

e.g. Is Stephen very handsome? Yes, he is. / No, he isn't.

T8 | Speaking: Prepare a description of someone in class or a famous person

Notes here

Tell your class your description.

The other students have to guess who it is you are describing. They should write the person's identity on a piece of paper as they listen to your description.

At the end of the description collect the papers and see how many guessed correctly.

Unit 13 Force Structure

Present Tenses | Active And Passive Verb Forms

T1 | Speaking: Talk and Report

How many soldiers are there in your army?

How many brigades/divisions are there?

How many men are in a brigade/division?

T2 | Reading: Read and Answer

Read the text on the next page and find out how many men are in a US Army platoon, company etc.

T3 | Language Analysis: Analyse the Text

T4 | Listening: Listen and Make Notes

Listen to part of a talk about US army force structure. What new information that was not in the text is there? (See T13.1)

T5 | Speaking: Talk and Report

What are the differences between the US army and your army?

Language Reminder: Contrasts

In the US army a platoon consists of 16 to 44 men **whereas** in our army a platoon has 50 men.

Our army has three platoons in a company **but** the US army has three to five.

T6 | Grammar: Notice: Find these patterns in the text

(a) X consists of Y

(b) X is made up of Y

(c) X makes up Y

(d) X is composed of Y

(e) X is comprised of Y

T7 | Reading: Read and Think

Read Fact File FF13.1 in your Workbook. What are the differences between the British Army and your army?

T8 | Listen and Read: Listen to a reading of the texts in T2 and T7

Which words do you need to practice saying? Which words do you need to learn?

T9 | Writing: Write a text about the force structure in your army

T10 | Consolidation Tasks

US Army Force Structure

In the US Army there are a number of different formations. The smallest is the squad, which consists of 8 to 12 soldiers. A squad is typically commanded by a corporal, sergeant or staff sergeant. It's exact size will depend on operational requirements.

A platoon consists of two to four squads and has 16 to 55 soldiers. A platoon is led by a lieutenant with an NCO as second in command.

A company is made up of three to five platoons (60 to 250 soldiers). A company is commanded by a captain, or major with a first sergeant as the commander's principle NCO. In the artillery the unit of equivalent size is called a battery. Two to six companies make up a battalion, with 300 to 1,000 soldiers. A battalion is commanded by a lieutenant colonel with a command sergeant major as principle NCO.

A brigade combat team is comprised of two to seven combat battalions, that is 3,000 to 5,000 soldiers. A brigade is usually commanded by a colonel with a command sergeant major as senior NCO. An infantry brigade combat team consists of seven battalions: one cavalry (Reconnaissance, Surveillance, And Target Acquisition: RSTA) battalion, one brigade support battalion, one engineer battalion, three infantry battalions and one field artillery battalion. Three brigades normally make up a division with 10,000 to 15,000 soldiers. Commanded by a major general, divisions conduct major tactical operations.

An army corps is composed of two to five divisions and is typically commanded by a lieutenant general. There are 20,000 to 50,000 soldiers in an army corps. Two or more corps (40,000 + soldiers) combine to make an army. A field army is typically commanded by a lieutenant general or higher.

[From FM 7-20; FM 7-8; FM 3-96; FM 3-94]

Unit 14 Forces: Belligerents and Others

Present Tenses | Active And Passive Verb Forms | Modals | Conditionals

T1 | Speaking: Talk and Report

Look at P14.1. What can you see?

T2 | Vocabulary: Opposing Forces

Which of these words describe **opposing forces** to you in a conflict?

enemy	insurgents	blue	the opposition	warring parties/factions
military	terrorists	NGOs	partisans	non-combatants
civilians	government	allies	aid agencies	(freedom) fighters
militia	diplomats	police	belligerents	security forces
guerrillas	combatants	red	para-military	illegal combatants
observers	friendlies	rebels	peacekeepers	international organisations

T3 | Reading: Check the meaning of the words in T1 and answer the questions

In any conflict there are a number of participants. The forces opposing you are always the **enemy**, and you are their **enemy**. If you are a neutral observer though the forces fighting each other are **belligerents**. The **government** and **rebels** are both **belligerents**, for example, as they are both fighting. Two countries fighting each other are also **belligerents**. In a multi-sided civil war where the government has collapsed, the belligerents might be called **warring factions** or **warring parties**. There might be a number of different **warring factions** fighting the **government** and/or each other. Groups opposed to the government are called the **opposition**. **Civilians** are people who are not fighting and are not in any **military** or **para-military** or **civilian police force**. They are **non-combatants**. Anyone fighting is a **combatant**. **Para-militaries** can be organised by a government to support the **security forces** or they might be organised by the **opposition** to fight against the **government**. Security forces include all those forces supporting the government – the army, navy, air force, police, para-militaries and militia. The forces opposing a government might be considered **freedom fighters, fighters, insurgents, guerrillas, partisans, terrorists** or **rebels** depending on your viewpoint. If you support the government they will be **insurgents, fighters, terrorists, guerrillas, partisans** or **rebels**. If you do not support the government they will be **freedom fighters**, who you might also call **rebels, guerrillas, partisans** or **insurgents** but <u>not</u> **terrorists**. **Rebels** are rebelling against the government. **Guerrillas** or **partisans** are irregular soldiers who use guerrilla warfare, harassing the enemy by surprise raids and sabotage. **Insurgents** are people who rise up in forcible opposition to the government. **Insurgents** might also be **terrorists** if they use terror attacks against **civilian** targets. **Illegal combatants** are people who should not be fighting. The **government** will consider **insurgents** and **terrorists** as **illegal combatants**. One side in a conflict might have **allies** helping it against its **enemy**. Forces on your side, or at least not against you, might be considered **friendlies**. The **government** might form a **militia** - a body of citizens enrolled for military service but only used in emergencies. Some citizens might organise a local **militia** to defend themselves against the **government** or other **factions**. Other parties involved in a conflict might be trying to help: **aid agencies** and other **NGOs**, like the Red Cross. Other outsiders to the conflict might be representatives of **international organisations** like the EU, UNO and African Union. There might be **diplomats** trying to resolve the conflict or **observers** monitoring ceasefires and elections. Or **peacekeepers** keeping **warring factions** apart and patrolling war-torn regions and helping with aid distribution. **Former warring parties** are belligerents who have stopped fighting. Finally, in a war game **blue** forces are the 'good guys' and **red** the 'bad guys'. Non-combatants might be labelled 'greens'. Unknowns are 'yellow'.

1. You are the government: Who are the 'good guys'? Who are the 'bad guys'?
2. You are rebels: Who are the 'good guys'? Who are the 'bad guys'?
   Who are 'neutral'?

T4 | Speaking: Agree on a translation for the words in T1

T5 | Language Analysis: Analyse the Text

T6 | Listen and Read: Listen to a reading of the text in T3

Which words do you need to practice saying? Which words do you need to learn?

T7 | Listening: Listen and Make Notes

Listen to this talk about a conflict.
Make notes under two headings: **1. Facts 2. Opinions**
Listen and write down the facts the speaker says and his opinions.
Listen again and write down the exact words which tell you - fact or opinion.
Check with your partner. Then check with T14.1.

T8 | Speaking: A Conflict

Think of a conflict your know about. Prepare answers to these questions.

1. Where and when is/was the conflict?
2. Who is/was involved and what is happening/happened in the conflict?

Tell the class about the conflict.

Unit 15 Checking Questions

T1 | Speaking: Talk and Report

Look at P15.1. What can you see?

T2 | Grammar: Question Word Order

Order the words to make questions:

1. do what leave time we?
2. get do we back when?
3. are how patrol people going on many the?
4. are what we ambushed if?
5. casualties if we get what?
6. take to kit do what we need?
7. to radio use what are frequency we going?
8. going we where are?
9. sign call what is your?
10. do we get separated do what if we?
11. name is the operation what of this?
12. cover we air have will?
13. take much how should ammunition we?
14. much take food and how water should we?
15. many there checks how radio are?
16. is map target what reference the?
17. the how mission long is?
18. mission the what is objective?
19. of it mission what type is?
20. do intel have good we?

T3 | Grammar: Question Analysis

1. Which questions are about facts now?
2. Which questions are about the future?
3. Which questions are about the past?
4. Which questions are about hypotheticals?

T4 | Listening and Speaking: Practice the Questions

Work as a class or groups. One student reads out a situation from Cards 1 – 12 (from your teacher). The other students then ask questions. Try to ask as many questions as possible, as quickly as possible. The student has to answer the questions. Then a new student reads out the next situation.

Unit 16 Time and Time Zones

Present Tenses | Time Words

T1 | Vocabulary: Put the words on the timeline

Copy the timeline and moon/sun table into your notebooks.

00:01	12:00	23:59

Moon | _____ > _____

Sun | _____ > _____

Add these words to the timeline and moon/sun table.

midnight	afternoon	dawn	evening	dusk	pm
twilight	morning	am	moonset	sunrise	midday
sunset	moonrise	noon	daybreak	night	daylight

T2 | Listening: Listen and Check

Listen to a talk about time words to check your timeline and to find out the difference between astronomical, nautical and civil twilight.

T3 | Listening: Transcript Tasks 1

Complete Transcript Tasks 1 on page 31. Listen to check. (See T19.1) Also see P16.1.

T4 | Speaking: Talk and Report

What time zone are you in? What is Zulu time?

T5 | Listening: Listen and Make Notes

Look at the diagram on page 30 and then listen about time zones. Make notes about the cities marked on the diagram.

T6 | Listening: Transcript Tasks 2

Complete Transcript Tasks 2 on page 31. Listen to check. (See T19.2)

T7 | Speaking: Date Time Group: DDHHMM(Z)MONYY

Study the example:

081330(Z)FEB16   DD (08) HHMM (1330) (Zulu) MON (Feb) YY (16)

8th 13.30 hours Zulu time zone (= GMT) February 2016

What is the Time Date Group right now where you are? Check with your partner.

T8 | Speaking: Talk and Report

What do you think of the concept of 'summer time' or 'daylight saving time'? Think of reasons for and against and compare your ideas with the class.

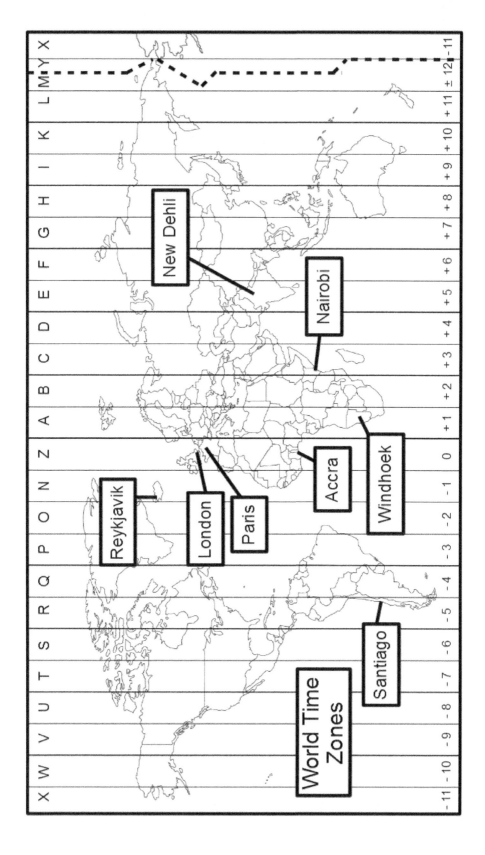

World Time Zones

New Dehli
Nairobi
Reykjavik
London
Paris
Accra
Windhoek
Santiago

Transcript Tasks 1

1. Listen to part of the talk again and mark down the / pauses / and <u>underline</u> the words which are most stressed. The first part is done as an example.

> / the <u>day</u> begins at 0001 <u>hours</u> / just a <u>minute</u> after <u>midnight</u> / this is when the morning starts this period is known as "am" which means ante meridiem the time period before midday ante meridiem means "before midday" it is still night though the night lasts until dawn

2. Complete the extract with the correct verb form. Listen to check.

> Then there [1] _____ a period of twilight before sunrise. There [2] _____ three classifications of twilight. Morning astronomical twilight [3] _____ when the sun [4] _____ 18 degrees below the horizon and rising. Nautical twilight [5] _____ when the sun [6] _____ 12 degrees below the horizon and rising. And civil twilight [7] _____ when the sun [8] _____ 6 degrees below the horizon and rising. Nautical twilight [9] _____ a danger time for attacks and many armies [10] _____ it a rule for all soldiers to stand-to ready for an attack during the period of nautical twilight to sunrise or sunset.

Transcript Tasks 2

Complete the extracts with the correct word form. Listen to check.

> Zulu Time is world time, so it also [1] _____ as UTC (Universal Time (Co-ordinated)). And this is the [2] _____ as GMT, which is Greenwich Mean Time – the time [3] _____ London, [4] _____ the winter. The zero degree meridian crosses [5] _____ Greenwich [6] _____ London, England. UTC uses the 24-hour system [7] _____ time notation. 1:00 a.m. [8] _____ UTC is expressed as 0100. Fifteen minutes [9] _____ 0100 is expressed as 0115; thirty-eight minutes [10] _____ 0100 is 0138. The time one minute [11] _____ 0159 is 0200. The time one minute [12] _____ 1259 is 1300. This continues until 2359. One minute later is zero hundred, and the start of a new day.

> Accra, [13] _____ Ghana, is always [14] _____ Zulu time. Windhoek, the capital [15] _____ Namibia is [16] _____ Alpha time: Zulu + 1 from April to September and [17] _____ Bravo time from September to April. Nairobi [18] _____ Kenya is [19] _____ Charlie time all year round. The time [20] _____ New Delhi, India, is India Standard Time which is Zulu + 5.5 hours: that is [21] _____ the Echo Star Time Zone. Santiago [22] _____ Chile is either [23] _____ Quebec time – Zulu -4 or, [24] _____ the summer, [25] _____ Papa time: Zulu -3.

Unit 17 Talking about Formation Purpose

Present Tenses I Active and Passive Verb Forms I Modals (can)

T1 I Speaking: Talk and Report

The US army is organised into Brigade Combat Teams (BCTs).

Why do you think this is?

T2 I Reading: Read to Check

Read about the text about the Brigade Combat Team on the next page to check your ideas. What is its purpose?

T3 I Reading: Read Again and Answer

1. What are the three kinds of BCTs in the US Army?
2. Why are there these three kinds of BCTs?
3. Why does each BCT have its own recon and artillery battalions?
4. Why does each battalion in a BCT have its own headquarters?
5. What are 'organic support and fire units'?
6. What advantages are there to a BCT?

T4 I Language Analysis: Analyse the Text

T5 I Listen and Read: Listen to a reading of the text

Which words do you need to practice saying? Which words do you need to learn?

T6 I Speaking: Talk and Report

How are units organised in your army below divisional level?

Discuss with your partner then present your findings to your teacher

T7 I Writing: Write a Report

Write a short report about the organisation and purpose of units in your army.

Structure your report like this:

Paragraph 1: Introduction to the report

Paragraph 2: Unit Formation 1

Paragraph 3: Unit Formation 2

Paragraph 4: Unit Formation 3

Paragraph 5: Unit Formation 4

Paragraph 6: Summary

T8 I Consolidation Tasks

The Brigade Combat Team

The Brigade Combat Team (BCT) is a modular organization below division level which is designed for the full spectrum of operations. They fight battles and engagements by employing the tactical advantages of a combined arms force structure. A BCT consists of one combat arms branch maneuver brigade (three Infantry, Stryker or Armoured battalions), and its assigned organic support and fire units.

The **infantry brigade combat team** contains almost 4,500 soldiers. There are three infantry battalions (usually motorised infantry in Humvees), supported by one cavalry battalion (Reconnaissance, Surveillance, and Target Acquisition: RSTA), one brigade support battalion, one engineer battalion, and one fires battalion. All infantry BCTs are capable of air assault. Each battalion in the BCT has its own headquarters. The brigade support battalion includes a distribution company, field maintenance company, medical company and forward support companies to support the work of recon, engineers, infantry and field artillery.

Stryker brigade combat teams, with over 300 Stryker infantry fighting vehicles, have three infantry battalions, one reconnaissance squadron, one fires battalion, a brigade support battalion, headquarters and headquarters company and a brigade engineer battalion and is an intermediate force between the infantry and armored BCTs.

The **armored brigade combat team** is also a combined arms formation. An armored BCT consists of seven battalions. There are three combined arms battalions (tanks and IFVs), one cavalry battalion, one fires battalion, one engineer battalion and one brigade support battalion. Each ABCT has 90 M1 Abrams tanks, 90 M2 Bradley IFVs, and over 100 APCs.

A BCT is commanded by a colonel or a brigadier general. BCTs can conduct high tempo offensive operations against both conventional and unconventional forces. They can operate in multiple combat situations including offensive operations, mixed terrain defense, urban combat, mobile security missions, and stability operations. With organic reconnaissance capabilities, the enemy can be found and engaged effectively without delay. It also has organic self-contained close-fire support for a more precise and rapid response to threats. A BCT is highly mobile and all assets can be transported by organic motor transport, or by aircraft.

[Source: FM 3-96 Brigade Combat Team]

Unit 18 Forces: Mechanised Infantry

T1 | Speaking: Talk and Report 1

Look at P18.1. What can you see?

T2 | Speaking: Talk and Report 2

What is the difference?

- motorized infantry
- mechanised infantry
- armoured infantry

T3 | Reading: Read To Find Out

Read the text on the next page to find out if you were correct.

T4 | Reading: Read Again and Answer

1. When was motorised infantry first widely used?
2. What are the advantages of mechanised or armoured infantry?
3. Which is better: APCs or IFVs?
4. What is required to keep a mechanised or armoured infantry unit in the field?

T5 | Language Analysis: Analyse the Text

T6 | Listen and Read: Listen to a reading of the text

Which words do you need to practice saying?

Which words do you need to learn?

T7 | Listening: Listen and Make Notes

Listen to this talk.

Make notes under two headings: **1. Facts 2. Opinions**

Listen and write down the facts the speaker says and his opinions.

Listen again and write down the exact words which tell you - fact or opinion.

Check with your partner.

Then check with T18.1.

T8 | Consolidation Tasks

Motorised Infantry

Motorised infantry is infantry which is equipped with motor transport like trucks or jeeps. The vehicles provide the troops with transport so they can keep up with mechanised forces, like amoured formations. The "soft-skinned" vehicles do not offer protection from hostile fire. Motorized infantry can move to critical sectors of the battlefield faster, respond to enemy movements, and attempt to outmanoeuvre the enemy. Motorised infantry came into use in WWII during German Blitzkrieg operations but it was limited by the availability of transport like trucks and half-tracks.

Mechanised Infantry

Mechanised infantry uses APCs for transport and protection. Most APCs are fully tracked and are capable of cross-country mobility across rough ground. Most types of APC have support weapons, like machine guns, cannons, howitzers and/or anti-tank guided missiles, mounted on them to provide suppressive fire support and anti-armour capabilities. They are lightly armoured to provide protection during movement. Mechanised infantry can engage in rapid tactical movement either alone or in combination with armour.

Armoured Infantry

Armoured infantry is carried in Infantry Fighting Vehicles, which have more firepower than APCs. IFVs are either tracked or all-wheel drive vehicles with cross-country performance, armour protection and significant firepower. APCs generally carry more men than IFVs and require fewer crew but they are less well protected and have less firepower.

Mechanised or armoured infantry formations require manpower to crew APCs and IFVs, combat supplies (fuel and ammunition), and mechanics and recovery vehicles. There is still a role for light infantry fighting on foot so when the enemy is contacted, the infantry soldiers in trucks, APCs and IFVs have to dismount and engage the enemy with their individual weapons. Mechanisation, though, does protect soldiers during movement, provides fire support, and gives them the ability to manoeuvre more effectively as part of combined arms operations. In offence, APCs or IFVs allow the infantrymen to fight (and manoeuvre) mounted as long as possible and to dismount when confronted by close terrain, obstacles that prevent movement, or a strong anti-armour defence that cannot be bypassed or suppressed. In defence, APCs or IFVs allow the infantrymen to fight mounted or dismounted, and to manoeuvre for advantage.

Unit 19 Telling the Time

T1 | Speaking: Practice saying these numbers

0/zero/oh	1/one/wun	2/two/too	3/three/tree	4/four/fower
5/five/fife	6/six	7/seven	8/eight/ait	9/nine/niner

T2 | Speaking: Practice saying these numbers

10	11	12	13	14	15	16	17
18	19	20	21	22	23	24	25
26	27	28	19	30	31	32	33

T3 | Speaking: Practice saying these numbers

1st	2nd	3rd	4th	5th	6th	7th	8th
9th	10th	11th	12th	13th	14th	15th	16th
17th	18th	19th	20th	21st	22nd	23rd	24th
25th	26th	27th	28th	29th	30th	31st	

T4 | Dictation: Write down ten numbers: Dictate them to your partner

Write down the numbers your partner dictates to you.

T5 | Speaking: Practice saying these numbers.

33	tree tree
44	fower fower
85	ait fife
90	Niner zero
156	wun fife six
600	six zero zero
1700	wun seven zero zero
5000	five thousand
11000	wun wun thousand
895018	ait niner fife zero wun ait

T6 | Dictation: Write down ten more numbers: Dictate them to your partner

Write down the numbers your partner dictates to you.

T7 | Speaking: Decimals: Practice saying these numbers

    1.6   "wun decimal six"

    81.59   "ait wun decimal fife niner"

    7.189

    9.10

    678.34

    10.10

    1001.10

    345.678

T8 | Dictation: Write down ten decimal numbers: Dictate them to your partner

Write down the numbers your partner dictates to you.

T9 | Speaking: 24 hours: what time is it?

1 a.m.	01:00	zero one hundred (hours) oh one hundred (hours)
5.30 a.m.	05:30	zero five thirty (hours) oh five thirty (hours)
7.45 a.m	07:45	zero seven forty-five (hours) oh seven forty-five (hours)
10.15 a.m.	10:15	ten fifteen (hours)
1 p.m.	13:00	thirteen hundred (hours)
4.30 p.m.	16:30	sixteen thirty (hours)

T10 | Speaking: Practice saying these times using the 24 hour clock

2.45 a.m.	11.53 a.m.	6 a.m.	1.15 p.m.	8.05 p.m.	3.25 p.m	11.53 p.m.
1 a.m.	3.25 a.m.	6.35 p.m.	5. 12 p.m.	10.15 a.m.	10 p.m.	20.45 p.m.

T11 | Dictation: Write down ten times: Dictate them to your partner

Write down the times your partner dictates to you.

T12 | Speaking: Ask and Answer

Write five questions to ask your partner, like: *'What time do you get up?'*

1. _____

2. _____

3. _____

4. _____

5. _____

Unit 20 Leisure, Hobbies and Interests

Present Simple | Expressing Likes And Dislikes

T1 | Speaking: Talk and Report 1

Look at P20.1 and P20.2. What can you see?

T2 | Speaking: Talk and Report 2

Tell your partner 5 things you love doing in your free time.

Tell the class what your partner loves doing.

Language Reminder

I like/love/hate doing something.

I like walking.   I love climbing mountains.   I hate waiting for people.

T3 | Vocabulary: In my free time I *go/play/do*

Sort the words into the correct column in the table below.

clubbing	to concerts	out drinking	with my children
the piano	fishing	collect stamps	sing in a choir
shooting	board games	to the gym	to the movies
walking	repair cars	travel a lot	make things from wood
climbing	read novels	football	computer games
drawing	write stories	listen to music	voluntary work
cards	watch TV	swimming	spend time with my friends
cook	nothing	birdwatching	out with my friends
chess	woodwork	paint pictures	help my kids with their homework

I go	I play	I do	I

T4 | Vocabulary: Love and hate

Complete the table with things you like and dislike or like/dislike doing.

Like this:

> I like **computer games**.
> I don't like **watching TV**.

Very Positive	I love _____
	I really like _____
	I like _____
	I quite like _____
Slightly Positive	_____ is ok.
Neutral	I don't mind _____
Negative	I don't like _____ very much.
	I really don't like _____ at all.
Very Negative	I hate _____

T5 | Speaking: Talk and Report

Compare your list with your partner and then report:

> We **both** like [cooking].
> I like [playing football] **but** John [hates it]
> **Neither of us** likes [watching TV]

T6 | Vocabulary: What is stronger?

Look at the examples. Which word in **bold** is stronger?

1. I **love** Asian food in general but I absolutely **adore** Japanese food.
2. I **hate** rap music but I **loathe** hip hop music.
3. I **can't stand** waiting in queues but I **detest** queue jumpers.
4. I'm **keen on** music in general but I'm **crazy** about jazz.

Write sentences which are true for you, then tell the class.

T7 | Grammar: Changes

Look at the examples.

> Recently, I've **got/come** to like peas/eating peas.
> Recently, I've **started** walk**ing** to work.
> Recently, I've **started to** exercise more.
> Last week I **started** running every day.

Write sentences which are true for you, then tell the class.

Unit 21 Talking about Military Hardware 1

Present Simple I Noun Phrases I Numbers I Comparisons

T1 I Speaking: Talk and Report 1

Look at P21.1. What can you see?

T2 I Speaking: Talk and Report 2

Talk with your partner and list the equipment your army has in these categories:

APCs	trucks/lorries	helicopters	tanks
IFVs	other vehicles	ground attack aircraft	artillery

T3 I Vocabulary: Check you know the meaning of these words

tracks	wings	hardpoint	smoke dispenser	turret	cab
rotor	hatch	stub wings	armour/armor	fuselage	primary & secondary armament
canopy	barrel	wheels	external tanks	soft top	

Check with these pictures:

P21.2 Bedford I P21.3 Palladin I P21.4 Warrior I P21.5 Apache I P21.6 A10-A

T4 I Vocabulary: Which words can be used to describe the hardware from T3?

take-off weight	A10-A, Apache helicopter
top speed	
operational range	
flight crew	
service ceiling	
projectile	
cruising speed	
diesel engine	
6-speed manual transmission.	
ferry range	

T5 I Reading: Read and Match

Read the texts on the next page. Match the platforms **1 - 5** below to the descriptions on the next page.

1. Blackhawk helicopter
2. Puma IFV
3. M109A7 self-propelled howitzer
4. Bedford truck
5. Leopard 2 tank

T6 I Speaking: Underline and practice saying the numbers

1	This vehicle weighs 62.3 t and is 9.97 m long and 3.75 m wide. It has a crew of 4. It uses 3rd generation composite armour. The main armament is a 120 mm Rheinmetall L55 smoothbore gun with 42 rounds. The secondary armament consists of 2× 7.62 mm MG3A1 machine guns with 4,750 rounds. It has a liquid-cooled V-12 twin-turbo diesel engine producing 1,479 hp. The power/weight ratio is 17.7 kW/t. It has an operational range of 550 km and a top speed of 72 km/h.
2	This vehicle weighs 35.38 t and is 6.8 m long (9.7 m with gun forward) and 3.9 m wide. It is 3.7 m high. It has a crew of 4. The main armament is a 155 mm M284 cannon with a secondary M182A1 gun mount and an automated loader. It can fire the 155 mm cannon at a sustained rate of one round per minute with a maximum rate of fire of four rounds a minute. The cannon has a maximum effective range of 22 km with standard projectiles and 30 km with rocket-assisted projectiles. The Cummins diesel engine produces 600 hp and it has an operational range of 322 km and a top speed of 61 km/h.
3	This vehicle weighs 31.5 tonnes and is 7.4 m long and 3.7 m wide. It has a crew of 3 and can carry 6 soldiers. It uses modular composite armour The main armament is a 30 mm MK30-2 autocannon with 400 rounds. The secondary armament consists of a 5.56 mm HK MG4 machine gun with 2,000 rounds, a Spike LR anti--tank guided missile and a 6-shot 76 mm grenade launcher It has a MTU V10 892 diesel engine producing 1,100 hp. The power/weight ratio is 25.4 kW/t. Its top speed is 70 km/h, with an operational range of 600 km.
4	This vehicle has a flight crew of 2, with 2 gunners. It can carry 1,200 kg of cargo internally (for example 11 troops). It is 19.76 m long overall with a fuselage length of 15.27 m x 2.36 m. It is 5.13 m high. The rotor diameter is 16.36 m. Maximum take-off weight is 10,660 kg. Maximum speed is 294 km/h, with a cruising speed of 280 km/h. The combat radius is 592 km, while the ferry range is 2,220 km with stub wings and external tanks. The service ceiling is 5,790 m. It can be armed with machine guns or mini guns and has hardpoints for rockets, missiles and gun pods.
5	This vehicle is 6.53 m long, 2.48 m wide and 2.63 m high. It has a three person cab. It weighs 4.76 t empty and has a 6 t capacity. The Perkins Phaser diesel engine generates 135 hp, giving a maximum road speed of 87 km/h and a range of 600-800 km. It has a 4 x 4 configuration with a 6-speed manual transmission. It can carry general cargo, troops, ammunition, fuel, water, containers, shelters and other equipment.

Unit 22 Talking about Music

T1 | Speaking: Talk and Report 1

1. Who is your favourite singer? Why?
2. How many different types of music do you know?

T2 | Vocabulary: Types of Music

Do you recognise these types of music? Which do you like and dislike?

pop	rock	rap	hip-hop	metal
classical	house	punk	electronic	drum and base
techno	trance	folk	country & western	jazz
blues	Latin	Reggae	R&B	soul

[**Note:** Classic and Classical music are different. **Classic** music is synonymous with good music from several years ago. **Classical** music is music by composers like Mozart and Beethoven.]

T3 | Vocabulary: Music Words

Check you know the meaning of these words.

CD	track	song	lyricist	singer-songwriter
lyrics	band	musician	composer	session musician
score	group	orchestra	vocalist	backing group
album	single	pianist	conductor	melody/tune
bassist	guitarist	drummer	lead singer	(play) live music
on tour	solo artist	instrument	concert/gig	recording studio

T4 | Vocabulary: Complete the sentences 1-10 with a word from T3

1. Brahms is my favourite _____.
2. The Beatles were the most famous pop _____ in the sixties.
3. Ringo Starr was the _____ for The Beatles.
4. I hear they have gone into the _____ studio to record a new _____ of songs.
5. _____ often use _____ musicians when recording in the studio.
6. Sir Georg Solti _____ many famous _____.
7. Can you play a musical _____?
8. I hate songs where you can't hear the _____.

9. I prefer going to see a band play _____ in _____ than listen to recorded _____.

10. Paul Simon was a _____ and wrote and sang many popular songs.

T5 | Vocabulary: Describing Music

Check you know the meaning of these words and phrases

beautiful	haunting	peaceful	depressing	gives me a headache
annoying	relaxing	irritating	boring	wonderful
catchy	repetitive	exciting	awful	unoriginal

Are they positive or negative?

T6 | Reading: Read the Review

Read the review. Is it positive or negative?

> **Savane: Ali Farka Toure**
>
> The great blues guitarist Ali Farka Toure's posthumous album "Savane" is without question one of the finest efforts in his legendary discography, and per-haps the finest of his career. From the first track to the last, every sound on the record is a haunting pleasure. It is beautiful and emotive music: wholly entran-cing. A single string violin can evoke the desert while a harmonica player intro-duces the sound of the city. It's a work that deserves every bit of praise that it receives and who would go against Ali's own instinct that it is the best of all his albums.

T7 | Speaking: Talk and Report 2

Discuss these questions with your partner.

1. Do you play a musical instrument?
2. Have you ever tried to learn a musical instrument?
3. Is there a musical instrument you would like to learn?
4. Can you sing? What do you like to sing?
5. What kind of music do you most like to listen to? Why?
6. Who is your favourite group?
7. What is your favourite song? Why?
8. Would you like to be a rich and famous singer? Why? Why not?

Then tell the class what your partner told you.

Unit 23 Talking about Military Hardware 2

Present Simple | Noun Phrases | Numbers | Comparisons

T1 | Speaking: Talk and Report

What do you remember about the military hardware from **Unit 21**?

1. Blackhawk helicopter
2. Puma IFV
3. M109A7 self-propelled howitzer
4. Bedford truck
5. Leopard 2 tank

T2 | Reading: Read and Answer

Read the texts from **Unit 21** again and answer these questions:

Which platform:

1. is the longest?
2. is the smallest?
3. is the fastest?
4. is the slowest?
5. is the heaviest?
6. is the lightest?
7. is the widest?
8. is the narrowest?
9. has the longest range?
10. has the shortest range?
11. carries the largest crew?
12. carries the smallest crew?
13. can carry the most soldiers?
14. is the heaviest armed?
15. is the lightest armed?
16. is the heaviest armoured?
17. is the lightest armoured?
18. is the most useful?

T3 | Speaking: Questions and Answers

Work in pairs. Use the Unit 23 Fact Files from your Workbook.

One of you should choose the Challenger (FF23.1); one should choose the Abrams (FF23.2).

Ask each other questions.

Find out the information your partner has about their vehicle.

e.g. *What is the maximum speed of the Challenger?*

Make notes of the answers, then check with the Fact Files.

Repeat the task for the Warrior (FF23.3) and Bradley (FF23.4).

Then, discuss in groups: which is the better tank of the two; which is the better IFV?

T4 | Writing: Write a text about some military hardware

Use the Fact Files from your workbook and the texts from Unit 21 to help you:

FF23.1 Challenger | FF23.2 Abrams | FF23.3 Bradley | FF23.4 Warrior

---

Language Revision Tasks

Reorder the words in the sentences.

1. tried musical you have learn instrument ever to a?
2. second he commission a 2010 battlefield was to lieutenant awarded in.
3. was by I aunt up my brought uncle and.
4. in British transferred Rhine Minden base was Germany to serve he with the army to army of the.
5. 16 a of squads two soldiers to four and has platoon to 44 consists.
6. enemy opposing their you always the enemy, forces and the you are are.
7. are how patrol people going on many the?
8. much take food and how water should we?
9. combat infantry soldiers brigade contains almost the team 4,500.
10. trucks is infantry transport infantry which is with motor equipped like or motorised jeeps.
11. absolutely food food in general I I love adore Asian Japanese but.
12. 155 can minute fire the of round mm it at a sustained cannon rate one per

Check in Units 7 -21.

Unit 24 Functional English: Hypotheticals

T1 | Grammar: Would

You are going to practice talking about what you would do and say in hypothetical situations. These are not 'real' situations but they are <u>possible</u> situations.

One of you should be the question master. This student will look at the 20 situations in the Teacher's Book, and read out the situation to the class. The other students will work individually or in groups and take it in turns to answer questions.

Example:

> **Situation**
>
> You are a sergeant and you realise that the men and other NCOs do not like the new (and inexperienced) lieutenant.
>
> What would you do? Who would you talk to? What would you say?
>
> What would your orders be?

The student whose turn it is to answer (or the group's spokesperson) should say what they would do, who they would talk to and what they would say. Like this:

> I **would** talk to the men and tell them that it is not a crime to be an inexperienced lieutenant and tell them they should give him a chance. He will make mistakes but he is learning. I **would** tell the other NCOs to support the lieutenant. I **would** also talk to the lieutenant and suggest he asks the NCOs for advice more.

The other students or other groups can challenge the one answering. Like this:

> Really? Why **would** you do that?
>
> Do you really think that **would** work?
>
> What about [doing X], **wouldn't** that be better?

T2 | Grammar: Feedback

Your teacher will listen and prepare feedback on your answers:

1. Were the answers clear?
2. Were they grammatically correct?

When all the situations have been discussed the teacher will give feedback.

Unit 25 Forces: Armour

Present and Past Tenses

T1 | Speaking: Talk and Report 1

Look at P25.1. What can you see?

T2 | Before Reading: Answer the Questions

1. When were tanks first developed?
2. Who first developed tanks?
3. When were they first used successfully?
4. How are modern MBTs used?
5. What are the standard features of MBTs?

T3 | Reading: Read and Answer 1

Read the text on the next page to answer the questions in **T2** and see if you were right.

T4 | Reading: Read and Answer 2

Read the text again to answer these questions.

1. Which generals are mentioned in the text?
2. Which countries did they fight for?
3. Which tanks fought in the Battle of Kursk?
4. Who won the battle?
5. What was General Patton's greatest achievement?

T5 | Language Analysis: Analyse the Text

T6 | Listen and Read: Listen to a reading of the text

Which words do you need to practice saying? Which words do you need to learn?

T7| Listening: Listen and Make Notes

Listen to this talk.
Make notes under two headings: **1. Facts 2. Opinions**
Listen and write down the facts the speaker says and his opinions.
Listen again and write down the exact words which tell you - fact or opinion.
Check with your partner. Then check with T25.1.

T8 | Speaking: Talk and Report 2

Why is armour important? Can armour operate effectively without infantry? Can infantry operate effectively without armour?

T9 | Consolidation Tasks

Armour

Armoured warfare is the use of tanks to penetrate defensive lines. Tanks were first developed in Britain and France in 1915 to overcome the World War One stalemate of entrenched infantry protected by barbed wire and armed with machine guns.

British Mark I tanks first went into action as direct infantry support unsuccessfully at the Somme, on 15 September 1916. Then British tanks broke the German Hindenburg trench line system at the Battle of Cambrai in 1917 but the breakthrough was not exploited. British and French tanks were first successfully used en mass at the Battle of Soissons and the Battle of Amiens in 1918 and helped end the war.

During the Second World War tanks came into their own with German Blitzkrieg operations like the invasion of France under General Guderian in 1940 and Operation Barbarossa – the invasion of the Soviet Union in 1941. In North Africa, the German Afrika Corps under General Rommel fought the British and threatened British control of Egypt until the Second Battle of El Alamein in November 1942, when he was defeated by General Montgomery, commanding the British 8th Army and Commonwealth forces. The largest tank battle of the war was the Battle of Kursk – an engagement between German and Soviet forces on the Eastern Front during July and August 1943, when Soviet T34 and JS2 tanks beat the German Tiger and Panther tanks. The most famous American tank commander was General Patton who led the US 3rd Army. During the Battle of the Bulge in 1944, he disengaged 6 divisions from front line combat during the middle of winter, then turned north to relieve the besieged town of Bastogne.

Modern Main Battle Tanks

Modern MBTs are used in armoured units working in co-operation with infantry and ground attack aircraft, as part of combined arms formations. MBT performance is a compromise between the size of the main armament (90 to 120 mm), usually turret-mounted, the thickness of the armour protection (adding to the weight of the vehicle: 45-70 tons), and speed (max. 75 km/h). The main tank gun is used to engage tanks and fortifications, and soft targets such as light vehicles and infantry. Modern tanks have sophisticated fire-control systems designed to keep the gun stable and aimed at a target even when the tank is moving. Tank protection is in its armour, which can be steel, composite ceramic and alloys, explosive reactive armour, or slat armour, and electronic countermeasures against missile attack. Tanks usually have operational ranges of up to 550 km.

Unit 26 Watches

T1 | Speaking: Talk and Report

Why do people wear watches? How many reasons can you think of to wear a watch?

T2 | Vocabulary: What are the parts of a watch called?

Look at P26.1 in the Wiki. Can you name the parts of a watch?
Check with P26.2.

T3 | Prediction: Think about the answers to these two questions

1. What different types of watches are there?
2. What are the requirements for a military watch?

T4 | Reading: Now read the text and see if your agree with the writer

Not wearing a watch and relying on your mobile phone might be an option for civilians but its not an option for military personnel. A good quality, tough and reliable timepiece is an essential piece of kit for a soldier.

There are different types of watch to choose from: digital watches with just numbers on the watch face; analogue watches with numbers around the dial on the face and hands which show the time, and combinations of both. There are diver watches for underwater activities, pilot watches, so-called military watches, and dress watches for smart occasions. Some watches just tell the time. Other watches have chronograph functions – basically a stopwatch built in. Some watches include a barometer to measure air pressure, an electronic compass to show direction, or an altimeter to measure altitude, and many other functions.

How the watch is powered is a key factor. The traditional watch needs to be wound up every day by winding the crown on the side of the watch and this winds up a spring inside the watch. Other watches have automatic movements which use the movement of the wearer's wrist to wind up the watch. As long as the wearer continues to wear the watch it will be wound up and will continue to work. The third type of watch runs on batteries and has a quartz movement: these watches are very accurate as long as the battery lasts. Some are solar powered.

There are many requirements for a good military watch. It should be tough – shockproof – so that if it is dropped or knocked it will still keep good time. It should also be waterproof and not just water resistant. The glass on the watch face should be scratch proof. It should be reliable – it should keep good time. Often military watches have a rotating bezel like a diver's watch so you can measure elapsed time. The watch should also be readable in the dark: the face and the hands need to be painted with luminous markings which need to be charged up, or have embedded Tritium capsules, which is radioactive and emits light. The strap, or band, is important too. Leather isn't good in the wet so fabric or rubber is preferred.

Where you wear your watch is also important. Do you wear it on your right or left wrist? On top of the wrist or below? Or around your neck on a cord so the luminous markings do not show on night operations?

T5 | Language Analysis: Analyse the Text

T6 | Listening: Listen and Answer

Listen to this man talking about his watches.

Look at P26.3 and identify the watches he talks about.

Complete this table about the watches. Which is his favourite and why?

	Watch 1	Watch 2	Watch 3	Watch 4
Description				
Features				
When does he wear it?				
Opinion about the watch				

T7 | Grammar: Comparing

How does the man compare the watches? Write down the phrases he uses. Then check with T26.1

T8 | Grammar: Formulating Questions

Write questions about watches from the prompts below.

1. What | watch?   *What kind/make/type of watch is it?*
2. Is | waterproof?
3. How many | functions?
4. Is | quartz | automatic?
5. How | accurate/reliable?

T9 | Speaking: Talk and Report

Ask your parter the questions from T8 and the ones below. Then report to the class.

1. Why did you choose your watch?
2. Where do you wear it and why?
3. What features does it have?
4. Does it meet the requirements for a military watch?
5. Is this your only watch or do you have a collection?

T10 | Consolidation Tasks

Unit 27 Personal Equipment 1

Present Simple I Active and Passive I Modal Verbs

T1 I Speaking: Talk and Report 1

What personal equipment do soldiers in your army carry on active duty?

Make a list and compare it with your partner's list.

T2 I Vocabulary: Look at P27.1. Is this the same equipment as you carry?

Now look at P27.2 - 4.

Check you understand all the words.

Agree on a translation.

T3 I Reading: Read about the new British Army Virtus body armour system

Look at P27.5 – P27.8 as you read.

What are the advantages of the new body armour?

The new Virtus system uses the latest materials. It offers the same protection as Osprey body armour but it is significantly lighter, moves with the body more easily and has a slimmer profile. The system consists of a new helmet, a dynamic weight distribution system, and a Scalable Tactical Vest. The new, lighter Virtus helmet provides increased blunt impact protection. It has face and mandible guards for certain roles and a shape that is designed to work with the armour and daysack so weapons can be comfortably used even in a prone position. The helmet has a fixed shroud for mounting night vision goggles on, and a counterweight for neck comfort. It can be easily adjusted in the same way as modern cycling and climbing helmets. The sculpted rear of the helmet prevents interference with body armour or daysack when in a prone fire position. It provides more protection to the side of the head and is 350 g lighter than the Mark 7 helmet.

The Virtus system has an integral 'spine' called the '*dynamic weight distribution*' system. The device is linked to the user's waist belt and it helps spread the load of the body armour, a Bergen or daysack across the back, shoulders and hips. This makes it easier to carry heavy loads. It also ensures that they are carried close to the body and prevents excessive movement of the load.

The Scalable Tactical Vest (STV) can be used to carry loads with or without armour. The amount of protection employed can be scaled up or down to match the type of threat as a soldier can add or remove soft armour pads and hard ballistic plates. It can be used as a fragmentation vest with soft armour padding (a composite granular material); as a plate carrier with no soft armour; or as a full body armour system with soft and hard armour. Any combination of front, rear or side plates can be used. It is compatible with both Osprey and Enhanced

Combat Body Armour. Pouches are made from one piece of fabric and fold flat when empty. The system also employs a new quick-release mechanism – a pin positioned on the chest that when pulled releases the entire body kit.

[Source: Crown Copyright]

T4 I Language Analysis: Analyse the Text

T5 I Listen and Read: Listen to a reading of the text

Which words do you need to practice saying?

Which words do you need to learn?

T6 I Speaking: Talk and Report 2

What do you think of the **British Army Virtus body armour system**?

T7 I Speaking: Talk and Report 3

What equipment checks do you do before a patrol/attack etc.? Use P27.9 to help you.

Language Revision Tasks

Complete the collocations:

1. body _____
2. last _____
3. _____ time
4. in _____ background
5. two-_____ house
6. _____ fence
7. clean _____
8. physical _____
9. a _____ commission
10. promoted _____
11. volunteered _____
12. operational _____
13. _____ battalion
14. commanded _____
15. security _____
16. international _____
17. field _____ company
18. _____ operations
19. _____ supplies
20. maximum _____ of fire
21. barbed _____
22. front _____ combat
23. ground _____ aircraft
24. fire-_____ systems
25. _____ range

Check in Units 1- 27.

Unit 28 Socialising 1

T1 | Speaking: Talk and Report

Work with a partner. Look at P28.1. What can you see?

T2 | Vocabulary: What day is it?

Work with a partner and answer the questions.

1. What day is today? [e.g. Monday]
2. What day was yesterday?
3. What day was the day before yesterday?
4. What day is tomorrow?
5. What day is the day after tomorrow?
6. What day is this time next week?
7. What is the date today?
8. What is the date in a week's time?
9. What date is next Friday?
10. What date is 'a week on Tuesday'?
11. It is Monday. When is next weekend?
12. It is Friday. This weekend starts tomorrow. When is next weekend?

Check as a class.

T3 | Vocabulary: Check the words in bold

Read the dialogue and check the meaning of the words and phrase in bold.

> **Alex:** John, we should have a talk before the briefing on Friday. Are you **free** later today?
>
> **John:** Sorry Sir, I've got to take my platoon to the range and my sergeant is down sick. Could we **do it** tomorrow instead, Sir?
>
> **Alex:** No, I'm not **available** tomorrow. I've **arranged** meetings at the Staff College all day. It'll have to be Thursday then.
>
> **John:** All right Sir, I can **make it** then. What time sir?
>
> **Alex:** What about 1000? Would that **suit**?
>
> **John:** I'm **supposed to meet** my NCOs then sir, but I'll **postpone it/put it off** to the afternoon.
>
> **Alex:** That's **settled** then. We'll meet at 1000 on Thursday in my office. I'll send you an e-mail to **confirm** this afternoon.

T4 | Vocabulary: Complete the dialogue

Complete the dialogue with a word or phrase from T3 in the right form.

Andrew: Are you [1] _____ this evening John? Do you fancy going out for a drink?

John: Sorry Andrew. I'd love to – that's just what I need - but I've got to finish a report for tomorrow and I can't [2] _____ it any more. What about to-morrow?

Andrew: No, I'm afraid I'm busy tomorrow night. I've already [3] _____ to go to the Pearson's for dinner.

John: That's a pity. I'll have finished my report. What about Saturday night?

Andrew: Well I'm [4] _____ to be going out with Jake and Claire. But they haven't [5] _____ it yet.

John: Maybe I could tag along? I get on with them.

Andrew: All right then. That's [6] _____ . Saturday – about seven

John: Great, I'm looking forward to it already.

T5 | Listening: Listen and Answer 1

Listen to a dialogue. Two friends are arranging to meet.
What do they decide to do? When do they decide to meet? (See T28.1)

T6| Listening: Listen and Answer 2

Listen to a dialogue. Two friends are arranging to meet.
When do they decide to meet? What are they going to do?

T7| Listening: Transcript Task

Look at the transcript for T6 on the next page. Make sure you understand everything. Listen and mark where the speakers pause. Listen and mark which words the speakers stress most. Practice reading the dialogue with a partner.

T8 | Speaking: Write and practise a dialogue

Work with a partner.
Write a dialogue about making an arrangement to meet.
Practise your dialogue and then perform it to the class.

Transcript Task

John:	Hi Peter! How's it going?
Peter:	Fine, how are you John?
John:	I'm OK. Can't complain. Say, what are you up to at the weekend?
Peter:	Nothing planned at the moment. What do you have in mind?
John:	Well, do you fancy going up to the cabin by the lake and doing a bit of fishing?
Peter:	Yeah, that would be good. I haven't been for a while. What's the weather forecast, do you know?
John:	Let me check..... well it's supposed to be a bit rainy, cool too – about 10 °C.
Peter:	Hmm. Not much fun for a barbecue then.
John:	Yeah, well, but the fishing should still be OK. We might be able to shoot some rabbits as well. I've got a new .22 to try out.
Peter:	Really? Sounds good. I'll bring my rifle too. Shall we get an early start?
John:	Yeah, good idea. I'll pick you up at 6.30 and we should be at the lake at 8. The boat's all ready so we'll be fishing by 8.30. The sun hits the water about then.
Peter:	OK. Have you got any bait or do you want me to get some?
John:	You get the bait and I'll bring the beer. How about that?
Peter:	Sure. Sounds good.
John:	Great. I'm looking forward to it already.

Unit 29 Personal Equipment 2

Present Simple | Active and Passive | Modal Verbs

T1 | Speaking: Talk and Report 1

Look at P29.1. What can you see?

T2 | Speaking: Talk and Report 1

What do you remember about the **British Army Virtus body armour system**?

T3 | Speaking: Talk and Report 2

Tell your partner about your favourite piece of kit.

Language Reminder	
I have a/an X.	It's a good X because........
I've had it for Y years now.	It's been invaluable/very useful/vital.
My X has never let me down.	I wouldn't go on patrol without my X.

T4 | Listening: Listen and Discuss

Listen to a soldier talking about personal equipment. Make notes about what he says, and then discuss his ideas. Do you agree/disagree? Why? (See T29.1)

T5 | Speaking: What is important?

Work with a partner. Talk about what is important when buying the gear in P29.2 to P29.21.

Language Reminder
The most important thing to remember when buying a/an X is......
The key feature(s) of a/an X is/are......
A good X will have A, B, and C.
The best X will have A, B, C and D.
A good X should be Y and Z.
A/an X should be made of Y.
A/an X can be used for......
A/an X can be used to do Y.

T6 | Speaking: Briefing

Work individually. There are 20 One Slide Briefings. See **Unit 29 Briefing Slides.**

Each slide is a presentation of the equipment you discussed in **T5**.

Prepare your presentation of one slide.

Then present your slide to the class. Be ready to answer questions.

Unit 30 Forces: Paratroopers

T1 | Speaking: Talk and Report 1

Look at P30.1 – P31.4. What can you see?

T2 |Before You Read: Answer the Questions

1. When were the first paratrooper units formed?
2. Can you name four operations paratroopers were used in?
3. Were they successful operations? Why? Why not?

T3 | Reading: Read and find out the answers to the questions in T2

Paratroopers are trained to parachute into action behind enemy lines. They are often used to seize strategic objectives such as bridges or airfields to establish an airhead. They have a tactical advantage as they can use the element of surprise. They also force the enemy to use resources to protect areas against airborne assault.

The Soviets and Italians first formed parachute units before the Second World War. The first units of Italian parachutists were trained at the Military School of Parachuting in Castel Benito, near Tripoli in Libya. During the Second World War Italian parachutists fought on the ground in the North African campaigns against the British.

German Fallschirmjäger units made the first airborne assault during the invasion of Denmark on April 9, 1940 as part of Operation Weserübung. They took control of Masnedø Fort and Aalborg Airport. German parachutists were also used in the invasion of the Low Countries in 1940: They attacked Fort Eben-Emael in Belgium May 10, 1940, but they used gliders, not parachutes. They did use parachutes during the 1941 Battle of Crete, which they won, but they suffered very high casualties. The Germans lost their enthusiasm for airborne operations after Crete.

Britain's first airborne assault took place on February 10, 1941 when II Special Air Service, part of the Commandos, parachuted into Italy in Operation Colossus to blow up an aqueduct. After the invasion of Crete, the Parachute Regiment was formed out of Commando units. British, American, Canadian and Free French parachutists then made successful drops during the Normandy landings (Operation Overlord) in June 1944. Operation Market Garden against Arnhem in September 1944 was less successful, and the British 1st Airborne Division was destroyed before ground troops could relieve the cut-off paratroopers.

Paratroopers generally use circular parachutes opened by a static line attached to the plane. Some special forces units use "ram-air" parachutes, which are manoeuvrable and opened manually at the right altitude. Two techniques are used: **HALO** (high altitude – low opening) and **HAHO** (high altitude – high opening).

Paratroopers have to carry all their food and equipment and weapons. This means that they are limited in how long they can act as an effective fighting force without resupply. Staying together during the drop and landing on target on or near the objective is difficult (in one D-Day drop only 4% of the 82nd Airborne landed in the target area, while in another 75% did). Paratroopers are also extremely vulnerable to ground fire during the drop.

T4 | Reading: Read Again and Answer

1. What military capability do paratrooper units give you?
2. What are the risks of using paratroopers?

What do you think? Under what conditions should you **not** use paratroopers?

T5 | Language Analysis: Analyse the Text

T6 | Listen and Read: Listen to a reading of the text

Which words do you need to practice saying? Which words do you need to learn?

T7 | Listening 1: Listen and Make Notes 1

Listen to this talk about paratrooper training. Make notes. Check with T30.1

T8 | Listening: Listen and Make Notes 2

Listen to this talk. Make notes under two headings: **1. Facts 2. Opinions**
Listen and write down the facts the speaker says and his opinions. Listen again and write down the exact words which tell you - fact or opinion. Check with your partner. Then check with T30.2.

T9 | Speaking: Talk and Report 2

Would you like to be a paratrooper? Why? Why not?
What kind of ops are best for paratroopers?
Does your army have paratroopers? Does it need them?
What other elite forces does your army have?

T10 | Consolidation Tasks

Unit 31 Kit

Present Simple I Use To Do Something I Noun Phrases

T1 I Speaking: Talk and Report 1

Look at P31.1. Check you know what all the things are. Check with P31.2

T2 I Listening: Listen and Answer

Listen to the man talking about the equipment for his hobby.

1. Why does the man use a small bag?
2. Why is a backpack/rucksack a bad idea?
3. How many cameras and lenses does he have?
4. What accessories does he have in his bag?

T3 I Listening: Listen again and make notes

1. How does he describe the camera and lenses?
2. What is the other equipment used for?

T4 I Listening: Transcript Task

Complete the transcript on the next page. Put one word in each gap. Then listen again to check. Check with T31.1.

T5 I Grammar 1: Noun phrases: study the examples of adjectives in noun phrases

1. It's a **small mirrorless digital** <u>camera</u>.
2. I also take a couple of **spare fast 16 GB memory** <u>cards</u> as I take a lot of photos.
3. It's made of **heavy waxed** <u>cotton</u> and it's pretty waterproof.

Language Reminder: Adjective order

Adjectives have a set order before nouns. Generally the order is this:

opinion	size	age	shape	colour	origin	material	purpose	noun
beautiful	*big*	*old*	-	*black*	*French*	*leather*	-	*sofa*

Sometimes the order is slightly different, especially for specialised adjectives and nouns. Usually not more than two or three adjectives are used before the noun.

T6 I Grammar Practice: Reorder the adjectives in the noun phrases below

1. an battery high-capacity excellent lithium
2. toys plastic quality poor
3. an car sports unreliable
4. Swiss a wristwatch beautiful
5. jacket green a waterproof

The Photographer

This is my camera bag and all my camera gear. As you [1] _____ see I don't have much gear as I like to travel light. I [2] _____ street photography and nature photography and I walk a lot. A big bag on one shoulder is not a good idea – it's bad for your back. A rucksack is [3] _____ not a good idea as a thief might be able [4] _____ open the pockets when I am on the bus or tram. The camera bag is pretty small. It's made [4] _____ heavy waxed cotton and it's pretty waterproof. There's [6] _____ in the bag for my camera and two lenses and that's about it. This is my camera. It's a small mirrorless digital camera. I like it because it's retro and small and light and people don't take it [7] _____ as a camera. It's not like a big digital SLR. I have two lenses for it – this 18-55 mm zoom lens and this 55-200 mm telephoto zoom lens. I [8] _____ the 18-55 mm zoom most of the time, especially [9] _____ street photography. I [10] _____ the 55-200 mm lens [11] _____ take photos of wildlife. There are a couple of pockets in the bag – I [12] _____ them for accessories. I take a spare battery with me; some cleaning gear – I [13] _____ this lens pen and lens tissue [14] _____ keep my lenses clean. I also have a pen and notebook [15] _____ take notes of course. I also [16] _____ a couple of spare fast 16 GB memory cards [17] _____ I take a lot of photos. There's a back pocket on the bag here for maps or my smart phone. That's about it.

T7 | Grammar 2: Study the examples

1. a thief might be able **to** open the pockets
2. I **use** this lens pen **to** keep my lenses clean
3. I also **have/take** a pen and notebook **to take/make** notes of course.
4. There's a back pocket on the bag here **for** maps or my smart phone.

T8 | Grammar: Practice: Reorder the words in the sentences below

1. all gear room your there's here for.
2. ready I make have notes to my laptop.
3. my the information research I with to help need me.
4. are I use shots target to the check binoculars my on.
5. so I fire starter fire always start can a always magnesium me take with I a.

T9 | Speaking: Talk and Report 2

Make a list of things you need to do something, like a hobby or sport. Work in pairs. Show your list to your partner. Ask and answer about the items on the list e.g. *What do you need an X for? I use an X to/for ....*

Unit 32 Socialising 2

T1 | Speaking: Talk and Report

Work with a partner. Look at P32.1 – P32.5.

What can you see? Where are the people? What are they doing?

T2 | Grammar: Look at the examples

Which of these examples are about plans?

1. I went shopping yesterday.
2. I'm going camping with my kids in the summer.
3. I'm thinking of going to the cinema at the weekend. Do you fancy coming?
4. I was thinking about buying a new car.
5. I'm taking next week off.
6. I would like to have a holiday soon.
7. I'm enjoying my day off so far: I got up late; had a great breakfast and now I'm playing with the kids.
8. We're planning on going on safari to Namibia in summer.
9. Next week I hope to have time to finish repairing the roof.
10. I'm playing tennis with John tonight at seven.

T3 | Grammar: Study the Meaning 1

We can talk about plans, ideas and arrangements in different ways.

When we are thinking about ideas we can be **more** or **less positive** about them.

Reasonably positive:	**I'm thinking about going** to the cinema.
I have become less positive:	I **was thinking about going to** the cinema. [but now I'm not sure]
Potential: It's an option:	I **could go to** the cinema.

T4 | Grammar: Study the Meaning 2

There are different ways to **make suggestions**.

Making a suggestion:	Let's go to the cinema!
	How about going to the cinema?
	What about going to the cinema?
	Would you like to go to the cinema? [More formal]

T5 | Grammar: Study the Meaning 3

There is a process for **making decisions**:

Stage 1	Before the decision I consider my options	*I'm thinking about going to the cinema. But I could go to the opera. Or a bar.*
Stage 2	I make the decision	*Ok, I'll go to the cinema.*
Stage 3	The plan: I have decided	*I'm going to the cinema.*

T6 | Grammar: Study the Meaning 4

There is a process for **making arrangements.**

Stage 1	**Before** making an arrangement I consider our options:	Me:	*What to do? Play tennis with John (if he's free) or watch TV?*
Stage 2	I make a suggestion:	Me:	*John, **would you like to play** tennis this evening?*
Stage 3	The suggestion is accepted (or rejected):	John:	*Sure. That **would be** great.*
Stage 4	The decision: we **decide**:	Me:	*Super. **Let's meet** there are 7.*
		John:	*Ok. See you there.*
Stage 5	The arrangement: **after** we have decided:	Me to Eric:	*I'm playing tennis with John at 7.*

T7 | Speaking: Make plans and arrangements

1. Draw a calendar plan for the next two weeks.

Monday	
Tuesday	
Wednesday	
Thursday	
Friday	
Saturday	Sunday

Monday	
Tuesday	
Wednesday	
Thursday	
Friday	
Saturday	Sunday

2. Decide what you are going to do on five of the days e.g. go to the cinema, dentist, fishing etc.

3. Stand up, walk around and talk to everyone. Make an arrangement with five other people to meet and do something together. If you are busy at a certain time, tell the person asking what your plans are.

4. Report back to the class about what you plan to do and what arrangements you have made: *John and I are going to the cinema on Friday at 6 pm.*

Unit 33 Forces: Combat Engineers

Learn About Combat Engineers

T1 | Speaking: Talk and Report 1

Look at P33.1. What can you see?

T2 | Speaking: Talk and Report 2

1. What do combat engineers do?
2. How do they help the army fight wars?

T3 | Read and find out the answers to the questions in T2

Combat engineers are soldiers first and foremost and undergo basic combat training before doing specialised training. In some armies like the British Army they are known as "sappers"; in others like the Finnish army, "pioneers". They have a role across the battlefield: supporting the army during dry and wet gap crossing operations, building roads, building and destroying fighting positions and fortifications, clearing terrain obstacles and routes through minefields or using explosives to destroy bridges etc. They help the army to be mobile and help counter the mobility of the enemy.

Behind the front lines, engineers improve transport routes, construct camps and bases, build temporary airstrips, clear mines and conduct bomb disposal.

In the post-conflict reconstruction phase, engineers provide humanitarian support in areas like water production, electrical supply and infrastructure reconstruction, building hospitals etc.

Some of the skills engineers learn are:

*   Basic demolitions
*   Basic explosive hazards
*   Constructing wire obstacles
*   Fixed bridge building
*   Basic urban operations
*   Operating heavy equipment

Combat engineering areas of expertise include basic field engineering (from knots & lashings to building construction techniques), water supply, demolitions (using explosives), force protection (through the construction of protective structures and defensive obstacles), the location and clearance of explosive devices, and building bridges.

A combat engineer will need to be proficient in using a range of equipment from knives, entrenching tools and chainsaws to cement mixers, bulldozers, APCs (like the M1132 Engineer Squad Vehicle (ESV), which can be fitted with can be fitted with a bulldozer blade and mine-breaching devices), and bridging equipment like the Titan Armoured Bridge Layers, which is used to provide close bridging support.

[Text based on information from http://www.army.mod.uk/royalengineers/26391.aspx Crown Copyright]

T4 I Reading: Read Again and Answer

1. What is the difference between combat engineer, sapper and pioneer?
2. What is a wet gap crossing?
3. What do engineers do with fighting positions?
4. How do engineers help the air forces?
5. What kinds of things do engineers do after combat operations have finished?
6. Why should engineers be able to construct wire obstacles?
7. What is an ESV?

T5 I Language Analysis: Analyse the Text

T6I Listen and Read: Listen to a reading of the text

Which words do you need to practice saying? Which words do you need to learn?

T7 I Listening: Listen and Make Notes

Listen to this talk.

Make notes about Combat Engineer training and skills.

Training	Skills

Does the speaker agree with the text in T3? Check with your partner.

Then check with T33.1.

T8 I Consolidation Tasks

Unit 34 Talking about Individual Weapons

Present Simple | Present Perfect

T1 | Vocabulary: Parts of a Rifle and Pistol

What are the parts of a rifle and pistol called? Label the parts in P34.1 and P34.2. Check with P34.3 and P34.4. Also look at P34.5.

Cover up T3 before doing T2

T2 | Speaking: Individual Weapons

What individual weapons do these armies use?

US Army: _____

British Army: _____

Swiss Army: _____

T3 | Reading: Read the text to find out if you were right

The **US Army** uses the **M4** carbine. The M4 is chambered for a 5.56 mm NATO round, and is an air-cooled, gas-operated, magazine-fed carbine. It weighs 2.88 kg empty and 3.4 kg with a 30 round magazine. It is 840 mm long with the telescoping stock extended (756 mm stock retracted), with a barrel length of 370 mm. The rate of fire is 700–950 round/min and the muzzle velocity is 880 m/s. This gives it an effective range of about 500 m. It has standard iron sights and a Picatinny rail for other sights.

The **SA80 A2 L85 IW** has been the standard issue service rifle of the **British Armed Forces** since 1987. It is a bullpup design with the magazine behind the trigger, chambered for the standard 5.56 mm NATO round. The cyclic rate of fire is 610 to 775 rounds per minute. Muzzle velocity is 940 m/s and the effective range is up to 400 m. Its weight is 3.8 kg for the weapon only; 5.08 kg with SUS-AT (Sight Unit Small Arms Trilux) telescope and full 30 round magazine. The barrel length is 518 mm but it is 785 mm long (980 mm with bayonet) overall and can be fitted with a grenade launcher.

Switzerland uses the **SG 550** service rifle chambered in the 5.56 mm NATO round. It weighs 4.1 kg without the magazine. It is 998 mm long with a barrel length of 528 mm. It can be set on semi-automatic, 3-round burst or automatic fire. It can fire 700 rounds per minute; the standard magazine capacity is 20 rounds. It has a high muzzle velocity of 911 m/s and a good effective range of 600 m. It has standard dioptric sights and can mount optical and other sights on a

> Picatinny rail. A grenade launcher can be attached.

T4 | Language Analysis: Analyse the Text

T5| Listen and Read: Listen to a reading of the text

Which words do you need to practice saying? Which words do you need to learn?

T6 | Grammar: Comparisons: Complete the text below with these words

longer	shorter	higher	shorter	lower	both	lighter	compared

The American M4 carbine is [1] _____ than the British SL85 IW at 3.4 kg [2] _____ to 5 kg. They [3] _____use a standard 30 round magazine in the NATO 5.56 mm calibre. The M4 has a slightly [4] _____ muzzle velocity (880 m/s) than the SL85 IW (940 m/s) but a 100 m [5] _____ effective range even though the M4 barrel is much [6] _____ (370 mm) than the SL85 IW (518 mm). The M4's rate of fire is [7] _____ (700–950 round/min) than the SL85 IW (610 to 775 rounds per minute). The bullpup design of the SL85 IW makes it [8] _____ (780 mm) than the M4 with the stock extended (840 mm).

T7 | Speaking: What personal weapons do soldiers in your army use?

Work in groups. Prepare a briefing for your teacher on the personal weapons your army uses. In your briefing:

1. Describe the weapon.
2. Give technical details
3. Say what are the advantages and disadvantages of the weapon compared to the ones used in other armies.

T8 | Writing: Write a text about a weapon

Use these Fact Files from your Workbook: FF34.1 AK-74 | FF34.2 Makarov

FF34.3 SIG P75 | FF34.4 Glock 17

FF34.5 M9

Write texts about one or more of the weapons or write texts comparing two or more of the weapons and your army's individual weapons. You might want to use P34.6.

T9 | Speaking: Brief on an individual weapon from T8

Work alone. Make a short briefing on an individual weapon. In your briefing say: the weapon's name, the type, calibre, basic specifications and performance; finally, give your opinion about the weapon.

T10 | Consolidation Tasks

Unit 35 Films/Movies

T1 | Speaking: Talk and Report

What is your favourite movie? Why? What kind of film is it? Who stared in it? Tell the class about your partner's favourite film.

T2 | Vocabulary: Types of Film

Match the type of film below with the synopsis a – h.

western	thriller/action	horror	romantic comedy	war
samurai	musical	gangster	teen comedy	children's
romance	drama	historical	detective/whodunit	noir
cartoon	kung-fu	fantasy	science fiction	documentary

A	Ellen Ripley's escape vehicle is recovered fifty-seven years later and she is awakened from cryogenic stasis. Back on earth, nobody believes her story about the aliens on the planet LV-426. The Company had set up a colony on LV-426, however, all communication with the colony is lost. The Company sends Ripley with a team of tough, rugged space marines on a desperate rescue mission.
B	On October 3, 1993 nearly 100 U.S. Army Rangers, commanded by Capt. Mike Steele, were dropped by helicopter in the capital city of Mogadishu to capture two top lieutenants of a Somali warlord. This leads to a large firefight between the Rangers and hundreds of Somali gunmen, and the destruction of two U.S. Black Hawk helicopters.
C	NYPD cop John McClane goes to visit his wife Holly for Christmas in Los Angeles where she works for the Nakatomi Corporation. While they are at the Nakatomi headquarters for the Christmas party, a group of bank robbers led by Hans Gruber take control of the building and hold everyone, except John, hostage. John is forced to take matters into his own hands.
D	Vito Corleone is the ageing don of the Corleone family. His youngest son Michael returns home from WWII just in time to see the wedding of Connie Corleone (Michael's sister) to Carlo Rizzi. Michael just wants to live a normal life but becomes involved in a violent mob war against a drug dealer called Sollozzo which tears the Corleone family apart.
E	Abandoned in the jungle, baby Mowgli is raised by a family of wolves. As the boy grows older, the wise black panther Bagheera realizes Mowgli must be returned to his own kind in the nearby man-village. The young boy runs away from Bagheera and meets Baloo the bear. Mowgli is stolen by King Louis. He is

	rescued by Baloo and Bagheera but runs away again and finally has to face Shere Khan the tiger.
F	An ancient Ring of Power thought lost for centuries has been found, and through a strange twist in fate has been given to a small Hobbit named Bilbo. He eventually gives the ring to Frodo. When Gandalf the wizard discovers the Ring is in fact the One Ring of the Dark Lord Sauron, Frodo must make an epic quest to Mordor to the Cracks of Doom in order to destroy it once and for all and save Middle-Earth.
G	Five college students take time off to spend a peaceful vacation in a remote cabin in a forest. They discover a book and audio tape and read the incantations aloud. This releases the Evil Dead and the friends find themselves fighting to live until morning.
H	Ethan Edwards, returns from the Civil War to his brother's Texas ranch, hoping to find a home with his family. But Comanche Indian raiders kill his brother and his wife, and steal the children. Ethan sets out, along with his 1/8 Indian nephew Martin, on a years-long journey to rescue the surviving niece kidnapped by the Indians under Chief Scar.

T3 | Grammar: Which tenses are used in the reviews? Why?

T4 | Vocabulary: Talking about Films 1

Read the film review. Check you know the words in **bold**. Then answer the questions:

> The Godfather Part 2 **directed by** Francis Coppola is the second part of Mario Puzo's epic saga of the lives of the infamous Corleone family, which is now headed by Michael Corleone (**played by** Al Pacino). It is a film which outdoes its predecessor, "The Godfather". The film switches between the two parallel **storylines** of Michael's struggle over the family business and **flashbacks** of the life of young Vito Corleone (Robert De Niro, in a brilliant, **Oscar-winning performance**) and his rise to power. The film also **stars** Robert Duvall, Diane Keaton. Lee Strassberg and John Cazale give excellent **supporting performances.** Carmine Coppola's and Nino Rota's **score** is a **masterpiece** and the **cinematography** is superb. The film won six Oscars including Best Picture and Best Director.

1. Who wrote The Godfather Part 2?
2. Who starred in the film?
3. What kind of film is it?
4. Which awards did it win?
5. Have you seen the film? Would you like to see it?

T5 | Vocabulary: Talking about Films 2

Check you know the meaning of these words and phrases.

gripping	terrible	entertaining	laughable	incomprehensible
awful	violent	disappointing	a let down	a moving performance
boring	appalling	unbelievable	beautiful	a waste of time and money
exciting	rubbish	plot holes	nonsensical	the worst performance ever
fantastic	enjoyable	funny	powerful	badly/well written

Which are positive? Which are negative?

T6 | Vocabulary: Complete the sentences with words from T5

1. It was very _____ written. The plot was full of _____. I didn't understand it - it was completely _____.

2. I had great expectations for the film but it was very _____ and a complete waste of _____ and _____. I felt really let _____.

3. It was really _____ – hundreds of people were killed by the hero. Even though a lot of the stunts were completely _____ I loved it – it was _____.

4. She gave a really _____ performance. It was such a _____ and romantic story. I cried at the end.

5. I laughed all the way through the film. It was really _____ and _____. I really recommend you go and see it.

6. I didn't know what was going to happen next. It was really exciting and _____. I was really surprised at the ending.

T7 | Writing: Write a film review

Write a review of your **favourite** film. Include information about:

The plot	The stars and their characters	The director
Soundtrack etc.	Any awards that it won	Your opinion about the film

Use this structure to help you:

My favourite film is............................ It is a …........…........................... film. It stars .... as................................ It also stars................................as .... The film starts with .... Then...................... At the end............................ The cinematography is................ I ….................. the film score. The film won/didn't win................................ I …........... this film because …................................

Now write a review of the **worst** film you've ever seen.

T8 | Speaking: Tell the class about the worst film you've ever seen

Unit 36 Forces: Army Air Power

T1 | Speaking: Talk and Report

Look at P36.1 and P36.2. What is the connection between the two pictures?

T2 | Reading: Read And Answer

1. How can air power be used to support army operations?
2. What are "assets"?
3. What kind of aircraft can be used?
4. What is a FAC?
5. What three things does a FAC have to do?
6. What are the components of a US Army Division?
7. How many helicopters are there in a US Army full spectrum combat aviation brigade?

Air Power

Air power is used for many different kinds of army missions. It can be used to transport troops to and from the battlefield, to insert special ops forces behind enemy lines, for CASEVAC, and for reconnaissance and for close air support (CAS). An army unit might have its own organic aircraft or might have to call on special army units or on air force assets for support. Most army aviation uses helicopters but fixed wing aircraft like the A-10 A Warthog ground attack aircraft can also be used. High-altitude bombers can also be used for CAS because of the development of GPS guided weapons and laser-guided JDAM bombs.

Close Air Support

CAS is action by aircraft against targets in close proximity to friendly forces on the front line, or the Forward Edge of the Battle Area. Specialised personnel such as Forward Air Controllers (FACs) who are on the ground with the troops call in air strikes. The FAC directs air power to attack enemy targets, tries to avoid friendly fire incidents and makes sure that non-combatants are not targeted.

In the US army divisions are organised into a modular collection of brigade combat teams (BCTs), which can be deployed separately as required. The First Armoured Division, for example, has three BCTs, a combat aviation brigade (CAB), a division artillery brigade, and a sustainment brigade, which takes care of divisional support and logistics.

Combat Aviation Brigade

A full spectrum CAB fields military helicopters for a variety of missions. There are:

- Attack helicopters in an Attack Reconnaissance Battalion (three companies with 8 AH-64 Apaches each)
- Reconnaissance helicopters in an Attack Reconnaissance Squadron (three troops with 7 OH-58D Kiowa Warriors each)
- Medium-lift helicopters in an Assault Helicopter Battalion (three companies with 10 UH-60 Black Hawks each)
- Command capabilities in a Command Aviation Company or CAC (4 UH-60 Black Hawks and 4 EH-60s equipped with AN/ASC-38 Army Airborne Command and Control System [A2C2S])
- Heavy-lift helicopters in a Heavy Helicopter Company (three platoons with 4 CH-47 Chinooks each)
- MEDEVAC/CASEVAC capability in an Air Ambulance Medical Company or AAMC (five platoons with 3 HH-60Ms each).

A CAB also has a selection of UAVs such as the MQ-1C Gray Eagle and RQ-7B Shadow for reconnaissance. [Adapted from FM 3-04.111 Aviation Brigades]

T3 | Language Analysis: Analyse the Text

T4 | Listen and Read: Listen to a reading of the text

Which words do you need to practice saying? Which words do you need to learn?

T5 | Listening: Listen and Make Notes

Listen to this talk about an aircraft. Make notes about:

- Name of aircraft
- Weapons carried
- Special features
- Performance

Check with your partner. Then check with T36.1

T6 | Writing: Write a text about an aircraft

Use these Fact Files from your Workbook: FF36.1 Harrier | FF36.2 SU-25
FF36.3 Tornado | FF36.4 Super Étendard

Write texts about one or more of the planes or write texts comparing two or more of the planes.

T7 | Speaking: Brief on an aircraft

Work alone. Make a short briefing on an aircraft from T6 or another aircraft you know about.

In your briefing say: the aircraft's name, the type, basic specifications and performance; give your opinion about the aircraft.

T8 | Consolidation Tasks

Unit 37 Talking about Sport 1

T1 | Speaking: Talk and Report 1

Look at P37.1. What can you see?

T2 | Speaking: Talk and Report 2

1. Do you like to do sport? Which? Why?
2. Do you like to watch sport? Which? Why?

T3 | Vocabulary: Check the words and then complete the text with the words given

bat	batsmen	batter	classifying	courts	doubles
individual	kicking	pitches	racquets	score	team

There are many different ways of [1] _____ sports. There are [2] _____ sports using a ball like football (or soccer) , rugby, American football, field hockey. These are played on [3] _____ (in football and rugby) or on fields (in hockey and American football) and have goals at either end. The teams try to [4] _____ goals by putting the ball into the back of the net of the opposing goal (in football and hockey), or score a touchdown (in American football) or a try (in rugby), and then converting a kick between the goal posts for further points (in rugby), or [5] _____ the ball between the posts for a field goal. Other team sports with a ball also involve a [6] _____ – like cricket and baseball. Cricket is played by two teams of 11 players on an oval pitch. Two [7] _____ at a time go out to bat against the other team and try to score runs. A bowler bowls at one batsman, who tries to hit the ball away from the wicket. Each batsman has to safely run from one wicket to another to score one run. Baseball is played on a diamond with one [8] _____ facing the opposing team and trying to make a home run around the four bases. Other ball sports are played on [9] _____ with nets (like tennis, badminton and volleyball) or with baskets (like basketball), or in a walled court (like squash). Tennis, badminton and squash (played with [10] _____) can be an [11] _____ sport or played with a partner in [12] _____ . Volleyball and basketball are team sports.

T4 | Vocabulary: Check the words and then complete the text with the words given

competitions	consists	combines	distances
enclosed	events	over	road

Track and field sports (like athletics) include running various [1] _____ around a stadium track (like the 100 m sprint and 400 m races), or longer distance [2] _____ races like the 26 mile marathon. In the field [3] _____ by the track there are places for [4] _____ like the shot put, javelin, pole vault, long and high jump. A triathlon involves running, swimming and cycling; a pentathlon has [5] _____ in shooting, swimming, fencing, equestrianism, and cross country running. The decathlon takes place [6] _____ two days and [7] _____ ten track and field events. Day 1 [8] _____ of the 100 m sprint; long jump; shot put; high jump and 400 m race. Day 2 includes the 110 m hurdles, discus throw, pole vault, javelin throw and 1500 m race.

T5 | Vocabulary: Check the words, and then use them to complete the text

powered	shooting	endurance	indoor
variant	martial	strength	lifting

Water sports include swimming, water polo, rowing, canoeing and kayaking and sailing. There are [1] _____ sports like weight [3] _____ and [4] _____ sports like cycle road races, like the Tour de France, and ultra running competitions. Some sports use [5] _____ machines, like in motor racing – motorcars (like Formula 1 and NASCAR), and motorcycles – and in yachting – like the America's Cup. [6] _____ sports include swimming, gymnastics and ice-hockey and squash and badminton already mentioned. Football can also be played inside in its five-a-side [5] _____. Most [7] _____ arts competitions are held inside, like boxing, wrestling, karate, kung-fu, aikido, fencing, judo for example, though archery and pistol and rifle [8] _____ events can be done outside.

T6 | Listen and Read: Listen to a reading of the text

Which words do you need to practice saying? Which words do you need to learn?

T7 | Speaking: Talk and Report 3

1. Which of the sports above have you tried?
2. Which of these sports can you do in your town?
3. Which of these sports does your army have teams for?
4. Which of these sports are best for soldiers?
5. In which of these sports can men and women compete equally?

T8 | Consolidation Tasks

Unit 38 On the Range

T1 | Speaking: Talk and Report 1

Look at P38.1 and P38.2. What can you see?

T2 | Speaking: Talk and Report 2

1. Why do soldiers need to practice on a firing range?
2. What safety procedures are there on the range?
3. What should you do?
4. What should you **not** do?

T3 | Reading: Order these range rules. The first and last have been done for you.

	All shooters are responsible for their rounds staying within the confines of the range.
	Always keep firearms pointed in a safe direction i.e. away from people and at the target backstop or bullet trap down range.
	Always keep your finger off the trigger and outside the trigger guard, until ready to fire or until you hear the command "commence firing".
	Always keep your gun unloaded until you are in a position on the firing line and and the range has been cleared for live firing: when the range is declared "hot."
1	Always wear eye and ear protection.
	Be sure of the target and what is beyond it before you start shooting.
	Be sure the firearm and ammunition are compatible.
	Cold range: you must check with others to ensure firearms are unloaded, actions open and firearms laid down on the shooting bench (they are "benched") before going down range. No one is permitted to handle firearms or stand at the firing line while there is a cold range for any reason.
	Immediately stop shooting when anyone calls "cease firing."
	Know how the firearm operates.
	Never eat, drink or smoke on the firing line.
	Obey the range officer at all times.
	Only shoot at the target in line with your position on the firing line.
	Only shooters are permitted on the firing line.
	Only use one calibre of ammunition when shooting at one time. If you are using different firearms with different calibres, use one at a time and pack that firearm and ammunition away before using the next one.
	Shooters may only move safe guns to and from the firing line when the

	range is "hot."
	Check down range before the range is declared "hot". When the range is hot, that means shooters may fire.
18	You should wash your hands and face after shooting in cold water.

T4 | Vocabulary: Range Vocabulary

Explain these words and their purpose:

firing line/point	wind flags	bench	butt/backstop	target

T5 | Speaking: Talk and Report 3

What are the firearm qualification requirements in your army?

How much shooting practice do soldiers receive?

T6 | Vocabulary: Complete the text below with these words

pop-up	malfunction	engage	fundamentals	sight	expert	control
rounds	qualification	stances	reassemble	grip	squeeze	supported

After learning how to disassemble, clean, and [1] _____ your weapon, as well as safe handling and [2] _____ procedures you will learn and practice the four [3] _____ of Army marksmanship. The steady position teaches you how to correctly [4] _____ and handle your weapon during different firing and non-firing [5] _____. The aiming fundamental includes correct [6] _____ alignment and proper eye focus: you should focus on the front sight with the target blurry, and take into account factors like distance and the wind (shown by wind flags on the range). You must know and practice proper breath [7] _____ to hold your breath for a natural pause. When you fire a weapon you gently [8] _____ the trigger rather than pulling it. The US Army Marksmanship Qualification Course has 40 [9] _____ targets set up from 25/50 meters to 300 meters that you must [10] _____ in the order they show. There are 20 targets prone [11] _____, 10 targets prone unsupported, and 10 targets kneeling. At some points multiple targets will show at the same time and you have to engage all targets before they drop. You have forty [12] _____ for the forty targets. Hitting 23 to 29 of the targets will earn you the the marksmanship [13] _____. If you hit 30 to 35, you will qualify for the sharpshooter badge, but to get an [14] _____ badge, you must hit 36 to 40 of the targets.

[Source: Adapted from FM 3-22.9 Rifle Marksmanship]

Are these requirements the same as in your army?

T7 | Speaking: Prepare and present a training plan and schedule for your unit

Work in groups and draw up a firearms training plan. Present your plan the class.

T8 | Consolidation Tasks

Unit 39 Forces: Intelligence

Present Simple | Modal Verbs | Past Tenses | Active and Passive

T1 | Speaking: Talk and Report 1

Look at P39.1 – P39.4. What can you see? What is the connection?

T2 | Speaking: Talk and Report 2

1. Why is military intelligence important?
2. What sources of intelligence are there?

T3 | Reading: Read and find out the answers to the questions in T2

Military intelligence officers collect information and analyse it. They help commanders so that they have greater situational awareness and can make better decisions. They use intelligence systems and data from a range of sources. These sources include:

- **Imagery Intelligence**: The collection and analysis of photographs from satellites, reconnaissance flights and UAVs.

- **Human intelligence**: The collection and analysis of information from spies, informants, civil affairs interactions, interrogations of detainees and POWs, reports from the front line and reconnaissance patrols.

- **Signals intelligence**: The collection and analysis of information from voice and data transmissions.

An **All-Source Intelligence** specialist gathers information from intelligence, surveillance, and reconnaissance [ISR] operations and provides intelligence "product" and advice to commanders.

Counter-intelligence is about detecting and countering the intelligence operations of the opposition.

Intelligence Analysts and Officers use information to determine changes in enemy capabilities, their vulnerabilities, and probable courses of action in the future. They assess risks associated with enemy, friendly and neutral actors' courses of action, as well as trying to counter and neutralize intelligence threats. They need to determine the significance and reliability of raw intelligence.

There are three levels of intelligence. **Strategic intelligence** is about the state of a foreign nation's economy, their military capabilities, and a political assessment of their intentions, as well as an assessment of non-state actor capabilities and intentions. **Operational intelligence** supports a force commander during the operation. **Tactical intelligence** involves briefing patrols on the current situation and threats in the AOO. Intelligence officers debrief patrols after operations and analyse this information.

T4 | Reading: Read Again and Answer

1. How do military intelligence officers help with situational awareness?
2. Can intelligence eliminate uncertainty?
3. What is HUMINT?
4. What is IMINT?
5. What is SIGINT?
6. What is ISR?
7. What is "product"?
8. What kind of risks do intelligence officers assess?
9. Why does raw intelligence need to be assessed as being reliable?
10. What are the differences between strategic, operational and tactical intelligence?

T5 | Language Analysis: Analyse the Text

T6 | Listen and Read: Listen to a reading of the text

Which words do you need to practice saying? Which words do you need to learn?

T7 | Listening: Listen and Make Notes

Listen to this talk. Make notes under two headings: **1. Facts 2. Opinions**
Listen and write down the facts the speaker says, and his opinions. Listen again and write down the exact words which tell you - fact or opinion. Check with your partner.

T8 | Listening: Transcript Task

Complete the text with the correct verb forms and then listen to check.

There [1] _____ never be one hundred percent certainty about what the enemy will do. In World War 2 intelligence often suggested that Hitler [2] _____ do something, only for him to change his mind at the last moment. The intelligence officers [3] _____ blamed for not getting the dates of the invasion of Russia correct but they [4] _____ get the dates correct. Then the dates were changed as the operation [5] _____ postponed.

Check with T39.1

T9 | Speaking: Intel requirement

Work in groups. You are a company sized force on the front lines in a mountainous area of your country during a war with an enemy country. What intelligence do you need before you launch your next attack? Brief the class on your requirements.

T10 | Consolidation Tasks

Unit 40 Talking about Sport 2

Present Simple I Active and Passive I Modal Verbs

T1 I Speaking: Talk and Report 1

1. Which indoor sports do you remember from **Unit 37**?
2. Which outdoor sports do you remember?
3. Which martial arts do you remember?
4. Which team sports do you remember?
5. Which sports are in the Triathlon and Decathlon?

T2 I Vocabulary: Check the words and then complete the text with the words given

rifle	cold	depends	Biathlon

Winter sports include skiing (cross-country and downhill), ski-jumping, ice skating, snowboarding and the bobsled and luge. The winter [1] _____ combines cross-country skiing and [2] _____ shooting. Most winter sports are held outside and [3] _____ on snow and [4] _____ temperatures, except for ice-hockey and skating, which are held in ice arenas.

T3 I Vocabulary: Check the words and then complete the text with the words given

catch	cheat	drugs	inherent	rock	samples	scandals

Extreme sports have a high level of [1] _____ danger and includes such sports as wakeboarding, waterskiing, gliding, rallying, motocross, surfing, windsurfing, kiteboarding, parachuting, skateboarding, mountain biking, as well as non-vehicle extreme sports like [2] _____ climbing, canyoning, ice climbing, and parkour.

Doping [3] _____ where athletes try to [4] _____ by taking performance enhancing [5] _____ regularly hit certain sports like cycling and athletics. The sports governing bodies try to [6] _____ cheats by taking regular blood and urine [7] _____ from athletes in training and during competitions.

T4 | Vocabulary: Check the words and then complete the text with the words given

beat	final	hold	judges	lose
national	outstanding	part	physiotherapists	playing
referees	rules	stages	win	winning

Most organised sports have clubs and federations, who make the [1]_____ for the sports and [2] _____ competitions. Competitions can be local, regional, [3] _____ and international (like the European championships) as well as global – like the Olympics, Athletics World Championships and football World Cup. Clubs or individuals or teams take [4]_____ in the championships and there are usually [5] _____ to the competition. There might be many heats for runners leading up to a [6] _____ for the fastest, or rounds of competition leading to quarter-finals, semi-finals and finally the final, as in football. Matches and competitions are controlled by [7] _____ and linesmen (e.g. football), umpires (cricket), umpires and referees (tennis) and [8] _____ (athletics). Teams and sportsmen and women compete to [9] _____ the other team, player or athlete and [10] _____ the match, game, medal, trophy or competition. Professional teams and individual athletes have managers, coaches and [11] _____ to help them train and perform better. Some athletes and teams turn in an [12] _____ performance and win, while others are disappointing and [13] _____ or are defeated. The winners have the satisfaction of [14] _____while the losers have the satisfaction of [14] _____ the game.

T5 | Listen and Read: Listen to a reading of the texts

Which words do you need to practice saying? Which words do you need to learn?

T6 | Writing: Write about a sport you like

Include:

The sport's name	How it is played	Why it is a good to take part in
Who plays it	How you win	Why it is a good to watch
Where it is played	The equipment you need	What competitions are there

T7 | Speaking: Talk and Report 2

Talk to your partner and find out about their favourite sport. Ask your partner for details like where they play/do the sport, how often they play/do it, where they play/do it etc. Then tell the class what you found out.

T8 | Consolidation Tasks

Unit 41 Forces: Civil Affairs

Present Tenses | Active And Passive Verb Forms

"Civil Affairs Officers play a key role in peacekeeping operations, and are an essential part of our "peacekeeping toolkit", as we work with local communities and authorities to bring stability and help them build the foundations for lasting peace."

Hervé Ladsous Under-Secretary-General, Department of Peacekeeping Operations [DKPO]

T1 | Speaking: Talk and Report

Look at P41.1 and P41.2. What can you see?

T2 |Before You Read: Answer the Questions

1. What is civil affairs?
2. What do civil affairs officers do on peacekeeping missions?
3. Why might this be important?
4. Why might it be important to "win hearts and minds"?

T3 | Reading: Read and find out the answers to the questions in T2

In 2008, DPKO approved a Policy Directive on Civil Affairs for the first time. The policy sets out three core roles for civil affairs in UN peacekeeping. These depend on the operation context and mandate:

*   Role one: Cross-mission liaison, monitoring and facilitation at the local level
*   Role two: Confidence-building, conflict management and reconciliation
*   Role three: Support to the restoration and extension of state authority

Under role one, civil affairs components liaise with local communities and authorities on behalf of the mission. They coordinate with and facilitate the work of partners, gather information, monitor the situation on the ground and conduct analysis. Under role two, civil affairs undertakes a range of activities aimed at supporting the development of social and civic conditions for peace, as well as popular engagement and confidence ["hearts and minds"] in the peace process. This includes facilitating dialogue between interest groups, direct outreach to the population and working with civil society groups. Under role three, civil affairs components provide operational support to the restoration of state authority and administrative functions, in close coordination with other partners.

In each of the roles they perform, Civil Affairs Officers are primarily enablers, facilitators and problem-solvers. They look for opportunities to support the work of other actors (particularly local actors), to make connections and to help build on existing dynamics.

The activities of civil affairs are intended to support the implementation of the mandate as a whole, contributing to the core functions of multidimensional UN peacekeeping operations. Civil affairs can facilitate or directly implement tasks such as the protection of civilians. Civil affairs components can also directly implement specifically mandated tasks. These are often in areas that affect relationships between citizens, or relationships between citizens and the state.

[Adapted from p 23 UN DPKO/DFS Civil Affairs Handbook 2012]

T4 | Language Analysis: Analyse the Text

T5 | Listen and Read: Listen to a reading of the texts

Which words do you need to practice saying? Which words do you need to learn?

T6 | Vocabulary: Complete the phrases from the text

1.	core	_____
2.	range of	_____
3.	direct	_____
4.	operational	_____
5.	administrative	_____
6.	close	_____
7.	look for	_____
8.	build	_____
9.	core	_____
10.	affect	_____

Check with the text.

T7 | Listening: Listen and Make Notes

Listen to this talk.

Make notes under two headings: **1. Facts 2. Opinions**

Listen and write down the facts the speaker says and his opinions.

Listen again and write down the exact words which tell you - fact or opinion.

Check with your partner. Then check with T41.1

T8 | Consolidation Tasks

Unit 42 Forces: Special Forces 1

Past Tenses I Passive Verb Forms

T1 I Speaking: Talk and Report

Look at P42.1 – P42.4. What can you see?

T2 I Vocabulary: Complete the paragraph

Check you know the meaning of these words:

insurgency	unconventional	demolition	hostage	covert	counter

Complete the paragraph with the correct words.

Special Forces and Special Operations Forces are units trained to perform
[1] _____ missions like airborne operations, counter-[2] _____,
[3] _____-terrorism, [4] _____ operations, [5] _____ rescue, intelligence operations, and sabotage and [6] _____, support of air-force operations.

T3 I Reading: Read and Answer 1

Read the text and answer the questions below.

1.   Who first asked for (modern) special forces?
2.   What was the first unit formed?
3.   How many soldiers were in each Commando?
4.   Where were the Commandos trained?
5.   Are the Commandos special forces?

Before WW2 there were scout and ranger units in many armies, but modern
Special Forces date from 1940 when Winston Churchill called for "*specially
trained troops of the hunter class, who can develop a reign of terror down the enemy
coast.*" The first Commando raid took place on 23 June 1940, and a Special Service Brigade of 12 Commandos was formed. Each Commando had 450 men organised into 75 man troops divided into 15 man sections. Volunteers had to be
physically fit, and the training in the mountains of Scotland was rigorous and
realistic, with live fire exercises. They had to learn about weapons, land navigation, unarmed combat, small boat operations and about river crossings. Now,
the Royal Marine Commandos are considered to be a special-purpose infantry
unit rather than a Special Forces unit.

T4 I Reading: Read and Answer 2

Read the text and answer the questions below.

1.   Whose idea was it to form the Special Air Service?

2. Where did they first operate?

3. Was the unit successful?

4. What were the Chindits?

5. Where did the Americans get the idea for their Special Forces?

6. Who controls US Special Forces?

British Special Force units such as the Parachute Regiment, Special Air Service (SAS), and Special Boat Service (SBS) were formed in World War 2 by men who had served in, or were inspired by, the Commandos. The SAS was formed by David Stirling in North Africa. He convinced General Ritchie, Deputy Commander Middle East, to suggest the idea of a unit for missions behind German and Italian lines to the theatre commander, General Auchinleck. Its first mission, in November 1941, was a disaster: 22 men, a third of the unit, were killed or captured. Later, in 1942, the SAS attacked Bouerat and Benghazi harbours and Al-Berka airbase with better results. In Burma, the Chindits, long range penetration groups operating from bases deep behind Japanese lines, developed jungle warfare expertise which would be invaluable in later campaigns like the Malay counter-insurgency (1948-1960).

The United States Army Rangers were modelled on the British Commandos, and Merrill's Marauders, another American unit, were modelled on the Chindits and took part in similar operations in Burma. Modern US Special Operations Forces include the "Green Berets" - Army Special Forces, Army Rangers, Navy SEALs, Marine Special Operations, and Special Operations Aviation units. These all operate under the umbrella of the United States Special Operations Command (SO-COM), which oversees the various Special Operations Commands of the Army, Navy, Air Force and Marine Corps.

T5 | Language Analysis: Analyse the Text

T6 | Listen and Read: Listen to a reading of the texts

Which words do you need to practice saying? Which words do you need to learn?

T7| Listening: Listen and Make Notes

Listen to this talk. Make notes under two headings: **1. Facts 2. Opinions**. Listen and write down the facts the speaker says and his opinions. Listen again and write down the exact words which tell you - fact or opinion. Check with your partner. Then check with T42.1.

T8 | Speaking: Talk and Report

Does your army have special forces?

Brief your teacher on the units, strength, role and missions etc.

T9 | Consolidation Tasks

Unit 43 Describing People's Clothes

Learn how to describe what people are wearing and carrying

T1 I Speaking: Talk and Report 1

Look at P43.1. What can you see?

T2 I Vocabulary: Clothing

Check you know the meaning of these words. Look at the pictures (P) to help you.

waistcoat (GB) vest (US)	P43.2	jacket	P43.2/3/4/5/14	suit	P43.2
shirt (m.) blouse (f.)	P43.2/6	trousers	P43.2/6	t-shirt	P43.7
sweater/pullover/jumper	P43.8	fleece	P43.9	raincoat	P43.10
rain jacket	P43.11	skirt	P43.12	dress	P43.13

T3 I Vocabulary: What is the difference?

chinos jeans	trousers (GB) pants (US) slacks (US)	shorts (GB)	pants (GB) underpants (GB + US) (m.) shorts (US) (m.)	panties (f.)

T4 I Vocabulary: Islamic clothing: Check you know the meaning.

thawb/thobe	P43.15	burqa	P43.16

T5 I Speaking: Talk and Report 2

What clothes do people in your country wear? When do they wear them?

T6 I Vocabulary: Parts of Clothing

Check you know the meaning of these words. Look at the pictures (P) to help you.

lapel	P43.3/17	buttons	P43.3/6/7	collar	P43.4/5/6	cuff	P43.4/5/18
press-studs	P43.5	pocket	P43.4/5/6	loops	P43.6	zip/ zipper	P43.4/9
lining	P43.17	hood	P43.11/14	hem	P43.18	seam	P43.18
patch/badge	P43.18	velcro	P43.19				

What should you pay special attention to when searching someone at a checkpoint?

T7 I Vocabulary: Headgear

Check you know the meaning of these words. Look at the pictures (P) to help you.

baseball cap	P43.20	watch cap	P43.20	hijab	P43.22
broad-brimmed hat	P43.20	keffiyeh	P43.21	niqab	P43.23
turban	P43.24				

T8 | Vocabulary: Footwear

Check you know the meaning of these words.

walking boots	P43.25	high-heels	P43.26	sandals	P43.27	boots	P43.28
Wellingtons/ wellies	P43.29	flip-flops	P43.30	trainers	P43.31	shoes	P43.32

Which footwear do people in your country wear? When do they wear them?

T9 | Vocabulary: Accessories

Check you know the meaning of these words.

ring	P43.33	necklace	P43.33	bangle	P43.33	glasses	P43.34	gloves	P43.35
wallet	P43.36	bracelet	P43.33	earrings	P43.33	buckle	P43.37	belt	P43.37

Which accessories do men/women in your country wear? When do they wear them?

T10| Vocabulary: Bags

Check you know the meaning of these words. What is the difference?

handbag	P43.38	briefcase	P43.39	backpack	P43.40	shoulder bag	P43.41

T11 | Vocabulary: What is it made of?

Check you know the meaning of the words below and agree on a translation.

cotton	wool	nylon	polyester	leather	plastic	canvas	rubber

What are the clothes and footwear usually made of in your country? Think of five examples of things made of the material above: e.g. B*elts are usually made of leather*

T12 | Speaking: Describing clothing

Are there any clothes people in your country wear which are not in T3?
Explain to your teacher about these items of clothing.

Language Reminder
Men/women in my country/region wear a _____.
It is a kind of _____.
It is made of _____ (material).
It is usually _____ (colour).
You wear it _____(how you wear it).
It is worn every day/It is only worn on special occasions.
It is very comfortable to wear because _____.
I like/don't like wearing it because _____.

T13| Vocabulary: Writing a description

Look at P43.42 to P43.58. Choose a pictures. Write a description of what the person (or people) in the picture looks like *and* is wearing.

Unit 44 Forces: Special Forces 2

Present and Past Tenses | Passive Verb Forms | Prepositions

T1 | Speaking: Talk and Report 1

Look at P44.1 and P44.2. What can you see?

T2 | Speaking: Talk and Report 2

What do you remember about special forces from **Unit 42**?

T3 | Vocabulary: Complete the paragraph

Check you know the meaning of these words:

risk x 2	clandestine	conducted x 2	manned
unconventional	conventional x 2	strategic	

Complete the paragraph with the correct words.

> Special operations are military activities [1] _____ by specially designated, organized, trained, and equipped forces, [2] _____ with selected personnel, using [3] _____ tactics, techniques, and modes of employment. These activities may be [4] _____ across the full range of military operations, independently or with [5] _____ forces, to help achieve the desired end-state. Politico-military considerations may require [6] _____ or covert techniques and the acceptance of a degree of political or military [7] _____ not associated with operations by [8] _____ forces. Special Operations deliver [9] _____ or operational-level results or are executed where significant political [10] _____ exists.
>
> [NATO Allied Joint Publication (AJP) 3.5]

T4 | Grammar: Complete the paragraph with the correct propositions

at	by x 4	during	in x 7	of x 2	on x 3	out	to

> Famous operations and campaigns [1] _____ Special Forces include the successful anti-communist counter insurgency [2] _____ Malaya, Operation Entebbe – the hostage-rescue mission carried [3] _____ [4] _____ Israeli commandos [5] _____ Entebbe Airport [6] _____ Uganda [7] _____ 4 July 1976, the storming [8] _____ the Iranian Embassy [9] _____ the SAS during the Embassy siege (30 April [10] _____ 5 May 1980), the SAS Bravo Two Zero patrol [11] _____ the 1ˢᵗ Gulf War, the campaign [12] _____ US Special Forces [13] _____ the 2001 war [14] _____ Afghanistan, the SEAL raid to kill Osama bin Laden [15] _____ Abbottabad [16] _____ Pakistan [17] _____ May 2,

2011, and the SEAL rescue [18] _____ Captain Phillips [19] _____ the *Maersk Alabama* hijacking [20] _____ 12 April 2009.

T5 | Listening: Listen and Make Notes

Make notes about the operations and the speaker's opinion about them.

OPERATION 1	Operational Details:
OPERATION 2	Operational Details:
Speaker's Opinion:	

Check with your partner. Then check with T44.1.

Unit 45 Weapons and Platforms: Infantry Fighting Vehicle

Present Simple I Active and Passive I Modals I Comparatives

T1 I Speaking: Talk and Report 1

Look at P45.1. What can you see?

T2 I Speaking: Talk and Report 2

1. What are the characteristics of an IFV?
2. What is a "technical"?

T3 I Reading: Read and answer the questions in T2

An infantry fighting vehicle (IFV) is an armoured fighting vehicle (AFV) used to carry a combat infantry squad into battle and provide direct fire support using an integral or organic cannon of at least 20 mm calibre. IFVs have more armour than APCs and some have ports which allow soldiers to fire their personal weapons from inside. IFVs give protection to soldiers during movement and provide fire support. They give a squad the ability to manoeuvre more effectively as part of combined arms operations. IFVs transport infantrymen to the fight where they dismount and fight with the support of the IFV cannon and other weapons.

Most IFVs are tracked and can be armed with a 20 to 40 mm caliber autocannon, coaxial machine guns, anti-tank guided missiles (ATGMs), and smoke and grenade launchers. Some IFVs have modular armour of various thicknesses which can be changed for specific roles or missions. IFVs can engage unarmoured and lightly armoured vehicles, strong points, infantry, helicopters and low-flying aircraft. There are some Heavy Infantry Fighting Vehicle's (HIFV) based on MBT chassis but, generally, IFVs are not a match for MBTs. They offer a good compromise between mobility, protection, and firepower and are especially useful in low intensity conflicts and peacekeeping operations.

Insurgents, guerrillas, and militias might improvise a fighting vehicle (a non-standard tactical vehicle - NSTV) by modifying a civilian vehicle such as a Toyota Hilux or other such flat-bed pick-up truck. They mount a machine gun, anti-aircraft gun, anti-tank weapon, mortar, or other support weapon on the back of the vehicle, and some protective armour may be added. These are generally known as "technicals", but are also known as "battlewagons" or "gunwagons". While they provide speed and mobility for light troop deployment and a degree of fire support, as well as prestige for the users, they cannot match tanks or IFVs in an engagement. They are also extremely vulnerable to air strikes as they have little to no armour protection. Regular special operations forces might also use NSTVs, which are inspired by SAS jeeps from WW2.

T4 | Reading: Read Again and Answer

1. What kind of weapons can an IFV have?
2. What kind of targets can an IFV engage?
3. What are IFVs used for?
4. What are "technicals" used for?
5. What are the differences between IFVs and improvised fighting vehicles?

T5 | Language Analysis: Analyse the Text

T6 | Listen and Read: Listen to a reading of the text

Which words do you need to practice saying? Which words do you need to learn?

T7 | Listening: Listen and Make Notes.

Listen to this talk. Complete the information below about the two IFVs.

IFV 1
Name:

Weight:

Max speed:

Range:

Armour protection:

Armament:

Other information:

IFV 2
Name:

Weight:

Max speed:

Range:

Armour protection:

Armament:

Other information:

Check with your partner. Then check with T45.1.

T8 | Speaking: Talk and Report

Discuss with your partner. Which is the best IFV from T7? Why?

T9 | Consolidation Tasks

Unit 46 Giving Directions in an Urban Environment

Present Simple | Present Continuous | Modal Verbs

T1 | Speaking: Talk and Report

Look at P46.1: what can you see? How would you give directions to points B, C and D from A? Check with P46.2.

T2 | Vocabulary: What do these words mean?

junction	crossroads	past	traffic lights	turning	exit

T3 | Vocabulary: Study the diagram below

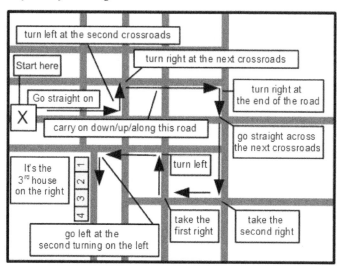

T4 | Listening: Listen and mark the route described

Look at the map on the next page. Listen to the directions from **Point A**. Draw the route on the map. Where do you end up? Check with the key in P46.3 and T46.1.

T5 | Vocabulary: Complete the text below

Complete the text and draw the route on the map. Where are you? Check with P46.4.

on	along	down	follow	hand
out	side	take	turn x 4	turning x 3

Start at **I**. Go [1] _____ of the house and [2] _____ left down the street. You are heading SSE, almost south. [3] _____ left at the junction and head down to the main road. [4] _____ right there and [5] _____ this road to the second [6] _____ to the right. [7] _____ right here and walk [8] _____ this road, to the west, to the third [9] _____ to the right. [10] _____ the third [11] _____ to the right and walk [12] _____ the road. There are

two big buildings [13] _____ the right-[14] _____
[15] _____ of the road. You want the smaller of these two buildings.

T6 | Speaking: Give Directions

Draw a route on the map from one point to another. Do **not** do show the route to your partner. Give directions to your partner. Your partner should draw the route on their map. Compare maps to check. Then change roles: listen to your partner and draw their route on your map. Repeat for more practice.

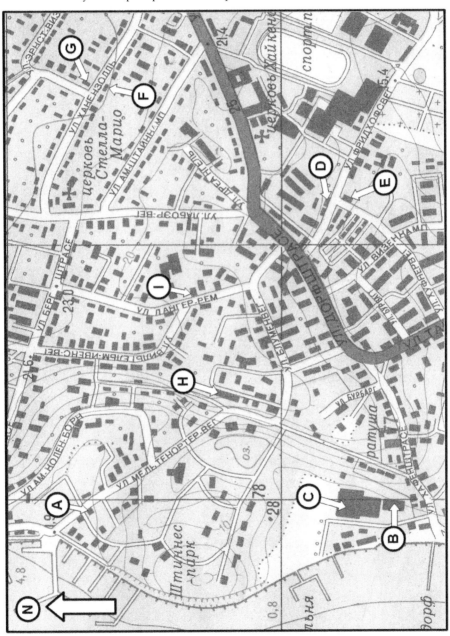

Unit 47 Weapons and Platforms: Main Battle Tanks

Learn More About Tanks

T1 | Speaking: Talk and Report

Look at P47.1. What can you see?

T2 | Vocabulary: Check you know the meaning of these words

coaxial gun	hatch or cupola	gun turret	drive sprocket	continuous track
sights	hull	link	side skirt	engine compartment
main gun	road wheel	muzzle	driver's hatch	radio antennae
range	turret ring	periscope	rounds	crew
primary	secondary	armour	armament	projectile

Use pictures P47.2 and P47.3 to help you.

T3 | Vocabulary: Complete the text with words from T2 and other words

Most modern MBTs look very similar with two continuous linked [1] _____ on either side of the vehicle rather than wheels, and a [2] _____ mounted main gun. The [3] _____ turns on a [4] _____ which gives it 360 degrees of traverse. The [5] _____ compartment is usually at the rear of the tank [6] _____. Access to the tank is through [7] _____ which can be sealed and the tanks provide protection against NBC warfare. Driver, gunner and commander can see through [8] _____ and a range of optical and thermal [9] _____. MBT performance is a compromise between the size of the main [10] _____, the thickness of the [11] _____ protection, and speed. The US Abrams, British Challenger 2 and Leopard 2 all have 120 mm main [12] _____ but the British L30A1 is a rifled [13] _____ with 49 [14] _____, while both the German and US guns are smoothbores with 42 [15] _____. All of these tanks have turret mounted main [16] _____ and two (Leopard and Challenger) or three (Abrams) machine guns as [17] _____ armament. Most MBT have a [18] _____ machine gun mounted next to the main gun which fires parallel to the main armament. The commander may have a [19] _____ gun by his [20] _____, or one mounted in a copula and this can be fired remotely. The Challenger 2 weighs 75 tonnes with add-on armour modules, which is [21] _____ than the Abrams (65 tonnes) and Leopard 2 (62.3 tonnes). The Leopard 2 emphasises [22] _____– 72 km/h – compared to the Challenger 2 (59 km/h) and Abrams (67 km/h). These three tanks all have a [23] _____ of four (commander, gunner, loader, driver), though some MBTs such as the French AMX Leclerc and Russian T-14 Armata have a [24] _____ of three and use an auto-loader. The Challenger and Leopard 2 both have an operational [25] _____ of 550 km compared to the Abrams' 426 km. Tank protection is in its [26] _____, which can be steel, composite ceramic and alloys, explosive reactive [27] _____, or slat [28] _____, and electronic countermeasures against missile attack. Most of the armour is concentrated at the front of the vehicle in a sloped glacis plate but the side and tracks can be protected by armoured [29] _____.

T4 | Reading: Read and Answer

Read the text in T3 and answer these questions:

1. What is the difference between the main armament of the Leopard, Abrams and Challenger tanks?
2. Which tank is the lightest/heaviest?
3. Which is the slowest/fastest?
4. Which has the shortest/longest range?
5. Which tank has an autoloader?

T5 | Listen and Read: Listen to a reading of the text

Which words do you need to practice saying? Which words do you need to learn?

T6 | Listening: Listen and Make Notes

Listen to this talk. Complete the information below about the two MBTs.

MBT 1
Name:
Weight:
Max speed:
Range:
Armour protection:
Armament:
Other information:

MBT 2
Name:
Weight:
Max speed:
Range:
Armour protection:
Armament:
Other information:

Check with your partner. Then check with T47.1.

T7 | Speaking: Talk and Report

Discuss with your partner. Which is the best MBT from T6? Why?

T8 | Consolidation Tasks

Unit 48 Knives

T1 I Speaking: Talk and Report 1

1. Why do soldiers need knives?
2. How many uses can you think of for a knife?

T2 I Vocabulary: What are the parts of a knife called?

Look at P48.1. Can you name the parts? Check with P48.2.

Now do the same with P48.3, and check with P48.4

T3 I Before You Read: Talk and Report 2

1. What different types of knives are there?
2. What are the requirements for a military knife?

T4 I Reading: Now read the text and see if your agree with the writer

---

Knives

The knife was one of the first tools invented by man. It remains a very useful thing to have on you and every soldier should have at least one on him at all times. The traditional military knife is the bayonet, which can be attached to the end of a rifle and used like a spear. Bayonets can also be used for everyday cutting jobs.

The simplest knife is a blade set in a handle (known as sheath knives because they are carried in a sheath to protect the wearer). The best knives have a full tang blade which extends all the way through the handle. Some blades have serrations (like those on a bread knife) to make cutting rope etc. easier. Blades also come in different shapes like the Bowie knife designed by legendary frontiersman Jim Bowie, and the triangular pointed tantō blade, which has a very effective stabbing point. Knife blades should be made of good quality carbon or stainless steel and should keep an edge well – that is, they should remain sharp. Hollow-handled knives with survival kits in the handle, or a compass in the butt, are gimmicks and should be avoided as they can break easily.

Folding knives (or jackknives) fold in the middle and the blade is folded back into the handle when not being used. These knives should have a lock so that the blade does not close suddenly on the user's fingers. Any lock can fail though, so these knives are not as safe as sheath knives. Other pocket knives, like the famous Swiss Army knives, can have a multitude of blades and tools, though the more tools these have, the thicker they are, and the less easy they are to use.

Military knives should be full tang (if a sheath knife), corrosion resistant, eas-

---

ily cleaned in the field, without serrations on the main cutting edge and should be capable of being used as an everyday tool as well as a weapon.

T5 | Language Analysis: Analyse the Text

T6 | Listen and Read: Listen to a reading of the text

Which words do you need to practice saying? Which words do you need to learn?

T7 | Listening: Listen and Answer

Listen to this man talking about his knives. Look at P48.5 and identify the knives he talks about. Complete this table about the knives.

	Knife 1	Knife 2	Knife 3	Knife 4
Name				
Description/Features				
When does he use it?				
Opinion				

Which is his favourite and why? What is his most useful knife? Why?

T8 | Vocabulary: What are the parts of a multi-tool called?

Look at P48.6. Can you name the parts? Check with P48.7.

What can you do with these tools? *With the screwdriver you can unscrew screws.*

T9 | Speaking: Talk and Report 3

Consider these different kinds of knives and multi-tools: sheath knife; Swiss Army pocket knife (P48.8); Swiss Army Tool (P48.9); Multi-tool; folding (jack-) knife. Discuss with your partner:

1. Which is the most useful one?
2. If you could only have two of them, which would you choose and why?
3. Tell the class your partner's answer and reasons. Do you all agree?
4. What knives are you issued with? Are they good knives?
5. If you could replace your service issue knife, what would you replace it with?

Language Reminder: is good enough for	
A/An X is good enough for Y.	*A multi-tool is good enough for most things.*
A/An X is best/excellent for Y.	*A multi-tool is great for everyday carry.*
A/An X is inadequate for Y.	*A multi-tool is inadequate for hunting.*
A/An X is not good enough for Y.	*A multi-tool is not good enough for me.*

T10 | Consolidation Tasks

Unit 49 Weapons: Artillery

Learn About Artillery | Present Tenses | Modal Verbs

T1 | Speaking: Talk and Report

Look at P49.1 - 2. What can you see?

T2 | Vocabulary: Parts of a Mortar and Field Gun

What are the parts of a mortar and field gun called?

Label the parts in P49.3 and P49.4. Check with P49.5 and P49.6.

T3 | Reading: Read and Translate

Read the paragraph below and think of translations for the different kinds of artillery fire support in **bold**.

> Artillery is used to provide fire support to destroy, neutralize or suppress the enemy. This can include **counter battery fire** targeting the enemy's artillery, **counter preparation fire** to disrupt an imminent attack by the enemy, **covering fire** to protect your troops, **defensive fire** to protect a unit which is under attack, **final protective fire** to stop the enemy from breaking through defensive lines, **harassing fire** fired randomly to disrupt the enemy, **interdiction fire** to deny the enemy the use of an area or position, **preparation fire** delivered before an attack to weaken the enemy position, **neutralization fire** to make a target temporarily ineffective or unusable, and **suppression fire** to keep the enemy from taking effective action.   [Based on NATO AAP-06]

T4 | Reading: Read and Answer

Read about the three classes of artillery weapons – guns, howitzers and mortars.
What are the advantages and disadvantages of each class?

> Artillery includes three classes of weapons – guns, howitzers and mortars. Guns and howitzers are very similar but guns are smooth-bores, have a lower elevation (under 45 degrees) than howitzers and can be used for direct fire e.g. against tanks or fortifications. Howitzers are rifled and can be fired at a high angle (45 – 70 degrees) and are employed for indirect fire. Both guns and howitzers can either be towed or self-propelled, or placed as a static part of fortifications. A towed gun fires from the ground while a self-propelled gun is a vehicle which can move around the battlefield and has some degree of armour protection. Guns and howitzers can have large calibres and have longer ranges than mortars.
>
> A mortar is a device consisting of a steel tube ranging in calibre from 60 mm to 120 mm, a base plate, and a bipod, and it fires bombs short ranges. The mortar tube is set at an angle of between 45 and 85 degrees to the ground by the gunner,

depending on the distance to target, and the assistant gunner drops the bomb into the tube. The bomb hits a fixed firing pin at the bottom of the tube, which detonates a charge in the bomb which fires the projectile. Most mortars are man-portable and provide infantry units with their own artillery. Mortars can be used for targets which are close by, elevated, and behind fortifications and obstacles and they are highly effective when used from concealed positions. The main disadvantage of mortar use for infantry is that the mortar and its rounds have to be carried.

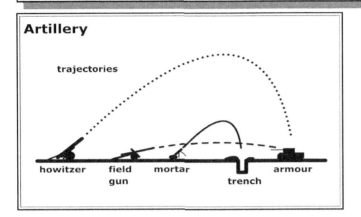

T5 | Language Analysis: Analyse the Text

T6 | Listen and Read: Listen to a reading of the text

Which words do you need to practice saying? Which words do you need to learn?

T7| Listening: Listen and Answer

What is a field artillery team? Listen and be ready to explain the diagram below.

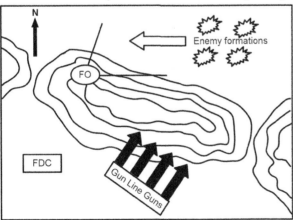

T8 | Speaking: Talk and Report 2

What artillery does your army have? Brief your teacher on your army's capabilities.

T9 | Consolidation Tasks

Unit 50 Weapons and Platforms: Helicopters

Learn About Helicopters

T1 | Speaking: Talk and Report

Look at P50.1. What can you see?

T2 | Vocabulary: Check you know the meaning of these words

aft rotor	cabin door	cannon	canopy	cockpit
elevators	engines	forward rotor	landing gear	landing skids
pylons	radar dome	ramp	rotor blade	sensor turret
stub wings	tail rotor	undercarriage	weapon pods	windows

Use these pictures to help you: P50.2 – P50.5

T3 | Reading: Read and Answer

1. Which kind of helicopter can carry the most troops?
2. Which can carry the most weapons?
3. Which can engage enemy armour?
4. Which can engage enemy forces on the ground?
5. Which has the best radar?
6. Which has the longest ferry range?
7. Which can carry the heaviest load?
8. Which is the fastest?
9. Which is the slowest?

There are many different kinds of helicopter. A transport helicopter is defined as heavy lift (like the Boeing CH-47 Chinook) or medium lift (like the Sikorsky UH-60 Black Hawk). An attack helicopter (sometimes called a helicopter gunship), like the Boeing AH-64 Apache, is used to engage targets such as enemy infantry and armoured fighting vehicles, including tanks. There are also single-engine, single-rotor helicopters used for observation, utility, and direct fire support, like the Bell OH-58 Kiowa.

The **Chinook** is a twin-engine, tandem rotor heavy-lift helicopter. It has a crew of three: pilot, copilot, and flight engineer/loadmaster. The Chinook's primary roles are troop movement, ferrying artillery and battlefield resupply. It can carry a load of up to 10,886 kg of cargo. It has a wide loading ramp at the rear of the fuselage and can accommodate 33–55 troops and their personal equipment and weapons. Its maximum speed is 170 knots (315 km/h) and it has a range of 741 km, but with a ferry range of 2,252 km with additional fuel tanks. It can be armed with three 7.62 mm M240 medium machine guns – one on the loading ramp and the other two shooting through shoulder windows.

The **Black Hawk** is a four-bladed, twin-engine, medium-lift utility helicopter. It is crewed by two flight crew and two crew chiefs/gunners. It can carry cargo and act as a weapons platform. It has a maximum speed of 159 knots (294 km/h), a combat radius of 592 km, and a ferry range of 2,220 km with external tanks. The Black Hawk can carry 12 troops or 6 stretchers (up to 1,200 kg of cargo) internally or 4,080 kg of cargo externally. It can be equipped with two 7.62 mm M240 machine guns, two 7.62 mm M134 miniguns or two 12.7 mm GAU-19 Gatling guns, and has two hardpoints on each stub wing for 70 mm Hydra 70 rockets, Hellfire laser guided missiles or Stinger air-to-air missiles, and gunpods.

The **AH-64 Apache** is an American four-blade, twin-turboshaft attack helicopter with a two-man crew in a tandem cockpit. It has a maximum speed of 158 knots (293 km/h), a range of 476 km, and a ferry range of 1,900 km. There is a nose-mounted sensor suite for target acquisition and night vision systems. It is armed with a 30 mm M230 chain gun carried under the forward fuselage. It has four hardpoints (two on each side) mounted on stub-wing pylons, for carrying a mixture of AGM-114 Hellfire missiles, AIM-92 Stingers and Hydra 70, CRV7 70mm, and APKWS 70 mm air-to-ground rockets. The AH-64D and E versions both feature the advanced Apache Longbow Fire-Control Radar (FCR) housed in a dome located above the main rotor.   [Data sources: Lockheed Martin; Boeing]

T4 | Language Analysis: Analyse the Text

T5 | Listen and Read: Listen to a reading of the text

Which words do you need to practice saying? Which words do you need to learn?

T6 | Listening: Listen and complete the table about an aircraft

Name	Type	Crew	Performance	Armament

T7 | Speaking: Prepare a briefing on a helicopter using Fact Files FF50.1 – FF50.5.

Use the T6 transcript (T50.1) to help you prepare your talk.

T8 | Consolidation Tasks

Unit 51 Talking About Animals And Their Dangers

Present Simple | Animals | Adjectives

T1 | Speaking: Talk and Report 1

Look at P51.1 – P51.14. What animals can you see?

Check with P51.15 – P51.28.

Where can these animals be found?

T2 | Vocabulary: Types of Animals 1

Are the animals in the photographs in T1 pets, domesticated or wild animals?

Complete the text below with the correct word: **wild | pets | domesticated**

[1] _____ are animals like cats and dogs, and they are tame and are found in the home. [2] _____ animals include pets like cats and dogs but also farm animals like cows, pigs and horses; some of these are not really tame (though some are) but they are not wild either. [3] _____ animals live in the [4] _____ and are not tame.

T3 | Vocabulary: Types of Animals 2

Look at the list of animals on the next page. Decide if they are <u>usually</u> pets [**P**], farm animals [**F**] or wild animals [**W**]. The first one is done as an example.

T4 | Speaking: Talk and Report 2

1. Which of the wild animals might make good pets?
2. Which of the animals are the 5 most dangerous animals? Why?

T5 | Vocabulary: Animal Attacks

Check you know the meaning of these words: **bite |sting | gore | trample | infect**

Discuss with your partner: Which animals from T3 can bite, sting, gore, trample or infect you?

T6 | Vocabulary: Adjectives

Check you know the meaning of these words.

beautiful	disgusting	ugly	delicious	favourite
creepy	frightening	tasty	amazing	aggressive

How would you describe the animals in T3?

Choose ten of the animals and write a sentence about each one.

The wildebeest is an ugly animal but it's quite tasty.

Then tell your partner. Do you agree with your partner's opinions?

List of Animals – are they pets, farm or wild animals?

snake	W	lion	
elephant (African)		fox	
cape buffalo (Africa)		rhino	
goat		leopard	
cow		water buffalo (S.E. Asia)	
jaguar		wolf	
sheep		polar bear	
scorpion		spider	
chimpanzee		oryx	
springbok		gorilla	
giraffe		deer	
cat		leech	
jackal		hyena	
wildebeest		dog	
crocodile		hippo	
mosquito		elephant (Asian)	
grizzly/brown bear		cheetah	
tick		kangaroo	

T7 | Speaking: Talk and Report 3

1. What is the most dangerous animal in Africa?
2. What is the most dangerous animal in Europe?
3. What is the most dangerous animal in South-east Asia?
4. What is the most dangerous animal in South America?
5. Why are these animals dangerous?

T8 | Listening: Listen and Answer

Listen to the speaker and answer the questions in T7 again.
Do you agree with the speaker?

T9 | Speaking: Talk and Report 4

1. What is the most dangerous animal you have encountered?
2. Have you ever been bitten, stung or attacked by an animal? What happened?

Tell the class what your partner told you.

Unit 52 Phase 1 Test 1: Grammar Test

T1 | Grammar: Complete the text with the words given

This test covers some things you have learnt on the course so far and also previews some things you will learn during the rest of the course.

Complete the text with these words in the correct form.

assign	assignment	attack	attend	attend	basic
combat	command	commission	cover	draft	drew
encircle	enlisted	exposed	flank	fortify	go
promote	regular	remain	repel	retire	rifle
seriously	serve	training	treatment	wounded	wounded

Lieutenant Colonel Charles Chris Hagemeister (US Army, Retired) [1] _____ the Nation in both the [2] _____ and commissioned ranks. He was both a reserve and [3] _____ Army officer. His [4] _____ included tactical and training units, in peacetime and in combat. He [5] _____ _____ into the United States Army in March 1966 and entered service in May 1966 at Lincoln, Nebraska. He went through [6] _____ training at Fort Polk, Louisiana, and completed advanced individual training as a [7] _____ medic at Fort Sam Houston, Texas, in November 1966.

LTC Hagemeister [8] _____ _____ to the 1st Battalion, 5th Cavalry of the 1ˢᵗ Cavalry Division in the Republic of Vietnam. He was a Specialist 4 (SPC) at the time, supporting a platoon in A Company in Binh Dinh Province on 20 March 1967 during the Vietnam War. SPC Hagemeister's platoon suddenly came under heavy [9] _____ from three sides by an enemy force occupying well concealed, [10] _____ positions and supported by machine guns and mortars. After SPC Hagemeister saw two of his comrades [11] _____ wounded in the initial action, he unhesitatingly and with total disregard for his safety raced through the deadly hail of enemy fire to provide them medical aid. SPC Hagemeister learned that the platoon leader and several other soldiers also had been [12] _____. He continued to brave enemy fire and crawled forward to render lifesaving [13] _____. While attempting to evacuate the seriously wounded soldiers, SPC Hagemeister was taken under fire at close range by an enemy sniper. SPC Hagemeister seized a [14] _____ from a fallen comrade and killed the sniper and three other enemy soldiers who were attempting to [15] _____ his position. He then silenced an enemy machine gun that covered the area with deadly fire. Unable to remove the [16] _____ to a less [17] _____ location and aware of the enemy's efforts to isolate his unit, he dashed through the heavy fire to secure help from a nearby platoon. Returning with help, he placed men in positions to [18] _____ his advance as he moved to evacuate the wounded forward of his location. He then moved to the other [19] _____ and evacuated additional wounded men, despite the fact that his every move [20] _____ fire from the enemy. SPC Hagemeister's repeated heroic and selfless actions at the risk of his life saved the lives of many of his comrades and inspired their actions in [21] _____ the enemy assault. SPC Hagemeister received the Medal of Honor on 14 May 1968.

After his service in Vietnam, Hagemeister (then Specialist 5) served at McDonald Army Hospital in Fort Eustis, Virginia, and then as a medical platoon sergeant in C Company, 1st Battalion, US Army Medical Training Center at Fort Sam Houston, Texas. Hagemeister received a direct [22] _____ in the US Army Reserve as an armor officer. After [23] _____ at Fort Knox, Kentucky he was assigned to Fort Hood, Texas where he served as a platoon leader, cavalry troop executive officer, and squadron liaison officer. In 1970 Hagemeister went to Schweinfurt, Germany where he [24] _____ Headquarters and Headquarters Troop, 3rd Squadron, 7th Cavalry of the 3rd Infantry Division where he was also the Squadron Intelligence Officer. After [25] _____ the Armor Officer Advanced Course and the Data Processing Course Hagemeister [26] _____back to Fort Hood in September 1977. There he served in the Communications Research and Development Command as the Tactical Operations System Controller. In 1980 he returned to Fort Knox and served as the Chief of Armor Test Development branch and later became the Chief of Platoon, Company, and Troop Training.

Hagemeister became a Regular Army officer on 15 December 1981 and was later [27] _____ to Major. Following this promotion, Hagemeister became the executive officer for the 1st Battalion, 1st Training Brigade at Fort Knox. He then [28] _____the US Army Command and General Staff College at Fort Leavenworth, Kansas. He [29] _____ at Fort Leavenworth as the Director of the Division Commander's Course and then as the Author/Instructor for Corps Operations, Center for Army Tactics in the Command and General Staff College. LTC Hagemeister [30] _____ from the Army in June 1990.

[Adapted from US Army FM 7-21.13]

T2 | Speaking: Discuss the Text

Check the answers and discuss the text with your teacher.

Do you understand everything?

Unit 53 Phase 1 Test 2: Reading Test: Exercise Cambrian Patrol

T1 | Reading: Read and Answer

Read the texts below to answer these questions:

1. What is Exercise Cambrian Patrol?
2. Where is it held?
3. When is it held?
4. Who is it for?
5. How much gear does each patrol member have to carry?
6. What do participants get if they complete the course?
7. How long and how far does the patrol have to travel?
8. What do they have to do during the patrol?
9. What will they get marks for?
10. Will they be assessed on First aid and CASEVAC procedures?
11. In 2013, which service sent the most patrols to the exercise?
12. In 2013, how many other countries sent teams?

Exercise Cambrian Patrol is an annual international Mission and Task Orientated patrolling exercise. It is the premier patrolling event of the British Army and is held in Wales each autumn. It is hosted by HQ 160 Infantry Brigade. Units which participate cover a 50-mile (80 km) course through the rugged Cambrian Mountains of mid-Wales. in less than 48 hrs while performing numerous types of military exercises. The exercise has been running for over 50 years and is the British Army's principle All Arms patrols exercise. It is open to all three services (Regular and Reserve) as well as international participants.

The Cambrian Patrol is an exercise and not a competition. It is conducted for the benefit of units and there is no final order of merit but there are four categories of Awards. These are:

1. Gold: 75% or more of the points available.
2. Silver: 65-74% of the points available.
3. Bronze: 55-64% of the points available.
4. Certificate: Completed the exercise in the time allowed and scored less than 55% of the points available

The exercise is designed to be within the capability of any well-led and well-trained patrol from any Arm or Service. The exercise is the same for Regular and Reserve Forces and also draws participants from foreign countries.

The exercise has a time limit of 48 hrs, during which each patrol will cover approximately 55 kms (average climb and descent is over 1000 m) carrying approx 25 kgs per person. During the course they will have to successfully complete

---

various tasks. The exercise is designed to be arduous and all participants must be prepared both mentally and physically for the challenge. Patrol performance is assessed throughout and scores are awarded based on the conduct of the patrol, quality of patrol reports and performance on each task/activity. Marks are awarded for:

1. Military skills (approx.70% of total marks).
2. Orders (approx.15% of total marks).
3. Debrief (approx.15% of total marks).

Military skills that *may* be assessed during Cambrian Patrol are:

1. Dismounted Close Combat Skills.
2. Obstacle crossing drills.
3. First aid and CASEVAC procedures.
4. Recognition of aircraft, vehicles, weapons, mines and other equipment.
5. CIED/Minefield Clearance drills.
6. Patrol Techniques incl. Harbour Drills
7. Captured Persons (CEPERS) Handling.
8. Helicopter drills.
9. Media handling.
10. Chemical, biological, radiological and nuclear (CBRN) drills.
11. Radio communications skills.
12. Artillery Target procedures.
13. Live Firing Grouping & Zeroing

Exercise Cambrian Patrol 2013 saw nine patrols achieve the top award, but almost 20% of the patrols failed to complete the mission. In addition to the nine golds, there were 37 silver, 21 bronze, 16 certificates and 17 withdrawals

Teams from the UK included 55 Regular army patrols, 12 Reserve and 16 teams from the University Officer Training Corps.

International troops from Norway, New Zealand, Ukraine, Pakistan, Italy, Germany, Denmark, Canada, Albania, Netherlands, Republic of Ireland, India, Australia, Estonia, Poland, Greece and France, all took up the challenge in the harsh and demanding terrain amid the Welsh Cambrian Mountains.

Texts written from information from Crown Copyright sources:
http://www.army.mod.uk/events/23232.aspx;
http://www.army.mod.uk/news/25847.aspx

Unit 54 Phase 1 Test 3: Writing Test: PKO Report

T1 | Reading: Read And Make Notes

Reread the **Peacekeeping Fact Files 1 – 12** in your Workbook and make notes on these questions.

1. Which is the longest/shortest UN Peacekeeping mission?
2. Which is the biggest/smallest mission?
3. Which mission has the most troops?
4. Which mission has the most military observers?
5. Which mission has the most police?
6. Which mission has the biggest number of civilian personnel?
7. Which mission has the most volunteers?
8. Which is the most/least dangerous mission in total fatalities?
9. Which is the most/least dangerous on an annual basis?

Also make notes on the different missions. Can you group them by mission?

T2 | Writing: Write a Report

Now write a short report about the UN Peacekeeping Missions you have read about. Use this plan:

Introduction: Which missions are you going to write about? What kind of missions are they?

Part 1 The Missions: Which are the longest/shortest and biggest/smallest?

Part 2 Personnel: Facts and figures about the personnel.

Part 3 Fatalities: Facts and figures about fatalities.

Conclusions: Summarise your findings.

Unit 55 Phase 1 Test 4: Speaking 1: Personnel Biographies

Give A Briefing About The Biography Of A Soldier

T1 | Speaking: Briefing Preparation

Work individually.

There are 30 One Slide Briefings.

See **Unit 55 Phase 1 Speaking Test 1 Briefing Slides.**

Your teacher will assign you a briefing slide.

Prepare your briefing of the slide. You will have to make up details of the soldier's career to present to the class.

Use this Speaking Frame to help you.

Language Reminder: Speaking Frame

This is [*name*].

He/She is a/an [*rank/job*].

He/She is currently based in/at [*place*].

He/She is responsible for [*X*].

[*Name*] joined the army in [*date*].

He/She did his/her basic training in [*place*].

After completing basic training [*Name*] was posted to [*place*] as a/an [*rank/job*].

There he/she [*did what?*]

After [*amount of time*], [*Rank and Name*] was promoted to [*rank*] and posted to [*place*].

There [*Rank and Name*] was responsible for [*X*]

[*Rank and Name*] served for [*amount of time*] in [*place*] and then ....

T2 | Speaking: Briefing

Present your soldier's career to the class.

Be ready to answer questions.

T3 | Listening: Make Notes

You should make notes of your colleagues' briefings. Your teacher will collect these notes to rate your listening and note-taking skills.

T4 | Speaking: Questions and Feedback

Ask questions about your colleagues' briefings.

Then give them feedback on their briefings.

Your teacher will give you feedback on your briefing [see p. xiii]

Unit 56 Phase 1 Test 5: Speaking 2: IFV Briefings

Give A Briefing About Infantry Fighting Vehicles

T1 | Speaking: Briefing Preparation

Work individually.

There are 10 One Slide Briefings of Infantry Fighting Vehicles.

See **Unit 56 Phase 1 Speaking Test 2 Briefing Slides.**

Your teacher will assign you a briefing slide.

Prepare your briefing of the slide.

T2 | Speaking: Briefing

Brief the class on your IFV.

Be ready to answer questions.

T3 | Listening: Make Notes

You should make notes of your colleagues' briefings.

T4 | Speaking: Questions and Feedback

Ask questions about your colleagues' briefings.

Then give them feedback on their briefings.

Your teacher will give you feedback on your briefing.

T5 | Speaking: Discussion

Now discuss the following questions as a class. Use your notes from T3 to help you.

1. Which IFV can carry the most troops?
2. Which has the best armament?
3. Which has the best armour?
4. Which has the furthest operational range?
5. Which is the fastest?
6. Which is the heaviest?
7. Which is the longest?
8. Which is the highest?
9. Which is the narrowest?
10. Which is the best IFV?

Phase 2

Units 57 to 175	Radio English
	Medical English
	Terrain
	Land Navigation
	Disposition of Forces
	Survival
	Bases
	Convoys
	Checkpoints
	Patrols
	Orders
	and more

Unit 57 Using the Radio 1: The Radio NET

Learn To Make Radio Calls In English

T1 | Speaking: Talk and Report

Look at P57.1. What can you see?

T2 | Speaking: Radio PRO Words and Net Procedures

When you call someone on the radio you say their call sign **first** and then your call sign. Like this:

[Call sign B2:] *A1. This is B2. Over.*

You say '**over**' to show you have finished talking.

'over' is a radio PROCEDURE [PRO] word.

There is a list of PRO words in your **Workbook.**

The NCS [or 0 : Zero] is the Net Control Station.

They control the operation of the radio net which can have two or more radio stations.

Important Note:
You can omit call signs when there are only two stations on the Net.
The receiving station can omit 'THIS IS' in good conditions when responding to a call.
[Sources: Units 57, 58 and 60: FM 6-02.53]

T3 | Speaking: Stetting up the Net

The NCS sets up the Net. Other stations join the Net. Like this:

Call Sign NCS: NET, this is NCS, over.

Call Sign A1D: NCS, this is A1D, over.

Call Sign A2D: NCS, this is A2D, over.

Call Sign NCS: NET this is NCS, out. [If NCS has no traffic]

[Note: the last letter of the call sign determines the answering order. The stations in the next respond alphabetically. A3D will answer before A2E and A2E will answer before BIF. If two stations in the net have the same last letter [A1D and A2D] the answering order will depend on the numerical sequence: A1D answers before A2D.]

Work in threes: practice the radio call above. Practice again with different call signs. Decide on your call signs first, then practice. Demonstrate the calls to the class.

T4 | Speaking: Radio Checks

The NCS can ask for radio checks. Like this:

Call Sign NCS: NET, THIS IS NCS. RADIO CHECK, OVER.

Call Sign A1D: NCS, THIS IS A1D. ROGER, OUT.

Call Sign A2D: NCS, THIS IS A2D. WEAK READABLE, OVER.

Call Sign A2E: NCS, THIS IS A2E. ROGER, OUT.

Call Sign NCS: NET, THIS IS NCS. ROGER, OUT.

Work in fours: practice the radio call above. Decide on your call signs first, then practice. Practice again with different call signs. Demonstrate the calls to the class.

T5 | Speaking: Authenticate

When a station joins the Net, NCS can ask them to authenticate, which is use a codeword paired with the challenge codeword. Like this:

Call Sign B4G: NCS, THIS IS B4G. REPORTING INTO THE NET, OVER.

Call Sign NCS: B4G, THIS IS NCS. AUTHENTICATE, OVER.

Call Sign B4G: NCS, THIS IS B4G. I AUTHENTICATE [PARIS], OVER.

Call Sign NCS: B4G, THIS IS NCS. I AUTHENTICATE [TEXAS], OVER.

Call Sign B4G: NCS, THIS IS B4G. ROGER, OUT.

Work in pairs: practice the radio call above. Decide on your call signs first, then practice. Practice again with different call signs and codewords. Demonstrate the calls to the class.

T6 | Speaking: Permission

When a station wants to enter a Net which they do not normally operate in they have to request permission. Like this:

Call Sign D4H: NCS, THIS IS D4H. REQUEST PERMISSION TO ENTER NET, OVER.

Call Sign NCS: D4H, THIS IS NCS. IDENTIFY YOUR STATION, OVER.

Call Sign D4H: NCS, THIS IS D4H. REFER TO [CALL SIGN] I AM PREPARED TO AUTHENTICATE, OVER.

Call Sign NCS: D4H, THIS IS NCS. AUTHENTICATE CAMERON, OVER.

Call Sign D4H: NCS, THIS IS D4H. I AUTHENTICATE NEW YORK, OVER.

Call Sign NCS: D4H, THIS IS NCS, PERMISSION TO ENTER NET, OUT.

Work in pairs: practice the radio call above. Decide on your call signs first, then practice. Practice again with different call signs. Demonstrate the calls to the class.

T7 | Speaking: Preliminary Call

A preliminary call (the first line below) will be transmitted when the sending station wants to know if the receiving station is ready to receive a message. Like this:

Call sign A24:   B4G THIS IS A24. IMMEDIATE (PRECEDENCE), OVER.

Call sign B4G: A24, THIS IS B4G, OVER.

Call sign A24:   B4G THIS IS A24. MESSAGE. NUMBER ONE. PRIORITY TIME [TDG]. FROM [COMMANDER'S FULL CALL SIGN] TO [COMMANDER'S FULL CALL SIGN]. BREAK. [TEXT OF MESSAGE]. BREAK, OVER.

Call sign B4G: A24, THIS IS B4G, ROGER, OUT.

Or like this:

Call sign A24:   B4G THIS IS A24. MESSAGE, OVER.

Call sign B4G: A24, THIS IS B4G, OVER.

Call sign A24:   B4G THIS IS A24. [TEXT OF MESSAGE], OVER.

Call sign B4G: A24, THIS IS B4G, ROGER, OUT.

[Note: when communications reception is good and contact has been continuous, a preliminary call is optional.]

Work in pairs: practice the radio call above. Decide on your call signs first, then practice. Practice again with different call signs. Demonstrate the calls to the class.

T8 | Speaking: Leaving the Net

When a station wants to leave the Net they should ask NCS to do so. Like this:

Call Sign A24:   NCS THIS IS A24, REQUEST PERMISSION TO CLOSE DOWN (OR LEAVE NET), OVER.

Call Sign NCS: A24 THIS IS NCS, ROGER, OUT.

Work in pairs: practice the radio call above. Decide on your call signs first, then practice. Practice again with different call signs. Demonstrate the calls to the class.

T9 | Speaking: Closing Down

The NCS can close down a Net: Like this:

Call Sign NCS: NET, THIS IS NCS. CLOSE DOWN, OVER.

Call Sign A1D: NCS, THIS IS A1D. ROGER, OUT.

Call Sign A2D: NCS, THIS IS A2D. ROGER, OUT.

Call Sign B2D: NCS, THIS IS B2D ROGER, OUT.

Work in pairs: practice the radio call above. Decide on your call signs first, then practice. Practice again with different call signs. Demonstrate the calls to the class.

Unit 58 Using the Radio 2: PRO Words

Learn To Use Pro Words In Radio Calls

T1 | Vocabulary: Key PRO Words 1

Match the PRO words and their meanings.

OUT	I have received your signal, understand it and will comply.
OVER	I have received your last transmission satisfactorily.
ROGER	This is the end of my transmission to you and a response is necessary. Go ahead; transmit.
WILCO	This is the end of my transmission to you and no answer is required or expected.

1. What is the difference between 'OVER' and 'OUT'?
2. Can we say 'OVER AND OUT'?
3. What is the difference between 'ROGER' and 'WILCO'?
4. Can we say 'ROGER WILCO'?

T2 | Vocabulary: Key PRO Words 2: I SAY AGAIN

When you want to repeat something very important you should say: **I SAY AGAIN**.

Like this: '*AT THE RAILWAY STATION. I SAY AGAIN. AT THE RAILWAY STATION*'.

Practice saying **I SAY AGAIN.**

Work in pairs. Write down 5 long words. Don't show your partner.

Say the words to your partner and then say **I SAY AGAIN** and say them again.

Like this: '*WASHINGTON, I SAY AGAIN, WASHINGTON*'.

Listen to your partner's words and write them down.

T3 | Vocabulary: Key PRO Words 3: I SPELL

When you want to spell something you should say the word and say: **I SPELL**..

Like this: ...*IN MANCHESTER. I SPELL. MIKE, ALFA, NOVEMBER, CHARLIE, HOTEL, ECHO, SIERRA, TANGO, ECHO, ROMEO*'.

Practice saying **I SPELL.**

Work in pairs. Write down 5 more long words. Don't show your partner.

Say the words to your partner and then spell them.

"*INTERNATIONAL. I SPELL. INDIA. NOVEMBER, TANGO.......*"

Listen to your partner's words and write them down.

T4 | Vocabulary: Key PRO Words 4: SAY AGAIN

When you do not hear something properly you can ask for it to be repeated.

Call sign A24: B4G, THIS IS A24. MESSAGE, OVER.

Call sign B4G: A24, THIS IS B4G, OVER.

Call sign A24: B4G, THIS IS A24. INSURGENTS SEEN MUMBLE MUMBLE MUMBLE, OVER.

Call sign B4G: A24, THIS IS B4G. SAY AGAIN ALL AFTER INSURGENTS, OVER.

Call sign A24: B4G, THIS IS A24. I SAY AGAIN: INSURGENTS SEEN MASSING NEAR STATION, OVER.

Call sign B4G: A24, THIS IS B4G, ROGER, OVER.

Work in pairs: practice the radio call above. Then practice again with different information which needs to be repeated. Demonstrate the calls to the class.

T5 | Vocabulary: Key Pro Words 5: WAIT, WAIT OUT, QUESTION and READ BACK

Sometimes you will need to ask a station to wait. If you just want to wait a few seconds, say: '**WAIT**'. If you want to wait longer, say '**WAIT OUT**' and then call the station back when you are ready. If you have a question you should use the word '**QUESTION**' and then ask your question. Like this: ...*QUESTION. IS THE AREA SECURE?* When you want to check the other station has understood your message you can ask them to '**READ BACK**' what you have told them.

Call sign A24: B4G, THIS IS A24. MESSAGE, OVER.

Call sign B4G: A24, THIS IS B4G. WAIT, OUT.

Call sign B4G: A24, THIS IS B4G, OVER.

Call sign A24: B4G, THIS IS A24. HAVE TAKEN OBJECTIVE BRAVO. ENEMY WITHDRAWING TO NORTH, OVER.

Call sign B4G: A24, THIS IS B4G. QUESTION: DO YOU HAVE ANY CASUALTIES?, OVER.

Call sign A24: B4G, THIS IS A24. NEGATIVE, OVER.

Call sign B4G: A24, THIS IS B4G, ROGER. PREPARE TO HOLD OBJECTIVE BRAVO UNTIL RELIEVED. READ BACK, OVER.

Call sign A24: B4G, THIS IS A24. I WILL HOLD OBJECTIVE BRAVO UNTIL RELIEVED, OVER.

Call sign B4G: A24, THIS IS B4G, OUT.

Work in pairs: practice the radio call. Then, practice again with different information. Demonstrate the calls to the class.

T6 | Speaking: Grid References

When you way grid references you should preface them with the word 'grid' and then say the numbers separately. Use falling intonation ↓ on each number:

....at Grid 6 ↓ 7↓ 8 ↓ 5 ↓ 4 ↓ 2 ↓ 9 ↓

Work in pairs. Look at your maps. Practice giving grid references to your partner. Choose five features on the map and tell your partner like this:

A1, this is B2. I am at the road junction at Grid 3 ↓ 4 ↓ 9 ↓ 5 ↓ 6 ↓ 0 ↓ Over ↓

Listen and find the feature on the map. Then say: **B2, this is A1. Roger. Out.**

Unit 59 Using the Radio 3: Incident Report and Other Reports

Practice an Incident Report

You will need to be familiar with all the kinds of reports you need to make when on active duty e.g. Contact Report, FIREP, SITREPS etc.

T1 | Vocabulary: Study the Incident Report Form

Look at the Incident Report Form below. Check you understand everything.

INCIDENT REPORT				
From:		Task No:		
To:		Precedence:		
DTG		Classification:		
1	PURPOSE OF REPORT			
2	TIME OF INCIDENT			
3	LOCATION OF INCIDENT			
4	DESCRIPTION OF INCIDENT: A. TYPE / DESCRIPTION OF INCIDENT B. REPORT SOURCE C. CORRELATION WITH OTHER INCIDENTS D. ASSESSMENT (1) EST. HOSTILE FORCES INTENTIONS (2) OWN MEASURES TAKEN (3) OWN MEASURES TO BE TAKEN			
5	PSO FORCES INVOLVED A. OWN FORCES B. OTHER AGENCIES			
6	ANY OTHER RELEVANT INFO			

Key: DTG: date time group; PSO: Peace Support Operation; Est.: estimate

[Form: courtesy of MAF]

T2 | Speaking: Complete the form and make a radio call

Work in pairs: prepare a radio call based on the Incident Report Form

Use a blank Incident Report Form from your Workbook.

Practice and then demonstrate your call to the class.

Listen to the other calls and write down the information you hear.

Check your notes with the original form.

Unit 60 Using the Radio 4: MEDEVAC/CASEVAC

T1 | Vocabulary: Study the Emergency CASEVAC/MEDEVAC Form

Look at the CASEVAC/MEDEVAC Form below. Check you understand everything.

EMERGENCY CASEVAC/MEDEVAC REQUEST				
MEDEVAC **9 Liner Request**		DTG		UNIT
1	**LOCATION**	1		
2	**CALL SIGN & FREQ.**	2		
3	**No. of Patients /Precedence**	3		
	A	B	C	D	E
	URGENT (2hr)	URGENT (2hr)	PRIORITY (4hr)	ROUTINE (24hr)	CONVENIENCE
4	**SPECIAL EQUIPMENT REQ'D**	4		
	A	B	C	D
	NONE	HOIST	EXTRACTION	VENTILATOR
5	**NO. OF PATIENTS/TYPE**	5		
	L		A	
	LITTER		AMBULATORY	
6	**SECURITY AT PZ/LZ**	6		
	N	E	P	X
	NO ENEMY	ENEMY IN AREA	POSSIBLE ENEMY	ARMED ESCORT REQUIRED
7	**PZ/LZ MARKING METHOD**	7		
	A	B	C	D	E
	PANELS	PYRO	SMOKE	NONE	OTHER
8	**NATIONALITY STATUS**	8		
	A	B	C	D	E
	MISSION MILITARY	MISSION CIVILIANS	MILITARY/ NON MISSION	CIVILIAN/ NON MISSION	EPW
9	**PZ/LZ TERRAIN/OBSTACLES**	9		

[Form: courtesy of MAF]

T2 | Listening: Listen to Radio Call 1

Listen and write down the nine lines of information.

Check with your partner. Listen again if necessary.

Check as a class. Check with T60.1 if necessary.

T3 | Listening: Listen to Radio Call 2

Listen and write down the nine lines of information.

Check with your partner.

Listen again if necessary.

Check as a class.

Check with T60.2 if necessary.

T4 | Vocabulary: Complete the radio call below

Call sign ZY5: B20, [1] <u>THIS</u> IS ZY5, OVER.

Call sign B20: ZY5, THIS IS B20, [2] _____ . OVER.

Call sign ZY5: B20, THIS IS ZY5, [3] _____ URGENT CASEVAC, OVER.

Call sign B20: ZY5, THIS IS B20, [4] _____ SHAKESPEARE, OVER.

Call sign ZY5: B20, THIS IS ZY5, I [5]_____ MACBETH, OVER.

Call sign B20: ZY5. ROGER, SEND [6] _____ OVER.

Call sign ZY5: B20. ROGER, NINE LINER AS [7] _____ , [8] _____ ,

ONE, 657345, BREAK

TWO, 69 DECIMAL 45, ZY5, BREAK

THREE, ALPHA 1, CHARLIE 2, BREAK

FOUR, DELTA 1, BREAK

FIVE, LIMA 1, ALFA 2, BREAK

SIX, ECHO, BREAK

SEVEN, BRAVO WHITE, BREAK

EIGHT, ALFA 3, BREAK

NINE, FROM THE SOUTH. OVER.

Call sign B20: ZY5. WE WILL SEND CASEVAC IMMEDIATELY. STAND BY.[9] _____

Call sign ZY5: B20. [10] _____ . [11] _____ .

Check with your partner. Then listen to check. [see T60.3]

T5 | Speaking: Prepare a CASEVAC/MEDEVAC Radio Call like the one above

Work with a partner.

Script a radio call modelled on the one above.

Demonstrate your call to the class.

The class listens and completes a CASEVAC/MEDEVAC Form (see Workbook).

Check the CASEVAC/MEDEVAC Forms.

Unit 61 Using the Radio 5: Call for Fire

Practice Calls for Fire

T1 | Speaking: Talk and Report 1

You want to call for indirect fire to support your unit.

What information should you give the Fire Direction Centre (FDC)?

T2 | Speaking: Read and Talk and Report 2

Calls for fire must include the following three elements:

- Observer identification and warning order.

- Target location.

- Target description.

Discuss with your partner: why are these elements important?

T3 | Speaking: Talk and Report 3

What type of fire missions are there?

T4 | Vocabulary: Complete the text with the correct words

Complete the text with these words:

clears	direct	direction	enemy	engaged
identified	known	location	quickly	type

Observer Identification and Warning Order

Observer identification tells the fire [1] _____ center (FDC) who is calling. It also [2] _____ the net for the duration of the call. The WARNO tells the FDC the [3] _____ of mission and the method of locating the target. The types of indirect fire missions are adjust fire, fire for effect (FFE), suppress, and immediate suppression.

Adjust Fire: Use this command when uncertain of target [4] _____. Calling an adjust fire mission means the observer knows he will need to make adjustments prior to calling a fire for effect.

Fire for Effect: Use this command for rounds on target, no adjustment. An example of this situation is if it is [5] _____ that the target is in building X. Building X is easily [6] _____ on the map as Grid ML 12345678910.

Suppress: Use this command to obtain fire [7] _____. The suppression mission is used to initiate fire on a preplanned target (known to the FDC) and unplanned targets.

Immediate Suppression: Use this command to indicate the platoon is already being [8] _____ by the enemy. Target identification is required. The term "immediate" tells the FDC that the friendly unit is in [9] _____ fire contact with the [10] _____ target. [All Texts Source: FM3-21.8]

T5 | Vocabulary: Read and Match

Target Description

The target description helps the FDC to select the type and amount of ammunition to best defeat the enemy target. Use the mnemonic **SNAP**:

Match **SNAP** with the examples:

Size and/or shape	"in the open,""dug in,"or"on a rooftop"
Nature and/or nomenclature	"stationary"or"moving"
Activity	"one enemy soldier" or "platoon of enemy soldiers"
Protection and/or posture	"T72," "sniper team," "machine gunner"

T6 | Vocabulary: Read and Answer

Read the example fire mission and answer the questions 1 - 4.

1. Who is calling the fire mission?
2. What kind of fire mission is it?
3. What is the target?
4. Where is the target?

Initial Fire Request from Observer to FDC	
OBSERVER:	Z57, THIS IS 271, ADJUST FIRE, OVER
FDC:	271, THIS IS Z57, ADJUST FIRE, OVER
OBSERVER:	Z57, GRID NK180513, OVER
FDC:	271, GRID NK180513, OVER
OBSERVER:	Z57, INFANTRY PLATOON IN THE OPEN, ICM IN EFFECT, OVER
FDC:	271, INFANTRY PLATOON IN THE OPEN, ICM IN EFFECT, OUT

Note: ICM = Improved Conventional Munitions e.g. Anti-Personnel (APICM), Dual Purpose (DPICM).

> **Message to Observer**
>
> After the FDC receives the call for fire, it determines if and how the target will be attacked. That decision is announced to the observer in the form of a message to the observer The observer acknowledges the message to observer by reading it back in its entirety.

Read the sample message and answer the question: how many shells are being fired?

Message to Observer	
FDC:	271, THIS Z57, 2 ROUNDS, TARGET IS AF1027, OVER
OBSERVER:	Z57, 2 ROUNDS, TARGET IS AF1027, OUT

Other PROWORD transmissions:

- **Shot.** The term SHOT, OVER is transmitted by the FDC after each round fired in adjustment and after the initial round in the fire for effect (FFE) phase. The observer acknowledges with SHOT, OUT.

- **Splash**. The term SPLASH, OVER is transmitted by the FDC to inform the observer when his round is five seconds from detonation/impact. The observer responds with SPLASH, OUT.

- **Rounds Complete**. The term ROUNDS COMPLETE, OVER signifies that the number of rounds specified in the FFE have been fired. The observer responds with ROUNDS COMPLETE, OUT.

- **Check Firing**. Stop firing.

- **End of Mission**. See T8.

T8 | Vocabulary: End of Mission

The Observer calls the end of mission with a Battle Damage assessment: "End of Mission Target # _____ BDA, Over." The FDC repeats the message with OUT.

T9 | Speaking: Prepare a Fire Mission Radio Call like the one above

Script a radio call modelled on the one above.

Demonstrate your call to the class.

The class listens and answers these questions after the call.

1. Who is calling the fire mission?

2. What kind of fire mission is it?

3. What is the target?

4. Where is the target?

See the **Call for Fire Form** in the **Workbook** – page 198.

Unit 62 Radio Simulation 1: Patrol

Practice Patrol Radio Calls

T1 | Speaking: Plan a Patrol

Work in groups.

Use your large-scale maps.

Plan a patrol through rough terrain; give a briefing and role play the radio calls as below.

Decide and make sure each of the group members knows what his role is.

Your starting point is at grid _____ (you decide the grid reference).

You have to organize the movement of a patrol to grid _____ (you decide the reference)

You have to decide the departure/arrival times.

Decide on the composition of the patrol.

Decide on three reporting points on your route.

> ### Language Reminder
>
> Use **present** and **future verb forms** to brief about the patrol.
> We **leave** at 0800.
> We **will arrive** back at base at 1100.

T2 | Speaking: Patrol Briefing

Brief the other groups about your patrol.

Take notes about the patrols.

Check your notes.

T3 | Speaking: Radio Call Demonstration

Prepare, practice and then demonstrate the four radio calls below to the class.

1. Report to the FOB about the departure of the patrol.

2. Do the first radio check at the first reporting point.

3. Do the second check at the second reporting point.

4. The patrol has been attacked from ambush. Report to the FOB. Two soldiers have been seriously wounded. Request CASEVAC/MEDEVAC.

The other groups will watch, listen, and give you feedback.

Unit 63 Radio Simulation 2: Convoy

T1 | Speaking: Plan a Convoy

Work in groups.

Plan a convoy, give a briefing and role play the radio calls as below.

Decide and make sure each of the group members knows what his role is.

Use your large-scale maps

Your starting point is at grid ____ (you decide the grid reference)

Organize the movement of a convoy to grid ____ (you decide the grid reference).

Decide on the departure/arrival time.

Decide on the number/type of vehicles in the convoy.

Decide on the number of personnel in the convoy.

Decide on the ROE for the convoy.

Decide on the five reporting points on your route.

T2 | Speaking: Convoy Briefing

Brief the other groups about your convoy.

Take notes about the convoys.

Check your notes.

T3 | Speaking: Radio Call Demonstration

Prepare, practice and then demonstrate the five radio calls below to the class.

1. Report to the FOB about the departure of the convoy.

2. Do the first radio check at the first reporting point.

3. Report arrival at the rest area.

4. Report departure from the rest area.

5. A traffic accident happens. Report to the FOB. Four soldiers have been seriously injured. Request CASEVAC/MEDEVAC.

The other groups will watch and listen and give you feedback.

Unit 64 Weather and Climate 1

Learn To Talk About The Weather

T1 | Speaking: Talk and Report

Look at P64.1, P64.2 and P64.3.

1. What can you see?
2. What is the weather like?
3. What's the weather like where you are today?

T2 | Vocabulary: Sort the words and phrases

What kind of weather these words and phrases are describing?

windy	sunny	freezing	snowing heavily
hot	sleet	raining	cloudy
gust	slush	spitting	clear blue skies
(a) blizzard	light	damp	(a) light/strong breeze
heavy	(a) shower	cold	freezing (rain)
dry	drizzling	chilly	prevailing (wind)
icy	boiling	humid	drifting snow
(a) gale	frosty	bitterly (cold)	pouring down
(a) downpour	(a) monsoon	biting	torrential

Rainy Weather	Windy Weather	Sunny Weather	Winter Weather

T3 | Vocabulary: The Climate

Write down words describing the typical weather for each month on the table on the next page. Mark the seasons on the table: winter, spring, summer, autumn, dry season, wet season etc.

Check with the class. *The weather in January here is cold* .... Do you all agree?

T4 | Speaking: Which season?

Work with a partner. Prepare a weather forecast for a typical day in one month in your country. Read it to the class. The class guesses which season/month it is.

	January	February	March	April	May	June	July	August	September	October	November	December
Season												
Average Temp.												
Precipitation												
Sun/clouds												
Wind												

Unit 65 Weather and Climate 2

T1 | Speaking: Test Your Partner

Work in pairs. Take it in turns to test your partner on the words from **Unit 64**.

"What does 'gale' mean?"

T2 | Listening: Listening Skills

Listen to these extracts. Mark where the speaker pauses / and <u>underline</u> which words they stress the most. The first one is done as an example.

1. /In <u>Astana</u> at the moment it's <u>clear</u> and <u>sunny</u>/
2. Cape Town is waking up to a beautiful day.
3. It is 4 degrees in Shanghai and overcast.
4. Today is forecast to be nearly the same temperature as yesterday.
5. It's clear and 19 degrees at the moment but this afternoon should see 26 degrees and yesterday's sunshine will continue.

T3 | Listening: Listen and Answer

Listen to the four weather forecasts. Complete the table.

	Forecast 1	Forecast 2	Forecast 3	Forecast 4
Weather now				
Weather later today				
Weather tomorrow				

T4 | Listening: Transcript Tasks

Complete the transcript tasks on Forecasts 1 – 3 on the next page. Complete the texts with the words given and then listen to check. Also check with T65.1 – T65.3.

T5 | Speaking: Talk and Report

Ask your partner these questions and then tell the class what they said.

1. What is your favourite time of year? Why?
2. What is your favourite kind of weather? Why?
3. What do you like doing when it rains?
4. What do you like doing when it's sunny?
5. Which do you prefer? Cold and damp? Or hot and humid? Why?
6. Which season is the best for visitors to your country? Why?
7. What was the weather like yesterday/last week?
8. What will the weather be like tomorrow/next week?

Transcript Tasks

chill	clouding	colder	from	minus x 6	rise	sharply	showers	warm

Forecast 1 In Astana at the moment it's clear and sunny. The temperature is [1] _____ 21 degrees but it feels [2] _____ – more like [3] _____ 27 degrees. Winds are [4] _____ the south-south-east: 15 to 30 km/h. The temperature should [5] _____ to [6] _____ 12 degrees in the mid-afternoon. It'll start [7] _____ over and you should expect late night snow [8] _____. There will be 2 -3 cms of snow. Tomorrow will be [9] _____ 8 in the morning, windy – 30 to 50 km/h - and with more snow showers. The temperature will drop [10] _____ again to [11] _____ 22 degrees in the evening but with the wind [12] _____ it will feel like [13] _____ 36. Keep [14] _____.

clear	cooler	gusts	reach	rise	sticky	warm x 2	windy x 2

Forecast 2 Cape Town is waking up to a beautiful day. It's sunny and [1] _____ – 20 degrees. It'll [2] _____ about 25 degrees this afternoon, so slightly [3] _____ than yesterday's high of 29 degrees. Humidity will [4] _____ during the day from a nice 55% now to a more [5] _____ 83% this evening. Tonight will be [6] _____ – about 18 degrees – but [7] _____ – southerly winds of up to 50 km/h at times. Thursday will continue [8] _____ – 28 degrees – and clear but still [9] _____, with [10] _____ up to 50 km/h again.

clear	develop	gusting	high	northerly	of	sunny	to	warm	windier

Forecast 3 It is 4 degrees in Shanghai and overcast. It's much cooler than yesterday's [1] _____ of 10 degrees so wrap up [2] _____. Occasional rain showers will [3] _____ later this morning bringing about 2 mm of rain. There are [4] _____ winds with gusts up to 30 km/h. The rain should end about 7 pm and the clouds should [5] _____ later tonight. The temperature will drop [6] _____ about minus 1 overnight. Thursday will be nicer – at least it will be [7] _____ all day – but still cool with a high [8] _____ 6 degrees expected. It'll be a bit [9] _____ too with north west winds [10] _____ up to 40 km/h at times.

Unit 66 Weather and Climate 3

Read About The Climate In Three Cities Around The World

T1 | Speaking: Talk and Report

What do you know about these cities?

London, England | Timbuktu, Mali | Singapore

Where are they? What is the climate like in each city?

T2 | Reading Puzzle

Read through this text to extract paragraphs about the three cities above. Note that the sentences are in the correct order for each paragraph.

> **London**, the capital of England and the United Kingdom, has a temperate oceanic climate. **Timbuktu**, a city in Mali, Africa, has a hot desert climate. **Singapore**, the city-island state in South-east Asia, lies 1 degree north of the equator and it has a tropical rainforest climate with no distinctive seasons. The weather is hot and dry throughout much of the year. It has regular but light precipitation (40 to 68 mm per month) throughout the year (total: 600 mm) with most rain falling from October to January. Average daily maximum temperatures in the hottest months of the year – April, May and June - are over 40 °C. June to August are the warmest months with average highs of 22 – 23 °C and average lows of 14 – 15 °C. It has uniform temperature (usually ranging from 22 to 36 °C), and high humidity, which averages around 79% in the morning and 73% in the afternoon. Summer temperatures rarely exceed 33 °C, though the highest temperature ever recorded in London was 38.1 °C one August. The lowest temperatures occur during the Northern hemisphere winter – December, January and February but even then, the average maximum temperatures do not drop below 30 °C. Winter temperatures range from average lows of 2 °C to average highs of 8 °C December – February. The average annual rainfall is 182.8 millimetres; June to September are the wettest months with from 16 to 73 mm of rain per month. March, April and May are the hottest months with average high temperatures of 31.6 °C. November to January are the wetter monsoon season with 19 rainy days per month on average.

T3 | Listen and Read: Listen to a reading of the texts

Which words do you need to practice saying? Which words do you need to learn?

T4 | Speaking: Talk and Report

Which of these three cities would you most/least like to visit? Why?

T5 | Consolidation Tasks

Unit 67 Weather and Climate 4

Read About The Climate In Three Cities Around The World

T1 | Speaking: Talk and Report

What do you remember about the weather in London, Timbuktu and Singapore?

T2 | Listening: Listen to a talk about world climate zones and make notes

Make notes and complete the diagram below.

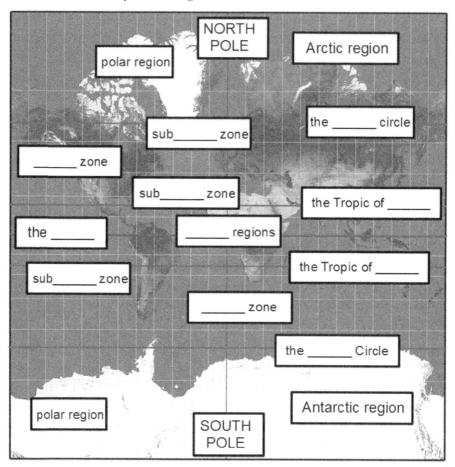

Check your notes with T67.1 and P67.1.

T3 | Listening: Listen to talks about these climate zones and complete the table

Climate Type	Characteristics
1. Temperate Maritime (e.g. London)	
2. Dry Continental (e.g. Timbuktu)	
3. Tropical (e.g. Singapore)	
4. Temperate Continental	

T4 | Listening: Transcript Tasks

Complete the transcript tasks on Talks 1 – 4 on the next page. Complete the texts with the words given and then listen to check. Also check with T67.2 – T67.5.

T5 | Speaking: A Weather Forecast

Write a **two-day** weather forecast for one of the three cities from **T2**.
Use the language of weather forecasts from **Unit 65.**

The forecast for this city is

Then tell your class the forecast.
The other students listen and decide which city the forecast is about.

T6 | Writing: Write a similar text about the climate of a city of your choice

T7 | Speaking: Talk and Report

Which of these four climates is best for you? Why?

Which would you find most difficult to live/operate in? Why?

Transcript Tasks: 1. Temperate Maritime

periods	slightly	snaps	falls	very	land	form	prevailing	over

Cool, temperate maritime climates are found on the western coast of Canada, in western Europe, in the [1] _____ south of Argentina and Chile, and in New Zealand. The [2] _____ winds move from the west to the east, moving [3] _____ the oceans. The winds bring wet and cool air to the [4] _____. As it reaches the land clouds [5] _____ and rain or snow [6] _____. There is [7] _____ more rain in winter than summer. The winters are mild with short cold [8] _____ below zero degrees Celsius. In summer there are short [9] _____ of hotter weather.

2. Dry Continental

rainy	severe	arid	deserts	most

Hot dry climates are typical of [1] _____ like the Sahara, and other semi-[2] _____ regions like in southern South America – in Chile and Argentina – in southern Africa, for example in Namibia, in [3] _____ of Australia and in the south western USA. Some of these desert areas might not receive rain for several years but then have a [4] _____ storm. Other areas might have a short [5] _____ season.

3. Tropical

seasonal	wet	rarely	length	round

In the equatorial regions near the equator there are hot regions with year-[1] _____ rain. The average temperature [2] _____ falls below 18 degrees Celsius and it is very [3] _____ with rainfall throughout the year. These regions are found in the northern parts of South America, in southern Central America, in central Africa e.g. the Congo, and in parts of South-east Asia. As the sun is always overhead the days are roughly the same [4] _____ and there are very small [5] _____ differences.

4. Temperate Continental

often	extreme	rapidly	climates	interior

The [1] _____ of continents like North America and Europe, as well as eastern Asia and northern Japan have cool temperate continental [2] _____. Continental climates have more [3] _____ temperatures than maritime climates. The land heats and cools more [4] _____ than the sea. Summers are warm or hot while winters are cold and [5] _____ very cold.

Unit 68 Weather and Climate 5

T1 I Speaking: Talk and Report

What do you know about these three cities? **Washington D.C. I Tripoli, Libya I Churchill, Canada**. Where are they? What is the climate like in each city?

T2 I Reading Puzzle

Read through this text to extract paragraphs about the three cities above. Note that the sentences are in the correct order for each paragraph.

Washington D. C., the capital of the USA, is in the humid subtropical climate zone. **Churchill**, a small town in northern Canada on the Hudson Bay, has a borderline subarctic climate. **Tripoli**, the capital of Libya, lies on the North African coast of the Mediterranean sea. It has long very cold winters, and short, cool to mild summers. Winter is usually chilly with light snow, spring is mild, summer is hot and humid, and autumn (or fall) is mild to warm. It has a hot semi-arid climate with long, hot and extremely dry summers and relatively wet and warm winters. Summer high temperatures often exceed 38 °C, while the record high is 48.3 °C. The shallow Hudson Bay freezes in winter making the winters colder than expected for its latitude. Average winter temperatures range from 4 °C in December to 1 °C in January and 3 °C in February, with record lows of – 26 °C recorded. Average July temperatures are between 22 and 33 °C. Temperatures can reach as low as 0 °C December to February but the average lows are around 9 °C for these months. Prevailing northerly winds from the Arctic cool the town to a –26.0 °C January daily average, with lows of – 30 °C, and a record low of – 45 °C . The average annual rainfall is less than 400 millimetres; October to January are the wettest months with 46 to 67 mm of rain per month. Snowfall is highest in January and February while the highest average rainfall occurs in May, June and August with 93 mm, and 96 mm and 99 mm respectively. In summer, when the Hudson Bay thaws, Churchill's temperature is an average of 12.7°C in July, though the record high is 36.9 °C. June to August is the hottest and most humid time of year with average temperatures of between 24 and 26 °C but with highs of 29 – 30 °C. Most rain falls in the summer months (June: 44 mm; July 60 mm; August and September: 70 mm), while in October and November 30 to 40 cms of snow falls.

T3 I Listen and Read: Listen to a reading of the texts

Which words do you need to practice saying? Which words do you need to learn?

T4 I Speaking: Talk and Report: Which city would you most/least like to visit? Why?

T5 I Consolidation Tasks

Unit 69 Weather and Climate 6

Read About The Climate In Three More Cities Around The World

T1 | Speaking: Talk and Report

What do you remember about the weather in Washington, Churchill and Tripoli?

T2 | Listening: Listen to talks about these climate zones and complete the table

Climate Type	Characteristics
1. Warm Temperate (e.g. Washington DC)	
2. Arctic/Subarctic (e.g. Churchill)	
3. Hot with seasonal rain (e.g. Tripoli)	
4. Monsoon	
5. Mountains	

T3 | Listening: Transcript Tasks

Complete the transcript tasks on Talks 1 – 4 on the next page. Complete the texts with the words given and then listen to check. Also check with T69.1 – T69.4.

T4 | Speaking: Presentation of a weather forecast

Work in groups. Prepare a **ten-day** weather forecast for one city from **Units 66** and **68**. Practice your presentation in your groups. Then present your city forecast to the class. Make notes on the other forecasts your hear. Then answer these questions from your notes. Check as a class to see if you agree.

1. Which city will be the warmest **on average** over the ten days?
2. Which city will be the coldest **on average** over the ten days?
3. Which city will have the most rain/snow on average over the ten days?
4. Which city will have the best weather?
5. Which city will have the worst weather?

Transcript Tasks: 1. Warm Temperate

adapted	tropical	around	mild	summers

There are warm temperate climates in south-eastern USA, in California, in Cape Province in South Africa, in countries [1] _____ the Mediterranean sea like Italy, and in southern Brazil. These regions have a Mediterranean climate of [2] _____ wet winters and warm or hot [3] _____. Some of these areas might have sub-[4] _____ climates – like Florida in the USA. The natural vegetation is [5] _____ to dry conditions with coniferous trees like the Aleppo pine and ever-green shrubs.

2. Arctic/Sub-arctic

precipitation	build	found	system	air

Cold climates are [1] _____ in polar regions in the Arctic and Antarctic. Antarc-tica, Greenland, northern Canada, northern Norway, northern Finland, and northern Russia are cold and very dry. For example a high pressure air [2] _____ sits above Antarctica's ice-sheets and stops warmer moist [3]_____ from coming in. So, it does not snow very much in Antarctica. The snow and ice [4] _____ up very slowly. Vostok station in Antarctica only receives 4.5 mm of [5] _____ annu-ally.

3. Hot With Seasonal Rain

migrate	wet	south	seasonal	annual

Also in the tropical zones there are hot climates with [1] _____ rains. These are semi-arid areas. These regions are found [2] _____ of the Sahara desert in the Sahel region of Africa, in East Africa, like Kenya and Tanzania, some coastal parts of central America and in parts of southern Brazil. In these regions most of the [3] _____ rainfall (up to 95%) falls during the [4] _____ season. The dry sea-son causes animals like zebras and wildebeest to [5] _____ long distances in search of food and water.

4. Monsoon

regions	dry	rains	heavy	wind

Hot climates with monsoon [1] _____ are found in South-east Asia, like in India, in Korea, southern Japan, and the northern tip of Queensland Australia. These climate [2] _____ have two seasons. There is a [3]_____ season and a wet monsoon season. The monsoon season is when the prevailing [4] _____ changes and wet air blows in from the sea and this brings [5] _____ rain.

Unit 70 Weather and Climate 7

Make Briefings On Weather Systems And Extreme Weather

T1 | Speaking: Group Briefings 1

There are six briefings to give on weather systems and extreme weather

1. Frontal systems
2. Thunderstorms
3. Hurricanes and Typhoons
4. Tornadoes
5. Blizzards
6. Monsoons

Work in groups. Your group will prepare one of the briefings.

Prepare the briefings using **Unit 70 Briefing Slides 1**. Remember you are working as teams, so help the presenter to give their best performance.

Practice your briefing.

Deliver your briefing.

Be ready to answer questions.

T2 | Feedback: Give feedback on your colleagues' briefings

Did you understand everything?
If not, what did you not understand?

T3 | Feedback: Your teacher will give you feedback on your briefing

T4 | Speaking: Group Briefings 2

Prepare a second set of briefings using **Unit 70 Briefing Slides 2**.

Follow the same procedure as above.

These briefings are about the climate in different parts of the world.

Brief your audience on the main climate features of the region shown on the slide.

Language Reminder

in the north/south/east/west etc.
Most of the country **has** a [tropical] climate.
The [north-east] **of** the country **has** a [tropical] climate.
This part of the country/region here **has** a [tropical] climate.
This [coastal] region **has** a [tropical] climate.
North/south/east/west **of** this we move **into** a region **of** [tropical] climate.

Unit 71 Terrain 1: Mountains 1

T1 | Speaking: Talk and Report 1

Look at P71.1 with a partner. How many things can you name? Check with P71.2.

T2 | Vocabulary: Check you know these words

Look at the pictures (P) to help you.

peak/summit	P71.2	lake	P71.2	mountain	P71.2
slope	P71.2	hill	P71.2	lake shore	P71.2
rock	P71.2	col/saddle	P71.3	arête	P71.3
ridge	P71.3	foothills	P71.4	rock face	P715
moorland	P71.6	rocky outcrop	P71.7	cliff	P71.7
scree slope	P71.8/24	shoulder	P71.9	pass	P71.10
gorge	P71.11	ravine/gully	P71.12	re-entrant	P71.13
escarpment	P71.13	spur	P71.14	horn/pyramidal peak	P71.15
plateau	P71.16				

T3 | Vocabulary: Complete the text with words from T2

A mountain [1] _____ is a series or chain of mountains that are close to-gether. Mountains themselves are landforms which are higher than the sur-rounding area. There might be lower [2] _____ near the mountain range itself. Some mountains form an [3] _____ ridge which rises up sharply from the lowlands.

Mountains usually have steep, sloping [4] _____ and sharp or rounded [5] _____. Mountain slopes can have steep [6] _____ or rocky out-crops on them and some slopes are covered with [7] _____ which makes walking difficult.

The side of a mountain is known as the flank. This might rise up to a rounded [8] _____ or up to a steeper ridge. The ridge will run to the highest point of the mountain called the [9] _____ or summit, or might run further as a ridge line which includes several peaks.

Some summits are called [10] _____ or pyramidal peaks. Mountain peaks have [11] _____ which are referred to by the direction they face e.g. the north face faces north.

There might be [12] _____ (or cols) in the ridge line where the elevation drops between two summits and this can be used as a [13] _____ to cross over the mountains. A [14] _____ is a lower summit of a mountain closely connected to the summit on the same ridge line. A small steep valley between two spurs is known as a [15] _____ or draw.

A [16] _____ is an area of relatively flat highland, also called a high plain or tableland.

T4 | Listen and Read: Listen to a reading of the texts

Which words do you need to practice saying?

Which words do you need to learn?

T5 | Vocabulary: Map Identification

Identify the features marked on map M71.1 . Check with the key: M71.2.

T6 | Speaking: Describing Mountain Features

Work in pairs.

Look at the photos (P71.17 - 24) and identify mountain features from T2.

Check with another pair to see if you agree.

Language Reminder
This **looks** like a/an _____.
This **might be** a/an _____.
What do you think? **Is** this a/an _____.
I'm **not sure** but this **could be** a/an _____.
I'm **sure this is** a/an _____.

T7 | Speaking: Talk and Report

1. Would you like to go on holiday to some mountains? Why/why not?
2. If yes, which ones? What would you do there?
3. Where would you stay?
4. What would you need to take with you? Why?
5. Would you like to do adventure training in a mountainous area? Why/why not?

T8 | Consolidation Tasks

Unit 72 Terrain 2: Mountains 2

Learn To Talk About Mountain Terrain

T1 | Speaking: Talk and Report 1

Look at P72.1. What can you see?

T2 | Vocabulary: Check you know these words

Look at the pictures (P) (including from **Unit 71**) to help you.

arête	P71.3	cirque	P71.3	V-shaped valley	P71.3
tarn	P71.5	moraine	P71.3	U-shaped valley	P71.3
cliff	P71.7	rocky outcrop	P71.7	scree slope	P71.9
headwall	P71.9	tree line	P71.10	waterfall	P72.2
hanging valley	P72.3	moorland	P72.3	pass	P72.3
gully	P72.3	lichen	P72.4	knife-edge ridge	P72.4
footpath	P72.5	peak/summit	P72.5	permanent snow	P72.6
morraine	P72.7	glacier	P72.7	watershed	

T3 | Vocabulary: Complete the text with words from T2

Many mountain ranges still have active glacier systems on them and these [1] _____ are still shaping the mountains by eroding the rock. A glacier can create a [2] _____ valley, while a river carves a [3] _____ valley. If an alpine glacier melts, an alpine lake can form in the [4] _____ left behind. The mountain side above the lake (or glacier) is known as the [5] _____. An [6] _____ is a steep-sided, sharp-edged bedrock ridge formed by two glaciers eroding away on opposite sides of the ridge. It is also known as a knife-edge ridge.

Mountain ranges can act as [7] _____ – water flows either side of the mountain ridge line into different river basins. Streams might cut deep [8] _____ into the rock as they flow down the mountainside and there might be high [9] _____.

Some mountains are covered in trees while others are higher in altitude and have a [10] _____ above which trees will not grow. Above this line there might be [11] _____ with grasses and heather plants. Above this there will be [12] _____ covered rocks. The permanent snowline is the point above which snow and ice cover the ground throughout the year.

T4 | Listen and Read: Listen to a reading of the texts

Which words do you need to practice saying? Which words do you need to learn?

Listen to a talk about the Rwenzori Mountains. Make detailed notes on:

Where the mountains are	Size of the range	Animals
Main peaks and altitude	Vegetation zones	National Parks

Check with the class.

T6 | Listening: Transcript Task

Complete the transcript task on Rwenzori Mountains talk below.

Complete the text with the words given and then listen to check.

Also check with T69.1.

Transcript Task

The Rwenzori Mountains, the Mountains of the Moon, are a [1] _____ of mountains in eastern equatorial Africa on the [2] _____ between Uganda and the Democratic Republic of Congo. The peaks are high enough to support [3] _____ and the mountain rivers feed source tributaries of the river Nile.

The range is about 120 kilometres long and 65 kilometres wide. It consists of six massifs separated by deep [4] _____. The highest [5] _____ is Mount Stanley at 5,109 metres high. The highest Rwenzori mountains are [6] _____ snow-capped. The mountains are in an extremely humid area and frequently enveloped in [7] _____. It rains almost every day of the year in the mountains.

There are 5 vegetation [8] _____ in the Rwenzori Mountains. These are the savannah grassland between 1000–2000 m, montane rain forest, at 2000–3000 m, then a bamboo forest zone between 2500–3500 m, and a [9] _____ heather zone with 6 m tall heather plants from 3000–4000 m, and finally the afro-alpine moorland zone above 4000m with moss and lichen covered rocks and [10] _____ snow. The Rwenzori mountains are known for their mountain elephants and mountain gorillas.

Much of the [11] _____ is covered by two national parks: the Rwenzori National Park in Uganda and the Virunga National Park in Congo.

T7 | Revision: Look at Maps M72.1 - 2 and identify mountain features with a partner

T8 | Speaking: Describing Mountain Features

Work in groups: describe one of the slides from **Unit 72 Briefing Slides Mountain Features**. These can also be seen as photographs: P72.8 – 11.

Remember you are working as a team: help the presenter to give their best performance. Practice your briefing. Then deliver your briefing. Be ready to answer questions. Give feedback on your colleagues' briefings. Did you understand everything?

T9 | Consolidation Tasks

Unit 73 Terrain 3: Mountains 3: Briefings

Brief The Class On A Mountain Range

T1 | Speaking: Group Briefing: Mountain Ranges

Work in groups to brief on one of the **Unit 73 Briefing Slides Mountain Ranges**.

There are 15 Briefings about Mountain Ranges

1. The Andes
2. The Rockies
3. The Pyrenees
4. The Atlas Mountains
5. The Alps
6. The Urals
7. The Himalayas
8. The Snowy Mountains
9. The Appalachians
10. The Scandinavian Mountains
11. The Carpathians
12. The Cairngorms
13. The Owen Stanley Range
14. The Southern Alps
15. The Semien Mountains

Remember you are working as a team so help the presenter to give their best performance.

Practice your briefing.

Deliver your briefing.

Be ready to answer questions.

T2 | Feedback: Give feedback on your colleagues' briefings

Did you understand everything?

If not, what did you not understand?

T3 | Feedback: Your teacher will give you feedback on your briefing

Language Reminder
The <u>X mountains</u> are located in _____
The <u>X mountains</u> are _____ km in length.
The highest peak is _____ at _____ high.
In summer/winter the weather is _____.
In summer/winter it is _____.
The biggest dangers are _____.

Unit 74 Terrain 4: Deserts 1

Learn To Talk About Desert Terrain

T1 | Speaking: Talk and Report

Look at P74.1 with a partner. How many things can you name? Check with P74.2.

T2 | Vocabulary: Check you know the meaning of these words

Look at the pictures to help you.

butte	P74.3	oasis	P74.3	mesa	P74.3
plain	P74.3	plateau	P74.3	dried up lake (playa)	P74.4
dried up river	P74.5	waterhole	P74.6	dry steam bed	P74.7
gulley	P74.8	rock outcrop	P74.8	boulder	P74.8
grove of trees	P74.9	mesa/tableland	P74.9	valley	P74.10
alluvial fan	P74.11	salt pan	P74.12	canyon/arroyo/gorge	P74.13

T3 | Vocabulary: Complete the text with words from T2

Sand and sand [1] _____ cover only about 20 percent of the Earth's deserts. Nearly 50 percent of desert surfaces are [2] _____ where the wind has exposed loose gravels consisting predominantly of pebbles. The remaining surfaces of arid lands are composed of exposed bedrock outcrops, desert soils, and fluvial deposits including alluvial fans, playas, desert lakes, and oases. [3] _____ outcrops commonly occur as small mountains surrounded by extensive plains. An [4] _____ is a vegetated area fed by springs, wells, or by irrigation. Most desert plants are drought- or salt-tolerant. Some store water in their leaves, roots, and stems. Other desert plants have long tap roots that penetrate the water table, anchor the soil, and control erosion. Rain does fall occasionally in deserts. Normally dry stream channels, called arroyos or [5] _____ , can quickly fill after heavy rains, and flash floods make these channels dangerous. Desert [6] _____ are generally shallow, temporary, and salty. When small lakes dry up, they leave a salt crust or hardpan. The flat area of clay, silt, or sand encrusted with salt that forms is known as a [7] _____ .

T4 | Speaking: Talk and Report

1. Would you like to go on holiday to a desert? Why/why not?
2. If yes, which one? What would you do there?
3. Where would you stay?
4. What would you need to take with you? Why?
5. Would you like to go on adventure training in a desert area? Why/why not?

T5 | Consolidation Tasks

Unit 75 Terrain 5: Deserts 2

T1 | Speaking: Talk and Report

Look at P75.1 with a partner. How many things can you name?

Check with P75.2.

T2 | Vocabulary: What is the difference?

Look at these pictures from **Unit 74** to help you.

horizon	P74.6	skyline	P74.8

T3 | Vocabulary: Match the words and definitions

bedrock	An area of bedrock above the surrounding land surface, not covered in soil or sand.
salt marshes	The solid rock which is found under soil or sand.
outcrop	A flat wet area where water has evaporated leaving a salt crust on the surface

T4 | Vocabulary: Complete the text with the words given 1

short-lived	salt-tolerant	evaporates	basins	flash

Mountain Deserts are characterised by scattered ranges or areas of barren hills or mountains separated by dry, flat [1] _____. High ground may rise gradually or abruptly from flat areas to several thousand meters above sea level. Most of the infrequent rainfall occurs on high ground and runs off rapidly in the form of [2] _____ floods. These floodwaters erode deep gullies and ravines and deposit sand and gravel around the edges of the basins. Water rapidly [3] _____, leaving the land as barren as before, al-though there may be [4] _____ vegetation. If more water enters the basin than evaporates, shallow lakes may develop: most of these lakes have a high [5] _____ content.   [Note: All Texts Source:FM -90.3]

T5 | Vocabulary: Complete the text with the words given 2

steep-walled	wadis	relief	plains

Rocky Plateau Deserts have relatively low [1] _____ separated by extens-ive [2] _____ with quantities of solid or broken rock at or near the surface. There may be [3] _____ , eroded ravines, known as [4] _____ in the Middle East and arroyos or canyons in the United States and Mexico.

T6 | Vocabulary: Complete the text with the words given 3

leeward	movement	gravel	life	terrain

Sandy or Dune Deserts are extensive flat areas covered with sand or [1] _____. Some areas may contain sand dunes that are over 300 meters high and 16 to 24 kilometers long. Ease of **[2]** _____ in such [3] _____ will depend on the windward or [4] _____ slope of the dunes and the texture of the sand. Plant [5] _____ may vary from none to scrub over 2 meters high.

T7 | Vocabulary: Complete the text with the words given 4

undrinkable	thick	desolate	arid	deposits

Salt Marshes are flat, [1] _____ areas, sometimes studded with clumps of grass but devoid of other vegetation. They occur in [2] _____ areas where rainwater has collected, evaporated, and left large [3] _____ of alkali salts and water with a high salt concentration. The water is so salty it is [4] _____. A crust that may be 2.5 to 30 centimeters [5] _____ forms over the saltwater.

T8 | Vocabulary: Complete the text with the words given 5

rainstorms	wide	broken	range	canyons

Broken Terrain All arid areas contain [1] _____ or highly dissected terrain formed by [2] _____ that erode the soft sand and carve out [3] _____ or wadis. A wadi may [4] _____ from 3 meters wide and 2 meters deep to several hundred meters [5] _____ and deep.

T9 | Listen and Read: Listen to a reading of the texts

Which words do you need to practice saying? Which words do you need to learn?

T10 | Speaking: Talk and Report 2

Which type of desert would be the easiest/most difficult to operate in? Why?

T11 | Writing: Write a description of P75.3 and P75.4

Use the picture description strategies from **Units 3** and **4**.
Show your teacher or partner for feedback.

T12 | Consolidation Tasks

Unit 76 Terrain 6: Deserts 3: Revision: Listening Tasks

T1 | Listening: Listen and Make Notes 1

Listen to this talk about the types of desert terrain and make notes.

Make detailed notes about the features of mountain, rocky plateau, sandy, and dune deserts.

[Check with T76.1]

T2 | Listening: Listen and Make Notes 2

Now listen to a talk about some specific terrain features of deserts.

Make detailed notes about wadis and salt marshes.

[Check with T76.2]

T3 | Listening: Listen and Make Notes 3

Now listen to a talk about some desert environmental features.

Make notes about the following points:

1.	Temperature:
2.	Desert winds:
3.	Sandstorms:
4.	Water:
5.	Plants:

[Check with T76.3]

T4 | Listening: Listen and Make Notes 4

Now listen to a talk about some other desert environmental features.

Make notes about the following points:

1.	Spiders, scorpions and centipedes:
2.	Dogs, rats and fleas:
3.	Snakes:

[Check with T76.4]

T5 | Listening: Listen and Make Notes 5

Now listen to a talk about some more desert environmental features.

Make notes about the following points:

1.	Heat:
2.	Radiant light:
3.	Sunburn:
4.	Wind:

[Check with T76.5]

Unit 77 Terrain 7: Deserts 4: Briefings

Brief About Deserts Around The World

T1 | Speaking: Group Briefings

There are eight briefings to give on desert areas (see **Unit 77 Briefing Slides**). Work in groups to prepare and deliver your briefings. Your teacher will give you feedback.

The deserts are:

1. Atacama
2. Namib
3. Kalahari
4. Gobi
5. Sahara
6. Arabian
7. Great Basin
8. Patagonia

Remember you are working as a team so help the presenter to give their best performance.

Practice your briefing.

Deliver your briefing.

Be ready to answer questions.

T2 | Feedback: Give feedback on your colleagues' briefings

Did you understand everything?

If not, what did you not understand?

T3 | Feedback: Your teacher will give you feedback on your briefing

---

Language Reminder

The X desert covers _____ square kms.

It is a _____ desert.

The X is on the west coast of southern Africa

The X is known for _____.

The highest/lowest temperature recorded is _____.

The main dangers to travellers are _____.

Unit 78 Terrain 8: Temperate Hills and Lowlands

T1 | Speaking: Talk and Report 1

Look at P78.1 with a partner. How many things can you name? Check with P78.2.

T2 | Vocabulary: Check you know the meaning of these words

Look at the pictures (P) to help you.

leaf	P78.3	tree branch	P78.3	tree trunk	P78.3
bushes	P78.3	twig	P78.3	farm	P78.4
foliage	P78.4	forest	P78.5	village	P78.5
wood	P78.5	dell	P78.6	footbridge	P78.7
quarry	P78.8	road bridge	P78.9	ditch	P78.10
fence	P78.11	undergrowth	P78.12	waterlogged ground	P78.13
grass	P78.13	coniferous leaf	P78.14	deciduous leaf	P78.14
clearing	P78.15	regrowth	P78.15	shrubland	P78.16

T3 | Vocabulary: Complete the text with words from T2 in the correct form

Temperate lowland and hilly rural areas are characterised by farmland and forest areas, with small settlements.

Farms are cultivated areas of [1] _____ with farm buildings. These [2] _____ are bordered by hedges or wire [3] _____, or by drainage ditches, or left without a boundary marker.

[4] _____ are large areas of trees, while [5] _____ are smaller areas. The trees might be coniferous or [6] _____ trees. [7] _____ are small isolated stands of trees.

Paths or [8] _____ can cross across the countryside linking roads and [9] _____, which are smaller than towns.

Hilly areas may be wooded or they may be covered in treeless moorland with low-growing vegetation like heather and grasses.

[10] _____ is rough ground with patches of bushes and some scattered trees. It is not farmed and may be forest regrowth after felling.

There might be different kinds of [11] _____, used to extract building materials.

Temperate lowland rural areas often seem safe but there are dangers – bears and snakes and ticks for example.

T4 | Listen and Read: Listen to a reading of the text

Which words do you need to practice saying? Which words do you need to learn?

T5 | Vocabulary: What's the difference?

Discuss the difference between these terms. Use the pictures to help you.

Decide on a translation or definition for each term.

trail	P78.17	
(foot)path	P78.17	
game trail	P78.18	
tarmac road	P78.19	
unpaved road	P78.20/1	
track	P78.22	

T6 | Vocabulary: Explain these terms

belt/line of trees	
patch of ground/saplings	
scattered bushes/trees	
bare ground	
dense bushes/undergrowth/trees	

T7 | Writing: Write descriptions of P78.23 - 35

Choose one or more of the photographs P78.23 -35. Write a description of the photo-graph. Show your text(s) to your teacher or partner for feedback.

T8 | Speaking: Talk and Report 3

1. Would you like to go on holiday to a lowland area? Why/why not?
2. If yes, which one? What would you do there?
3. Where would you stay?
4. What would you need to take with you? Why?
5. Would you like to go on adventure training in a forested lowland area?

T9 | Consolidation Tasks

Revision: Key Collocations		
1. dried up	a) dune	
2. water	b) channel	
3. arid	c) lake	
4. stream	d) table	
5. shallow	e) river	
6. sand	f) land	

Check with Units 74-5.

Unit 79 Terrain 9: Rivers and Lakes

Learn To Talk About Rivers and Lakes

T1 | Speaking: Talk and Report 1

Look at P79.1 with a partner. How many things can you name? Check with P79.2.

T2 | Vocabulary: Check you know the meaning of these words

Look at the pictures (P) to help you.

river channel	P79.3	embankment	P79.3	river bank	P79.3
rapids	P79.4	water meadow	P79.5	spring	P79.6
stream	P79.6	moss	P79.6	reeds	P79.7
lake	P79.7	weir	P79.7	fern	P79.8
flood water	P79.9	pond	P79.10	reeds	P79.11
shallow water	P79.11	deep water	P79.11	bog	P79.12
wetlands	P79.12	dam	P79.13	reservoir	P79.13
swamp	P79.14	waterfall	P79.15	whitewater	P78.16

T3 | Vocabulary: Complete the text with words from T1 and T2 and Unit 78

[1] _____ in hills feed [2] _____which join together to form rivers. [3] _____ streams and rivers join the main river of a river [4] _____. The joining of two rivers is known as the [5] _____.

Rivers may have water meadows which flood in the spring when the [6] _____ of the rivers burst or overflow.

Rivers may be crossed by [16] _____ bridges, or by [7] _____ for pedestrians. Rivers can be fast flowing with dangerous [8] _____ and waterfalls, or slow flowing with [9] _____. A canal is a kind of man-made river – they usually have a straight channel.

Lakes are also fed by streams and sometimes rivers, and are sometimes the main source of rivers which start at the [10] _____ mouth.

Wooded lake [11] _____ are good habitats for wildlife. [12] _____, artificial lakes, are made by constructing a [13] _____ and the water in the lake is used for hydro-electric power generation or as a water supply for towns and cities. Ponds are small lakes. Other wetland areas include [14] _____, areas of grasses, rushes or reeds found on the edges of lakes and rivers, and [15] _____, forested wetland.

A river's catchment area is all the land where water falls and flows into that one river. The watershed is the division between two catchment areas.

T4 | Listen and Read: Listen to a reading of the text

Which words do you need to practice saying? Which words do you need to learn?

T5 | Speaking: Talk and Report 2

Look at M79.1. What features can you identify? Check with M79.2.

T6 | Speaking: Describing River and Lake Features

Work in pairs.

Look at the photos (P79.17 - 26) and identify features. from T2.

Check with another pair to see if you agree.

Language Reminder
This **looks like** a/an _____.
This **might be** a/an _____.
What do you think? **Is** this a/an _____?
I'm not sure but this **could be** a/an _____.
I'm sure this is a/an _____.

T7 | Speaking: Talk and Report 3

1. Would you like to go on holiday to a river or lakeland area? Why/why not?
2. If yes, which one? What would you do there?
3. Where would you stay?
4. What would you need to take with you? Why?
5. Would you like to go on adventure training on a river or a lake? Why/why not?

T8 | Consolidation Tasks

Revision: Key Collocations			
1.	farm	a)	meadow
2.	treeless	b)	supply
3.	building	c)	materials
4.	rural	d)	moorland
5.	water	e)	buildings
6.	catchment	f)	areas
7.	water	g)	area

Check with Units 78-9.

Unit 80 Terrain 10: Tropical Forest 1

T1 | Speaking: Talk and Report

Look at P80.1 with a partner. How many things can you name?

Check with P80.2. Also study P80.3.

T2 | Vocabulary: Complete the text with the words given 1

floor	vegetation	number	dense	sunlight	primary

The climate varies little in **tropical rain forests**. Up to 3.5 meters of rain falls evenly throughout the year. Temperatures [1] _____ from about 32 degrees C in the day to 21 degrees C at night. The forest [2] _____ the bottom-most layer, of the forest only receives 2% of the [3] _____ through the canopy. This means the forest floor is relatively clear of [4] _____. The understory layer lies between the canopy and the forest floor. It is home to numbers of birds, small mammals, insects, reptiles, and predators. The canopy is the [5] _____ layer of the forest, forming a [6] _____roof of vegetation over the two lower layers. It contains the majority of the largest trees, which are typically 30–45 m in height. The emergent layer, above the canopy, contains a small [7] _____ of very large trees, called *emergents*, which reach heights of 45–55 m.

[Note: All Texts based on: MF 21-76]

T3 | Vocabulary: Complete the text with the words given 2

banks	sunlight	denser	regrowth	paddy

Secondary growth rain forest is very similar to rain forest but has [1] _____ vegetation as more [2] _____ reaches the lower levels of the forest. Secondary jungle is often [3] _____ of areas of forest which have be burned, cut or cultivated and then abandoned. It is also found along the edges of the jungle or on river [4] _____. In SE Asia forests are often cleared and the ground terraced to make [5] _____ fields.

T4 | Vocabulary: Complete the text with the words given 3

drought	story (storey)	strata

Semi-evergreen seasonal and monsoon forests have two [1] _____ of trees. Those in the upper story average 18 to 24 meters; those in the lower [2] _____ average 7 to 13 meters. The diameter of the trees averages 0.5 meter. Their leaves fall during a seasonal [3] _____.

T5 | Vocabulary: Complete the text with the words given 4

thorns	season	leafless	bare

In **tropical scrub and thorn forests** there is a definite dry [1] _____ when the trees are [2] _____. The ground is [3] _____ except for a few plants in bunches; grasses are uncommon. Most plants have [4] _____. A *wait-a-while* tree will force you to stop and unhook your clothing.

T6 | Vocabulary: Complete the text with the words given 5

intervals	soils	grassy

Tropical savannahs are found within the tropical zones in South America and Africa. They look like a broad, [1] _____ meadow, with trees spaced at wide [2] _____. Savannah [3] _____ are frequently red.

T7 | Vocabulary: Complete the text with the words given 6

obstacle	poor	tidal	thrive

Saltwater swamps are common in coastal areas subject to [1] _____ flooding. Mangrove trees, which can reach up to 12 m high, [2] _____ in these swamps and their tangled roots are an [3] _____ to movement. Visibility in this type of swamp is [4] _____, and movement is extremely difficult. Tides in saltwater swamps can [5] _____ as much as 12 meters.

T8 | Vocabulary: Complete the text with the words given 7

abundant	visibility	low-lying	islands	undergrowth

Freshwater swamps are found in [1] _____ inland areas. There are masses of thorny [2] _____ , reeds, grasses, and occasional short palms that reduce [3] _____ and make travel difficult. There are often [4] _____ that dot these swamps, allowing you to get out of the water. Wildlife is [5] _____ in these swamps.

T9 | Reading: Read the texts in T2 – T8 again and answer these questions

1. How much rainfall can fall in a tropical forest in a year?
2. What is the temperature range in a tropical forest?
3. Which is more difficult to travel through? Tropical or secondary forest? Why?
4. Which is more difficult to travel through? Saltwater or freshwater swamps?
5. Which of the ecosystems in T2 - T8 has the least number of trees?

T10| Listen and Read: Listen to a reading of the texts

Which words do you need to practice saying? Which words do you need to learn?

T11 | Speaking: Talk and Report 3

1. Would you like to go on holiday to a tropical area? Why/why not?
2. If yes, which one? What would you do there?
3. Where would you stay?
4. What would you need to take with you? Why?
5. Would you like to go on adventure training in a tropical area? Why/why not?

T12 | Consolidation Tasks

Unit 81 Terrain 11: Tropical Forests 2: Revision: Listening Tasks

Listen To Four Short Talks About Tropical Jungles

T1 | Listening: Listen and Make Notes 1

Listen to this talk about the types of tropical jungle. Make detailed notes about:

1. Primary jungles
2. Tropical rain forests
3. Deciduous Forests
4. Secondary jungles

[Check with T81.1]

T2 | Listening: Listen and Make Notes 2

Now listen to a talk about some common jungle features. Make detailed notes about:

1. Mangrove Swamps
2. Palm Swamps
3. Savannah
4. Bamboo
5. Rice Paddies
6. Plantations
7. Small Farms

[Check with T81.2]

T3 | Listening: Listen and Make Notes 3

Now listen to a talk about some dangers of the jungle. Make detailed notes about:

1. Mosquitoes
2. Wasps and bees
3. Centipedes and scorpions
4. Spiders
5. Ants
6. Leeches
7. Snakes
8. Humidity

[Check with T81.3]

T4 | Listening: Listen and Make Notes 4

Now listen to a talk about other dangers of the jungle. Make detailed notes about:

1. Large animals
2. Domesticated animals
3. Water
4. Fungal diseases

[Check with T81.4]

Unit 82 Terrain 12: Tropical Forests 3: Briefings

Brief About Tropical Forests

T1 | Speaking: Group Briefings

There are fifteen briefings to give on tropical areas.

1. The location of the tropical regions.
2. The Amazon
3. The Congo
4. The Orinoco
5. Myanmar
6. Fiji
7. Borneo
8. New Guinea
9. The Pantanal
10. Rwanda
11. Uganda
12. Sri Lanka
13. Queensland, Australia
14. Kenya
15. New Caledonia

Work in groups or pairs and prepare one of the briefings.

Use the **Unit 82 Briefing Slides Tropical Regions**

Remember you are working as a team: help the presenter to give their best performance.

Practice your briefing.

Deliver your briefing.

Be ready to answer questions.

T2 | Feedback: Give feedback on your colleagues' briefings.

Did you understand everything?

If not, what did you not understand?

T3 | Feedback: Your teacher will give you feedback on your briefing.

Language Reminder
The X̲ rainforest covers _____ square kms.
It is a _____ rain forest.
The X̲ is known for _____.
The highest/lowest temperature recorded is _____.
The main dangers to travellers are _____.

Unit 83 Terrain 13: River Estuaries And The Coast 1

Learn To Talk About River Estuaries And The Coast (Riverine)

T1 | Speaking: Talk and Report 1

Look at P83.1 with a partner. How many things can you name?
Check with P83.2.

T2 | Vocabulary: Check you know the meaning of these words

Look at the pictures (P) to help you.

island	P83.3	bay	P83.3	river mouth	P83.3
cape	P83.3	strait	P83.3	breakwater/mole	P83.4
harbour	P83.4	crane	P83.5	dock	P83.5
dry dock	P83.5	jetty	P83.6	marina	P83.6
lighthouse	P83.7	waves/surf	P83.8	beach	P83.8
seaweed	P83.9	cliff	P83.9	confluence	P83.10
estuary	P83.11	peninsular	P83.11	coastline	P83.12
marsh	P83.12	point	P83.13	channel	P83.13
spit	P83.13	inlet	P83.13	coral reef	P83.14
lagoon	P83.14	delta	P83.14	sediment	P83.14
buoy	P83.15	mangroves	P83.16	tidal/mud flats	P83.17

T3 | Vocabulary: Check with the Map

Look at map M83.1 and identify the features A- O.
Check with M83.2.

T4 | Vocabulary: Read and Complete

Look again at map M83.2 and complete this description of map with words from **T2**.

> The map shows the [1] _____ of the North River.
>
> The river runs from the west into Massachusetts Bay. The Herring River joins the North River as it turns south-east towards the bay and the South River runs north to meet the North river as it joins the sea. The [2] _____ of the two rivers is exactly where the main [3] _____ to the sea is. The main river channel is open at low tide. Smaller creeks also join the rivers and there are extensive [4] _____ in the estuary, together with a number of [5] _____ like Bear Island and Wills Island.
>
> You can see the tidal [6] _____ _____ which are revealed at low tide and covered at high tide. There is a sand [7] _____ running south along

the coastline from Rivermoor into the North River channel, and this spit has pushed the river south. North of Rivermoor the coast is mainly a [8] _____ until Pegotty [9] _____. There is a second cliff before the [10] _____ at Scituate. The harbour is protected by a [11] _____ and there is a light-house on Cedar Point.

T5 | Speaking: Describing Coastal Features

Work in pairs: Look at the photos (P83.18-21) and identify coastal features. from T2. Check with another pair to see if you agree.

Language Reminder
This **looks** like a/an _____.
This **might be** a/an _____.
What do you think? **Is** this a/an _____.
I'm **not sure** but this **could be** a/an _____.
I'm **sure this is** a/an _____.

T6 | Speaking: Test Your Partner

Look at maps M83.3, M83.4 and M83.5 and identify features from T2.

Test your partner: *What feature is at GRID 123456?*

T7 | Consolidation Tasks

Revision: Key Collocations		
1. rain	a)	season
2. forest	b)	floor
3. canopy	c)	growth
4. secondary	d)	drought
5. seasonal	e)	forest
6. dry	f)	layer
7. tropical	g)	swamps
8. saltwater	h)	zones
9. primary	i)	paddies
10. rice	j)	jungles

Check with Units 81-2.

Unit 84 Terrain 13: River Estuaries And The Coast 2

T1 | Speaking: Talk and Report 1

Look at P84.1 with a partner.

What terrain features can you identify?

T2 | Vocabulary: Watercraft: Check you know the meaning of these words

Look at the pictures (P) to help you.

yacht	P84.2	lifeboat	P84.2	rowing boat	P84.3
warship	P84.4	aircraft carrier	P84.5	catamaran	P84.6
fishing boat	P84.7	submarine	P84.8	hovercraft	P84.9
ferry	P84.10	pilot boat	P84.11	canoe/kayak	P84.12
tug	P84.13	barge	P84.13	container ship	P84.14
inflatable boat	P84.15	freighter/cargo ship	P84.16	motor boat	P84.17
life jacket	P84.18	oar	P84.18		

T3 | Speaking: Talk and Report 2

Which watercraft from **T2** have you seen?

Which have you been on/in? When?

Which would you like to go on? Why?

T4 | Listening: Listen to a man talking about his experiences travelling on water

Make notes about the man's experiences with boats of various kinds.

Type of Boat	When did it happen? What happened?

T5 | Speaking: Talk and Report 3

1. Would you like to go on holiday to a coastal area? Why/why not?
2. If yes, which one? What would you do there?
3. Where would you stay?
4. What would you need to take with you? Why?
5. Would you like to go on adventure training in a coastal area? Why/why not?

Unit 85 Terrain 15: The Urban Environment 1 Buildings 1

Learn To Describe Different Types Of Buildings Found In Urban Environments

T1 | Speaking: Talk and Report 1

Look at P85.1 with a partner. What can you see?

T2 | Vocabulary: Check you know the meaning of these words

Look at the pictures (P) to help you.

one-storey building	P85.2	two-storey building	P85.2	block of flats	P85.3
apartment block	P85.3	church/cathedral	P85.4	castle/citadel	P85.4
tower	P85.4	mosque/minaret	P85.5	garage	P85.6
detached house	P85.6	cafe	P85.7	shopping centre	P85.8
pub/bar	P85.9	palace	P85..13	foundation	P85.16
fire station	P85.22	bazaar	P85.23	market	P85.23
petrol/gas station	P85.24	school	P85.25	terraced house	P85.26

Which buildings do you <u>not</u> have in your town/city?

T3 | Vocabulary: Check you know the meaning of these words

Look at the pictures (P) to help you.

roof	P85.2	satellite dish	P85.2	floor	P85.2
gutter	P85.2	drainpipe	P85.2	balcony	P85.3
window	P85.4	wall	P85.4	garden	P85.6
escalator	P85.8	advertisement	P85.8	sign	P85.8
window box	P85.9	entrance	P85.9	steps	P85.10
fountain	P85.10	chimney	P85.11	arch	P85.12
shop window	P85.12	arcade	P85.12	courtyard	P85.15
passageway	P85.15	fence	P85.17	hedge	P85.17
bench	P85.18	playground	P85.18	scaffolding	P85.19
skip	P85.20	bin	P85.21	manhole cover	P85.21
market	P85.23	lawn	P85.27	greenhouse	P85.28
stairs	P85.29	stairwell	P85.29	square	P85.30
tunnel	P85.31	walkway	P85.31	underpass	P85.32
gate	P85.33				

T4 | Vocabulary: Check you know the meaning of these words

Look at P85.14 to help you.

concrete	wood	brick	stone

T5 | Vocabulary: Complete the description of P85.34 with words from T2 - T4

The picture shows a block of [1] _____ (or an [2] _____ block). It is made of [3] _____. It is a five [4] _____ building. There are four [5] _____ to the build-ing. There are [6] _____ up to each entrance. There are sixteen [7] _____ and you can see three [8] _____.

T6 | Vocabulary: Complete the description of P85.35 with words from T2 - T4

The picture shows two buildings. On the left there is a pink two [1] _____ wooden [2] _____ house. It has a [3] _____ door in the centre of the ground [4] _____ and two [5] _____ on each side of the door. On the second storey there are probably five [6] _____ – two are hidden by a tree. It has grey asbestos [7] _____ and two [8] _____. The building on the right is a [9] _____ three [10] _____ building. It also has an asbestos [11] _____ and two [12] _____. There are four satellite dishes. This building is a corner [13] _____. Across the street from the pink building there is a park bench and rubbish bin. Between the two buildings there is a narrow street or a passageway to a [14] _____where a car is parked.

T7 | Writing: Write a description of P85.36

Write a description of the photograph.

Show your text(s) to your teacher or partner for feedback.

T8 | Vocabulary: What is the difference?

estate | compound | housing estate

T9 | Speaking: Talk and Report 2

What kind of building do you live in?

What is your neighbourhood like?

What kind of building/area would you like to live in? Why?

Unit 86 Terrain 15: The Urban Environment 2 Buildings 2

Learn To Describe Different Types Of Buildings Found In Urban Environments

T1 | Speaking: Talk and Report 1

Look at P86.1 with a partner. What can you see?

T2 | Vocabulary: Describing position on a building 1

Look at the diagram on the right.

There are two systems of talking about the floors of a building. In Britain there is a ground floor and then the first floor. In other countries the ground floor is the first floor.

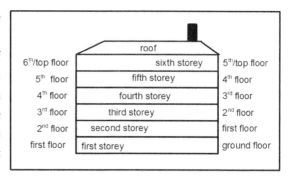

Which system is used in your country?

T3 | Vocabulary: Describing position on a building 2

When we give the position of a window on a building we say the storey and then describe the position of the window on that storey. Look at the diagram below.

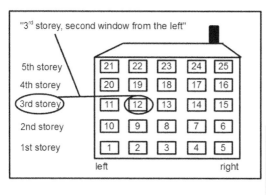

Which number windows are these windows?

1 First story, fourth **from** the right.

2 Second storey, third **from** the left.

3 Third story, first **from** the left.

```
Plural Spelling Note
British: storeys
US: stories
```

T4 | Speaking: Describing position on a building 3

Work in pairs. Take it in turns to describe the position of a window from P86.2 - 5.

Which window is your partner talking about?

T5 | Speaking: Talk and Report 2

Now describe the buildings in P86.2 – 5 using words from **Unit 85.**

Unit 87 Terrain 17: The Urban Environment 3 Roads etc. 1

Learn To Talk About Roads And Associated Features Of The Urban Landscape

T1 | Speaking: Talk and Report

Look at P87.1 with a partner. How many things can you name? Check with P87.2.

T2 | Vocabulary: Check you know the meaning of these words

Look at the pictures (P) to help you.

traffic lights/signals	P87.2	markings	P87.2	crossroads	P87.2
zebra/ pedestrian crossing	P87.2	sign	P87.2	exit	P87.3
roundabout	P87.3	pavement	P87.4	car park	P87.4
lamp post/street light	P87.4	parking space	P87.4	road	P87.4
roadworks	P87.5	barrier	P87.5	bollard	P87.5
bridge	P87.6	bench	P87.7	drain	P87.7
pedestrian zone	P87.7	advert	P87.7	rubbish bin/ trash can	P87.7
main road	P87.8	turn left	P87.8	turn right	P87.8
unpaved road	P87.9	verge	P87.9	bushes	P87.9
telegraph/utility pole	P87.9	ditch	P87.9	pavement/ sidewalk	P87.10
one way street	P87.10	No Entry	P87.10	parked cars	P87.10
bike rack/stand	P87.11	steps	P87.11	cables	P87.12
manhole cover	P87.12	traffic cone	P87.12	barrier	P87.13
courtyard	P87.13	passageway	P87.13	outside lane	P87.14
dual carriageway	P87.14	curb	P87.14	inside lane	P87.14
central reservation	P87.14	t-junction	P87.15	side street	P87.15
no through road	P87.16	embankment	P87.17	culvert	P87.17
ditch	P87.17	fire hydrant	P87.18	highway	P87.19
junction/interchange	P87.19	slip road/ramp	P87.19	motorway	P87.19

T3 | Vocabulary: Complete the description of P87.20

Use words from T1, T2 and other words.

> The picture shows a [1] _____ running through a city. The [2] _____ is running through a stone-lined channel. In the centre of the picture there is a stone [3] _____ crossing the river. There are some people walking across the

[4] _____. On the right bank of the river there is a [5] _____ with tram tracks and a tram. Between the road and the river there is a [6] _____. There are street [7] _____ lining the road. Cars and buses are also using this road. It is a [8] _____ street. On the other side of the river there is another [9] _____ and there is a glass fronted [10] _____. In the background there are trees – there is a small [11] _____. By the trees there seems to be a small [12] _____. And on this side of the river in the [13] _____ there are some tall [14] _____.

T4 | Vocabulary: Complete the description of P87.21 with words from T1 and T2

The picture shows a complicated road [1] _____. There is a road coming in from the left, meeting a road from the right to make a [2] _____. Just before the junction, on each road there is a zebra crossing. There are no [3] _____ lights.

To the left of this junction there is another [4] _____ to the right. Just after the turning there is another zebra crossing. The road from the right continues to the left of the photograph and there is a fourth zebra crossing there.

In the [5] _____ there are some trees and low [6] _____on the left, and on the right there is a white two [7] _____ building.

The road junction is protected with [8] _____ to stop [9] _____ crossing except at the zebra crossings.

In the foreground there are two flower beds with red flowers and there is a [10] _____ cover in the bottom right-hand corner of the photograph.

T5 | Writing: Write a description of P87.22 – 24

Use the picture description strategies from **Units 3** and **4**.
Show your teacher or partner for feedback.

T6 | Vocabulary: What is the difference?

road | street | avenue | highway | motorway | cul-de-sac | pavement | sidewalk

T7 | Revision: Giving Directions

Work in pairs. Look at Map M87.1 on the next page. Choose two points (A to I). Tell your partner the first point. Then give directions from there to the other point to your partner. See if your partner can follow your directions. (Reminder: See **Unit 46**)

T8 | Consolidation Tasks

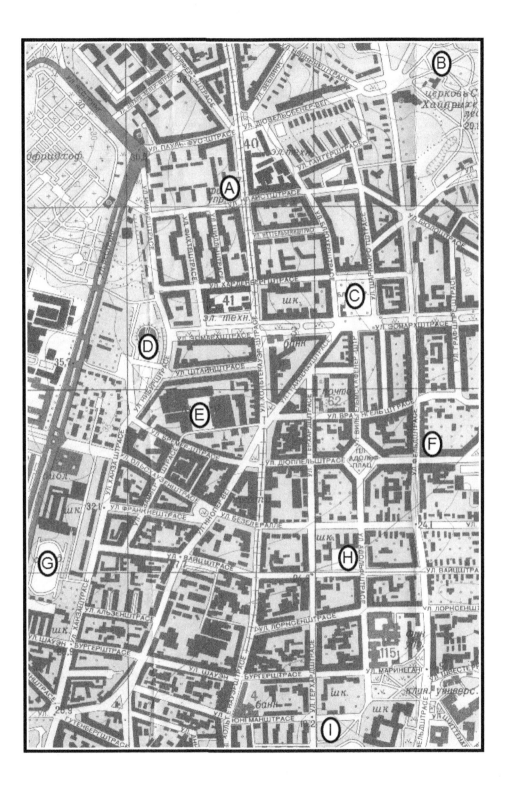

Unit 88 Terrain 18: The Urban Environment 4 Roads etc. 2

Learn To Talk About Roads And Associated Features Of The Urban Landscape

T1 | Speaking: Talk and Report 1

Look at P88.1 with a partner. What can you see?

T2 | Vocabulary: Check you know these vehicles

train	P88.2	bus	P88.3	ambulance	P88.4	tram	P88.5
coach	P88.6	tanker	P88.7	lorry/truck	P88.8	metro	P88.9
van	P88.10		fire engine/appliance		P88.11		

T3 | Speaking: Talk and Report 2

Which of the vehicles from T2 have you seen?

Which have you been on/in?

Which are most used where you live?

Which could be improved? How?

T4 | Vocabulary: Check you know the meaning of these words

Look at the pictures (P) to help you.

bus station	P88.12	platform	P88.12	bus bay	P88.12
departure board	P88.12	points	P88.13	train track	P88.13
engine/locomotive	P88.13	wagon/truck	P88.13	sleeper	P88.13
railway/train station	P88.13	rail/track	P88.13	platform	P88.13
marshalling yard	P88.13	bollard	P88.14	ramp	P88.14
bus stop	P88.14	bus shelter	P88.14	level crossing	P88.15
signal box	P88.16	bridge	P88.17	railing	P88.17
supporting piers	P88.17	abutments	P88.17	barrier	P88.17

T5 | Speaking: Revision Briefing

Work in groups.

Prepare a briefing on the slides in the **Unit 88 Briefing Slides**.

Use the words from **Units 85** to **88** and the picture description strategies from **Units 3** and **4**. Give a comprehensive description of what can be seen in the photographs.

Remember you are working as a team. Practice your briefing.

Deliver your briefing to other students/the class.

Be ready to answer questions.

Give feedback on your colleagues' briefings.

Did you understand everything?

If not, what did you not understand?

Unit 89 Terrain 19: The Urban Environment 5: 3-D 1

T1 | Speaking: Talk and Report 1

Look at the diagram in P89.1.

What elements are there in the three dimensional urban environment?

Why is it important to consider these three dimensions in the urban environment?

T2 | Vocabulary: Check you know the meaning of these words

approach	basements	buildings	built-up	cellars
concealment	counter-attacks	environment	fields	ground
level	lines	operations	outflank	points
positions	sewers	streets	vulnerable	weapons

T3 | Vocabulary: Complete the text with the words from T3

The urban environment is the most complex [1] _____ soldiers will operate in. Urban areas have three dimensions to consider.

Streets afford avenues of [2] _____ and are the primary means for rapid
ground movement in a [3] _____ area. Forces travelling along
[4] _____, however, are often channeled by [5] _____ and have
little space for maneuver off of the main thoroughfares.

Buildings themselves provide cover and [6] _____ . They limit or enhance
[7] _____ of observation and fire, and they restrict or block movement of
[8] _____ forces. Upper floors and roofs provide the urban threat forces
excellent observation [9] _____ and battle [10] _____ above the
maximum elevation of many [11] _____ of troops at ground level. Shots
from upper floors can strike friendly armored vehicles in [12] _____
points.

Conventional lateral boundary ([13] _____) will often not apply as threat
forces control some stories of the same building while friendly forces control
others. Below street [14] _____ , building [15] _____ can also
provide firing points below many weapons' minimum depressions and strike at
weaker armor on the underside of the vehicle.

Subterranean systems, such as [16] _____ , subways, connected
[17] _____ , and utility systems, like electric cable tunnels, can provide
covered and concealed access throughout the area of [18] _____ . They
can easily be employed as avenues of approach for dismounted elements. Both
attacker and defender can use subterranean routes to [19] _____ or turn
enemy positions and to conduct ambushes, [20] _____ , infiltration, and
sustainment operations.   [Based on: FM 3-06.11]

T4 | Vocabulary: Explain these collocations and phrases

1. primary means

2. main thoroughfare

3. maximum elevation

4. lateral boundaries

5. avenues of approach

6. threat forces

7. firing point

8. utility systems

9. concealed access

10. dismounted elements

11. subterranean routes

12. sustainment operations

T5 | Listen and Read: Listen to a reading of the text

Which words do you need to practice saying? Which words do you need to learn?

P6 | Speaking: Talk and Report 2

Work in pairs. Choose a photograph from **P89.2 – 28**.

Prepare a talk on the problems of operating in such an urban environment.

Language Reminder
The photograph **shows** _____.
In this area the buildings **are** _____.
Here, these tall buildings **dominate** this area.
This area is **overlooked by** these buildings here.
The **main difficulty** in this area **is** _____.
The **biggest problem** in this area **is** _____.
This area is **dangerous/safe** because it _____.
This area **has/does not have** lots of good cover.
In this area you are **exposed to fire from** _____.
There could be insurgents/enemy soldiers **in this area/on these roofs/ behind these buildings/in these buildings**........

T7 | Consolidation Tasks

Unit 90 Terrain 20: The Urban Environment 5: 3-D 2

Learn to talk about the three dimensional urban environment

T1 | Speaking: Talk and Report

What do you remember from Unit 89? What are the three dimensions in the urban environment? Why are they important? How do they make urban warfare difficult?

T2 | Vocabulary: Check you know the meaning of these words

market	bazaar	square	old city	citadel
museum	restaurant	cafe	temple	mosque
cathedral	castle	quarter	shopping centre/mall	
residential zone	industrial zone/park	suburbs	central business district	
square	office block	downtown	commercial buildings	
area	centre/center	district	county	region

T3 | Listening: Listen and Make Notes 1

Listen to the talk and make notes on the different parts of urban areas.

T4 | Listening: Transcript Task 1

Complete **Transcript Task 1** on the next page. Complete the text with words from T2 and then listen to check. Also check with T90.1

T5 | Listening: Listen and Make Notes 2

Listen to another talk and make notes to answer these questions.
1. What are the three *other* dimensions the speaker talks about?
2. Why are they important?

T6 | Listening: Transcript Task 2

Complete **Transcript Task 2** on the next page. Complete the text with the words given and then listen to check. Also check with T90.2

T7 | Speaking: Talk and Report

1. Do you agree with the speaker in T3?
2. What do you think are the most difficult aspects of urban operations?
3. Do you prefer urban or non-urban operations? Why?
4. What are the main differences between rural and urban operations?

T8 | Speaking: Intelligence Briefing

Work in groups. Prepare an intelligence briefing about the situation in one of the towns in **Unit 90 Briefing Slides.** Decide what the situation is in the town, describe the town and its environment, and the area around it. Listen to the other briefings and ask questions. Your teacher will give you feedback on your briefing.

Transcript Tasks: Task 1

In any urban area there are different zones. In the centre of a town or city there is an area called the [1] _____ in American English, or the town centre in British English. This is an area of city squares, [2] _____ buildings, shops, hotels and other commercial buildings. There might be local or national government [3] _____ spread through the centre of town. And the most important cultural buildings are usually found in the centre – buildings like theatres, the opera, and [4] _____. There might be an entertainment quarter with retail businesses, restaurants and [5] _____, casinos and bars. There might be a specialised central business [6] _____ where most of the banks, office blocks and expensive shops are. Some cities will have a large central market or [7] _____. The [8] _____ railway and bus stations are usually found in city centres. Historical cities may have an [9] _____ city, with the main [10] _____ , temple or mosque, or a [11] _____ or citadel in the centre. This might be the main tourist destination in the city.

The centre of the city might be surrounded by residential zones or districts where most people live. In these zones there will be small shops and even shopping [12] _____, or malls mixed in with the residential buildings. Further out there might be industrial [13] _____ where there are mainly factories; few people will live in these areas. There might be [14] _____ which are residential zones around the edge of the city. People may live in these suburban areas and commute into the city to work. There might be some out of town retail and industrial [15] _____ on roads going out of the cities.

Task 2

airspace	assets	control	day	forces
hostile	obstructions	population	space	terrain

There are three more dimensions to consider in urban operations. The first is the [1] _____ above the city or town. Airspace provides a rapid avenue of approach into the urbanized area. Aircraft must consider towers, signs, power lines, and other [2] _____ to flight. Towers and tall buildings can be used by threat [3] _____ as positions to attack air [4] _____.

In some cases, a sizable civilian [5] _____ may function as a fifth dimension to urban operations in urban [6] _____. This is especially true if the population or elements of it are [7] _____ to your forces or supportive of threat forces.

The final dimension is time. Because of the complexity of urban areas it is difficult to control the entire battle [8] _____ and to notice when changes have happened. An urban environment is different at night than by [9]. _____ Areas which are under control by day might not be under [10] _____ by night.

Unit 91 Terrain 21: Bridges, Dams and Airfield Briefings

T1 | Speaking: Talk and Report 1

Look at P91.1. What can you see?

T2 | Vocabulary: The Basics of Bridges

Bridges have three main parts:. Look at P91.2 and see what is in each part.
Complete the table below.

Foundation:	
Substructure:	
Superstructure:	

Instant Test: Test yourself with P91.3. Check with P91.4.

T3 | Vocabulary: Types of Bridges

There are four main types of bridges: suspension, truss, beam and arch.
Look at P91.5 and check you know the differences between them.

T4 | Vocabulary: Dams

Look at P91.6 and check you understand the key words.

T5 | Vocabulary: Airfields

Look at P91.7 and P91.8 and check you understand the key words.

T6 | Speaking: Briefings

Work in groups.
Prepare a briefing on the slides in the **Unit 91 Briefing Slides**.
Bridges and **Dams**: Each section of the briefing has two parts – a photograph of a bridge or dam, and a map of the bridge or dam and the surrounding area.
Airfields: There is one airfield map and four aerial photos.
Give a comprehensive description of what can be seen in the photographs and maps.
Imagine the bridge/dam/airfield is defended and it is your objective to take it.
Describe the disposition of the enemy forces defending the objective.

Remember you are working as a team: help the presenter to give their best perform-ance. Practice your briefing. Then deliver your briefing to other students/the class.
Be ready to answer questions.

T7 | Feedback: Give feedback on your colleagues' briefings

Did you understand everything? If not, what did you not understand?

T8 | Feedback: Your teacher will give you feedback on your briefing

Unit 92 Expressing Certainty and Uncertainty

Learn How To Express Certain And Uncertain Conclusions

T1 | Speaking: Talk and Report 1

Look at P92.1. What can you see?

T2 | Grammar: Facts and uncertainty 1

When we are sure about something we can express it as a fact:

> It _is_ raining.   We _are_ under attack.   Tanks _are_ coming.

When we are unsure about something we have to 'hedge'.

> I _think_ the sniper is in that tree over there.

T3 | Grammar: Facts and uncertainty 2

Look through the example sentences below.

Which are statements of certainty? Which are uncertain?

1. He has been promoted.
2. I'm not sure but I think we should go north-east.
3. He has been shot.
4. That might be true.
5. C Company is on your left flank.
6. That could be a minefield.
7. I think that is a bunker.
8. This looks like a residential area.
9. Intelligence suggests that the attack will come soon.
10. It's not very clear but this seems to be an industrial area.
11. It's probable that he has been killed.
12. It's possible that he survived the crash.

T4 | Vocabulary: Descriptions 1

If you are uncertain what something is, describe its shape, size, colour and position. Check you understand these words.

sort of	square	triangular	oval	circular
roughly	rectangular	cylindrical	oblong	conical

T5 | Speaking: Talk and Report

Look at P92.2.

How would you describe A – K?

Do not use the word for the thing even if you know it.

Check with P92.3.

T6 | Vocabulary: Descriptions 2

Complete the description below of P92.2 with a suitable word.

On the [1] _____ there is a light grey structure made out of [2] _____. It is [3] _____ and has a dark grey [4] _____ roof. Behind it, and slightly to the left, is another building which looks exactly the same. They are joined together by a metal [5] _____ which runs from the tip of each roof. Next to these two structures, on the left, is a square white [6] _____ with a dark grey roof. On the right side of this building there is a a dark grey rectangular [7] _____ structure which runs up to the tip of the first building with the conical roof. There is a similar structure running to the tip of the roof of the second cylindrical building. Behind the square white building is the largest building. It is a big [8] _____ building with a blue [9] _____ structure on the right on the wall facing us, as well as a tall, grey [10] _____ structure, on this same wall but on the left. Behind the building is a dark grey [11] _____ and another blue rectangular structure. In front of these are two large silver [12] _____ structures. The one of the left is slightly taller than the one on the right.

T7 | Speaking: Practice expressing certainty and uncertainty 1

Look at P92.4 to P92.8 in sequence.

Discuss P92.4 first, then P92.5 etc.

What can you see?

T8 | Listening: Listen for certainty and uncertainty

Listen to the briefing about P92.9.

1. What is the speaker certain about?
2. What is he uncertain about?

T9 | Speaking: Practice expressing certainty and uncertainty 2

Brief about one of the photographs in **Unit 92 Briefing Slides**. Make it clear whether you are certain or uncertain about the features you talk about.

Unit 93 Land Navigation 1: North and Grids

Learn About North And Giving Grid References In English

T1 | Speaking: Talk and Report

Why do soldiers need to be able to read maps? Give specific reasons.

T2 | Vocabulary: Points of the Compass

Draw a compass rose with the four cardinal directions and four intermediate points. Check with P93.1.

T3 | Vocabulary: Complete the text about the three norths: True, Grid and Magnetic

A compass points to _____ north. This is different from _____ north and _____ north, the north of the northing lines on a map. The difference between _____ north and _____ north is known as the magnetic declination.

T4 | Vocabulary: Parts of a Compass

Look at P93.2 and P93.3.

What are the parts of the compasses called?

Check with P93.4/5.

T5 | Speaking: Presentation

Work in groups.

Prepare a briefing about lensatic and Silva compasses: see **Unit 93 Briefing Slides**. Explain about the parts of the compass and how to use them.

Language Reminder

X is used for doing Y

X is used to do Y

You can use X to do/for doing Y

T6 | Vocabulary: Grid References 1

Maps are divided into numbered squares. These squares are made by the grid lines on the map. There are two kinds of grid lines: eastings and northings. **Eastings**: are lines that run **vertically** up and down the map. They increase in number the further you move east. **Northings**: are lines that run **horizontally** across the map. They increase in number the further you move north. Identify the **grid square marked X.**

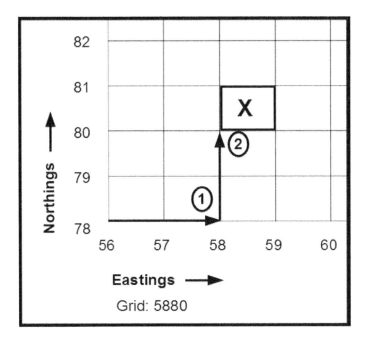

Grid: 5880

T7 | Vocabulary: Grid References 2: Six Figure References

Now imagine the square is divided into 10 x 10 smaller squares. Use these squares to calculate the 6 figure grid number as in the example below. Calculate the easting first and add it to the 4 figure grid reference and then the northing.

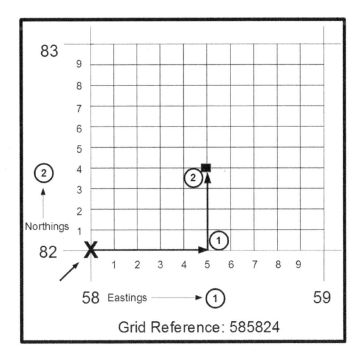

Grid Reference: 585824

T8 | Vocabulary: Grid References Test

Use the map below.

What are the grid references for points 1- 10?

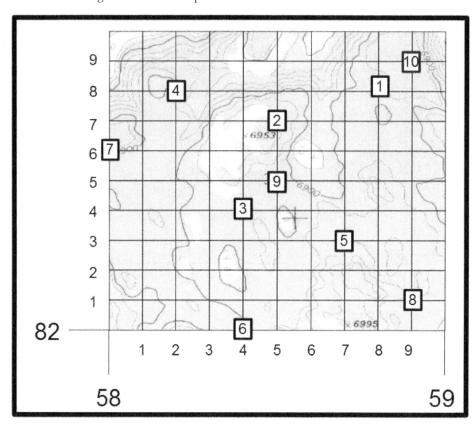

T9 | Speaking: Grid References

Work with a partner.

Use your maps.

Point to a place on the map and ask your partner to give you the six figure reference.

T10 | Consolidation Tasks

Unit 94 Land Navigation 2: Terrain Features

Learn To Read Terrain Features And Other Features From Maps

T1 | Speaking: Talk and Report

What terrain features do you remember from the units on mountainous terrain? Make a list with your partner. Check with **Unit 71/2**.

T2 | Vocabulary: Terrain Features and Maps 1

Study the diagrams in P94.1 – 8 and make sure you can identify these terrain features on maps.

T3 | Vocabulary: Terrain Features and Maps 2

Look at map M94.1 on the next page (or in the electronic map folder). What terrain features from **T2** can you find? Check the sample answers on M94.2.

T4 | Vocabulary: Other Features and Maps

Look at maps M94.3, M94.4, M94.5 and M94.6.

Identify these features:

church	cross-roads	drainage ditch	house	dam
culvert	wood	interchange	bridge	pond
t-junction	side road	embankment	lake	main road
stadium	cutting	railway station	park	cemetery

Check with maps M94.7, M94.8, M94.9 and M94.10.

Which feature is not on the maps?

T5 | Speaking: Talk and Report: Map Reading

Look at P94.9 Then look at M94.11. Identify the features A – E on P94.9 from the map. Check with P94.10.

Repeat the task with P94.11 and features A – H. Use M94.12, Check with P94.12.

T6 | Speaking: Map Interpretation

Work in Groups. Prepare a presentation on one of the 12 map slides in the **Unit 94 Map Interpretation Presentation.** Explain the map features from your maps to the class.

T7 | Vocabulary: Terrain and Other Features Quiz

Use your own maps or use the printable maps **M94.13** and **M94.14.**

Prepare a terrain and other features quiz for your colleagues.

Find ten terrain features on your map and decide on the grid reference.

Ask your colleagues: '*What terrain feature is at grid 457398?*'

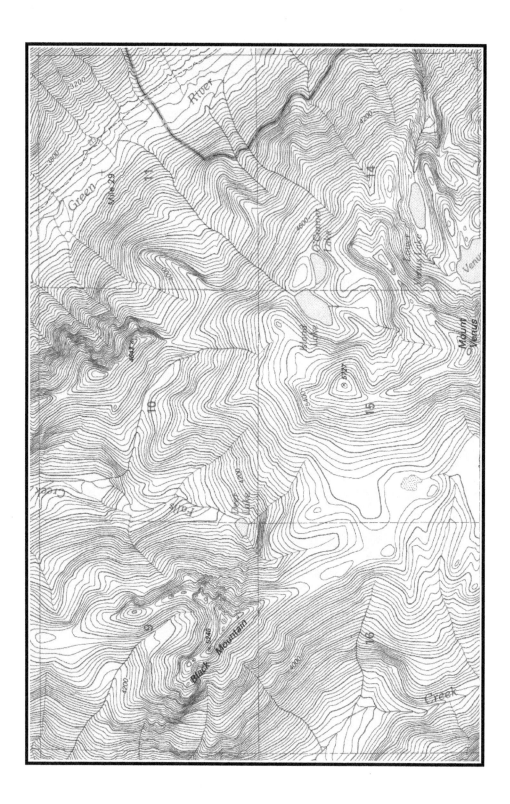

Unit 95 Land Navigation 3: Route Cards

Learn To Prepare A Route Card

T1 | Vocabulary: Route Card

Look at the route card and check you understand everything.

Route Card			Map Series		Sheet		Edition		Mag Variation	
Out / Back										
	From		To		Bearing (Mag)				Ground	
Leg	Location	Grid	Location	Grid	Grid	Mag	Distance	Time	Description	
1										
2										

T2 | Speaking: Plan a route and brief the class

Work in pairs.

Use your maps.

Plan a route with five legs from location Alfa to location Bravo.

You decide on location Alfa and Bravo.

Plan a different return route from location Bravo to location Alpha with 4 legs.

Complete a detailed Route Card for your route.

Use the blank Route Cards in your Workbook.

Brief the class on your route.

Listen to the other briefings.

Complete a route card for each route and mark the route on a map overlay.

Language Reminder

The <u>first</u> leg is from (location) at GRID _____ to (location) at GRID _____. The bearing is _____. It is _____ km/m. It should take _____ hours/minutes. The ground is _____.
The <u>second</u> leg is _____.

Unit 96 Land Navigation 4: Movement 1

Learn To Analyse Terrain For Movement In English

T1 | Speaking: Talk and Report 1

> Terrain should be analysed for **O**bservation and fields of fire, **A**venues of approach, **K**ey and decisive terrain, **O**bstacles, **C**over and concealment.

Why are these important?

Remember: **OAKOC**

T2 | Vocabulary: Check you know the meaning of these words

access	alleys	artificial	concealment	corridors
cover	cover	divert	factors	field
landmarks	obstacle	obstructions	position	protection
retention	route	routes	secondary	wadi

T3 | Vocabulary: Complete the text with the words from T2

Observation and Fields of Fire. The purpose of observation is to see the enemy (or various [1] _____) but not be seen by him. Anything that can be seen can be hit. Therefore, a field of fire is an area that a weapon or a group of weapons can [2] _____ effectively with fire from a given [3] _____.

Avenues of Approach. These are [4] _____ routes. They may be the routes you can use to get to the enemy or the routes they can use to get to you. Basically, an identifiable route that approaches a position or location is an avenue of approach to that location. They are often terrain [5] _____ such as [6] _____ or wide, open areas.

Key Terrain. Key terrain is any locality or area that the seizure or [7] _____ of affords a marked advantage to either combatant. Urban areas are often seen by higher headquarters as being key terrain because they are used to control [8] _____. On the other hand, an urban area that is destroyed may be an [9] _____ instead. High ground can be key because it dominates an area with good observation and fields of fire. In an open area, a draw or [10] _____ may provide the only cover for many kilometers, thereby becoming key. You should always attempt to locate any area near you that could be even remotely considered as key terrain.

Obstacles. Obstacles are any [11] _____ that stop, delay, or [12] _____ movement. Obstacles can be natural (rivers, swamps, cliffs, or mountains) or they may be artificial (barbed wire entanglements, pits, concrete or metal anti-mechanized traps). They can be ready-made or constructed in the [13] _____. Always consider any possible obstacles along your movement [14] _____ and, if possible, try to keep obstacles between the enemy and yourself.

Cover and Concealment. Cover is shelter or [15] _____ (from enemy fire) either natural or [16] _____. Always try to use covered routes and seek [17] _____ for each halt, no matter how brief it is planned to be. Unfortunately, two [18] _____ interfere with obtaining constant cover. One is time and the other is terrain. Concealment is protection from observation or surveillance, including concealment from enemy air observation. Before, trees provided good [19] _____ , but with modern thermal and infrared imaging equipment, trees are not always effective. When you are moving, concealment is generally [20] _____ ; therefore, select routes and positions that do not allow covered or concealed enemy near you.

[Adapted from: Fm 3-25.26 Map Reading And Land Navigation]

T4 | Vocabulary: Explain these words, collocations and phrases

1. field of fire
2. natural obstacle
3. artificial obstacle
4. ready-made
5. concealment
6. surveillance
7. air observation
8. thermal imaging equipment
9. infrared imagining equipment
10. concealed enemy

T5 | Listen and Read: Listen to a reading of the text

Which words do you need to practice saying? Which words do you need to learn?

T6 | Speaking: Talk and Report

Work in pairs. Use your maps. Decide on location Alfa and Objective Bravo. Plan a route with five legs from location Alfa to Objective Bravo. Complete a detailed Route Card for your route.

Brief the class on your route. Give **reasons** why you chose the route you did. Discuss key terrain, avenues of approach, cover etc.

Listen to the other briefings. Complete a route card and mark the route on the map for each briefing.

T7 | Consolidation Tasks

Unit 97 Land Navigation 5: Movement 2

Learn To Talk About Other Movement Factors

T1 | Speaking: Talk and Report

> Tactical factors other than the military aspects of terrain must also be considered in conjunction with terrain during movement planning and execution as well. These additional considerations are **M**ission, **E**nemy, **T**errain and weather, **T**roops, and **T**ime available.

Why are these important?

Remember: **METT-T**

T2 | Vocabulary: Check you know the meaning of these words

action	alternate	concealment	condition	consideration
down	effect	engaged	fighting	front
level	maneuver	mission	objective	reconnaissance
reduce	ridge	route	terrain	withdrawals

T3 | Vocabulary: Complete the text with the words from T2

> **Mission**. This refers to the specific task assigned to a unit or individual. Soldiers must get to the right place, at the right time, and in good [1] _____condition. Patrol missions are used to conduct combat or [2] _____ operations. During the map reconnaissance, the mission leader determines a primary and [3] _____ route to and from the objectives. Movement to contact is conducted whenever an element is moving toward the enemy but is not in contact with the enemy. Delays and [4] _____ are conducted to slow the enemy down without becoming decisively [5] _____ , or to assume another mission. To be effective, the element leader must know where he is to move and the route to be taken.
>
> **Enemy**. This refers to the strength, status of training, disposition (locations), doctrine, capabilities, equipment (including night vision devices), and probable courses of [6] _____ that impact upon both the planning and execution of the [7] _____ , including a movement.
>
> **Terrain and Weather**. The leader conducts a map reconnaissance to determine key terrain, obstacles, cover and concealment, and likely avenues of approach. Weather has little [8] _____ on dismounted land navigation. Rain and snow could possibly slow [9] _____ the rate of march, that is all. But during mounted land navigation, the navigator must know the effect

of weather on his vehicle.

Troops. Consideration of your own troops is equally important. The size and type of the unit to be moved and its capabilities, physical [10] _____ , status of training, and types of equipment assigned all affect the selection of routes, positions, fire plans, and the various decisions to be made during movement. On ideal terrain such as relatively [11] _____ ground with little or no woods, a platoon can defend a [12] _____ of up to 400 meters. The leader must conduct a thorough map reconnaissance and terrain analysis of the area his unit is to defend. Heavily wooded areas or very hilly areas may [13] _____ the front a platoon can defend. The size of the unit must also be taken into [14] _____ when planning a movement to contact. During movement, the unit must retain its ability to [15] _____ . A small draw or stream may reduce the unit's maneuverability but provide excellent concealment. All of these factors must be considered.

Time Available. At times, the unit may have little time to reach an [16] _____ or to move from one point to another. The leader must con-duct a map reconnaissance to determine the quickest [17] _____ to the objective; this is not always a straight route. From point A to point B on the map may appear to be 1,000 meters, but if the route is across a large [18] _____ the distance will be greater. Another route from point A to B may be 1,500 meters—but on flat [19] _____ . In this case, the quickest route would be across the flat terrain; however, [20] _____ and cover may be lost.

[Adapted from: Fm 3-25.26 Map Reading And Land Navigation]

T4 | Listen and Read: Listen to a reading of the text

Which words do you need to practice saying? Which words do you need to learn?

T5 | Speaking: FOB Patrol Challenge

Work in groups. Prepare a challenge for the other groups.

Use your maps. Decide on the FOB base location. Decide on the patrol mission: what is the objective? Decide on the forces available to the patrol leader. Decide on the dis-position and size of the enemy forces. Then ask another group to plan the patrol's primary and alternate route to and from the objective.

Be ready to deal with the challenge they have prepared for you. Brief them on your solution to their challenge.

Evaluate their solution to your challenge and give feedback.

T6 | Consolidation Tasks

Unit 98 Land Navigation 6: Difficult Terrain Briefings

Give A Briefing On Navigating In Difficult Terrain

T1 | Speaking: Group Briefings

There are thirteen briefings to give on aspects of navigation:

1. Moving by Dead Reckoning
2. Moving by Terrain Association
3. Direction: Shadow-Tip Method
4. Direction: Watch Method
5. Moving around an obstacle
6. Desert Terrain
7. Mountain Terrain
8. Jungle Terrain
9. Arctic Terrain
10. Urban Areas
11. Navigating in Vehicles
12. Night Navigation
13. Field Sketches

See **Unit 98 Briefing Slides**

[All briefing materials adapted from FM 3-25.26 Map Reading And Land Navigation]

Work in groups.

Prepare a briefing using the slides provided.

Remember you are working as a team: help the presenter to give their best performance.

Practice your briefing.

Deliver your briefing.

Be ready to answer questions.

T2 | Feedback: Give feedback on your colleagues' briefings

Did you understand everything?

If not, what did you not understand?

T3 | Feedback: Your teacher will give you feedback on your briefing

Unit 99 The Disposition of Forces 1

T1 | Speaking: Talk and Report

Look at P98.1 and P98.2. What can you see?

T2 | Vocabulary: Check you know the meaning of these words

antitank gun	light weapons	defensive position
armour/armor	machine gun	AT rocket launcher
artillery	mortar	howitzer
assembly area	objective	infantry
AT missile	platoon	section
squad	tank	

T3 | Vocabulary: Study the set of Symbols and Meanings below

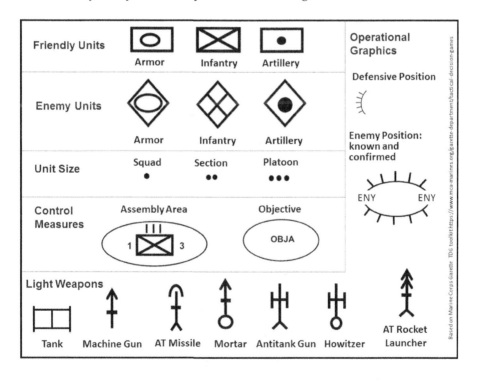

T4 | Writing: Write a description for a briefing

Look at M98.1 and Overlay below (or in the electronic Phase 2 Map Folder).
Complete this description of the disposition of forces.

We have a [1] _____ of 4 light tanks in defensive positions north of Pelican
Creek just east of Vermilion Springs. There are two light [2] _____ on a hill
at Grid 377878. South of the Creek there is an infantry [3] _____ with two
[4] machine guns, with two [5] _____ in support at Grid 373871, and two
light [6] _____ on the left flank on the Pelican Creek Trail. The enemy is in
defensive positions to the west. An armoured [7] _____ with three light
[8] _____ is in position to the east of Ebro Springs, between the Sulphur
Hills and Pelican Creek. South of the Creek there is an [9] _____ platoon
with three light [10] _____. Just north of the East Service Road, north of
Squaw Lake there is another light armoured [11] _____ with three
[12] _____.

Are there any errors in the map-overlay/description?

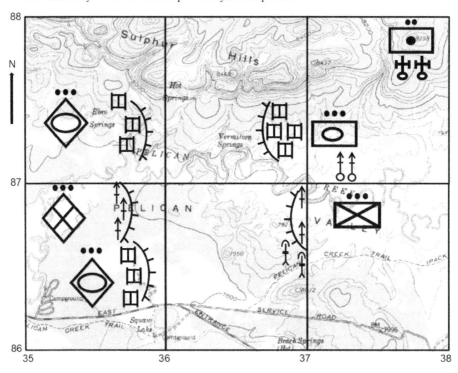

T5 | Speaking: Prepare a briefing

Use your maps. Prepare an overlay of disposition of forces using the symbols from
T3. Brief the class/group on the disposition of forces.

Unit 100 The Disposition of Forces 2

Present Tenses | Passive Verb Forms

T1 | Speaking: Test Your Partner

Draw a symbol from **Unit 99** and ask your partner what it means.

T2 | Vocabulary: Check you know the meaning of these words and phrases

amphibious armour	company
axis of planned advanced	mechanized infantry
battalion	medium weapons
battle position	motorised infantry
blocking position	regiment
boundary	

Which weapons do you remember from **Unit 99**?

Which other words do you remember from **Unit 99**?

T3 | Vocabulary: Study the set of Symbols and Meanings below

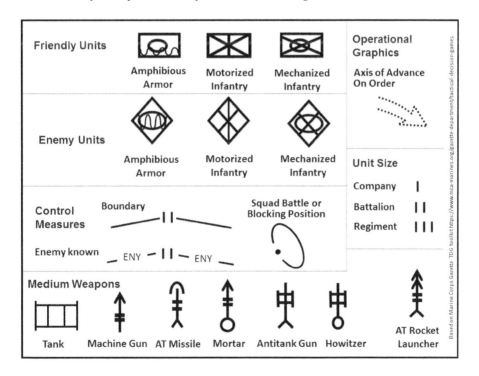

T4 | Writing: Write a description for a briefing

Look at M100.1 and Overlay below (or in the Phase 2 Map folder).

Write a description of the disposition of forces.

Display the descriptions on the walls of the classroom.

Go around and read all the descriptions.

Correct any mistakes.

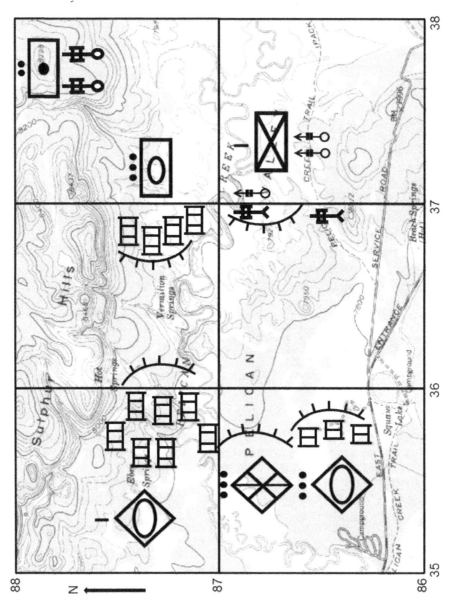

T5 | Speaking: Prepare a briefing

Use your maps. Prepare an overlay of disposition of forces using the symbols from **Unit 99** and **T3**. Brief the class /group on the disposition of forces.

Unit 101 The Disposition of Forces 3

Present Tenses | Passive Verb Forms

T1 | Speaking: Test Your Partner

Draw a symbol from **Units 99** and **100** and ask your partner what it means.

T2 | Vocabulary: Check you know the meaning of these words and phrases

air defence	checkpoint
airborne infantry	corps
axis of advance	division
battle position	force
blocking position	heavy weapons
brigade	rotary wing

Which weapons do you remember from **Units 99** and **100**?

Which other words do you remember from **Units 99** and **100**?

T3 | Vocabulary: Study the set of Symbols and Meanings below

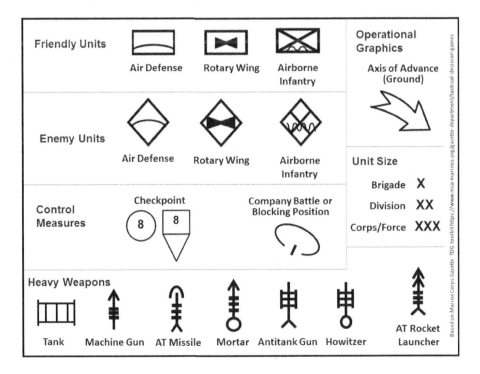

T4 | Writing: Write a description for a briefing

Look at M101.1 and Overlay below (or in the Phase 2 Map folder).

Write a description of the disposition of forces.

Display the descriptions on the walls of the classroom.

Go around and read all the descriptions.

Correct any mistakes.

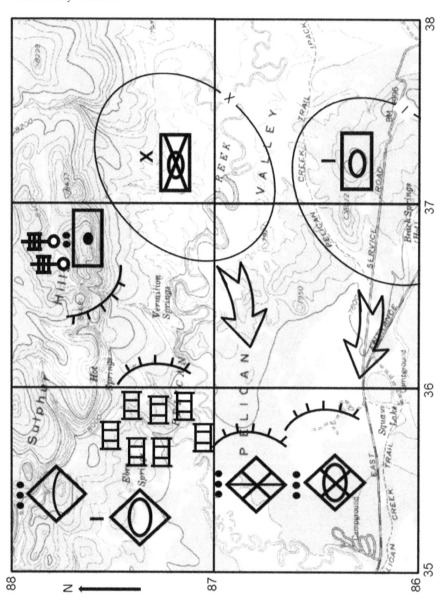

T5 | Speaking: Prepare a briefing

Use your maps. Prepare an overlay of disposition of forces using the symbols from
Units 99 - 100 and **T3**. Brief the class/group on the disposition of forces.

Unit 102 The Disposition of Forces 4

Present Tenses | Passive Verb Form

T1 | Speaking: Test Your Partner

Draw a symbol from **Units 99 – 101** and ask your partner what it means.

T2 | Vocabulary: Check you know the meaning of these words and phrases

battle position	fixed wing
blocking position	main
direction of attack	motor transportation
feint	recon
fire team	supporting
attack position	

Which weapons do you remember from **Units 99 – 101**?

Which other words do you remember from **Units 99 – 101**?

T3 | Vocabulary: Study the set of Symbols and Meanings below

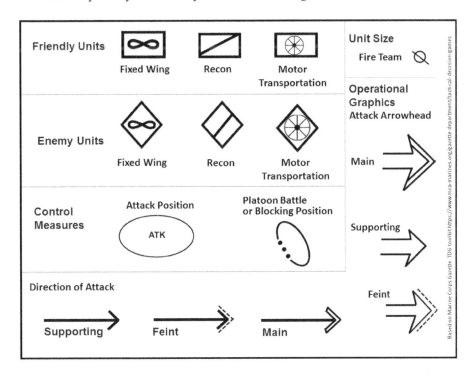

T4 | Writing: Write a description for a briefing

Look at the Map and Overlay below (or in the Phase 2 Map folder).

Write a description of the disposition of forces.

Display the descriptions on the walls of the classroom.

Go around and read all the descriptions.

Correct any mistakes.

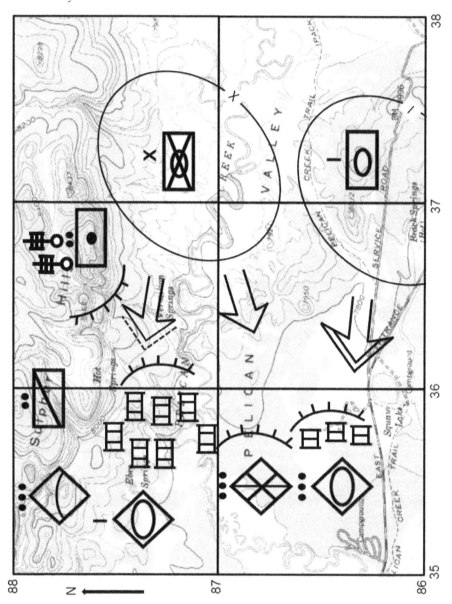

T5 | Speaking: Prepare a briefing

Use your maps. Prepare an overlay of disposition of forces using the symbols from
Units 99 – 101 and **T3**. Brief the class /group on the disposition of forces.

Unit 103 The Disposition of Forces 5

Present Tenses | Passive Verb Forms |

T1 | Speaking: Test Your Partner

Draw a symbol from **Units 99 – 102** and ask your partner what it means.

T2 | Vocabulary: Check you know the meaning of these words

ambush	linkup point
axis of advance	max effect
coordinating point	mechanized recon
engineers	phase line
heliborne	target

Which weapons do you remember from **Units 99 – 102**?

Which other words do you remember from **Units 99 – 102**?

T3 | Vocabulary: Study the set of Symbols and Meanings below

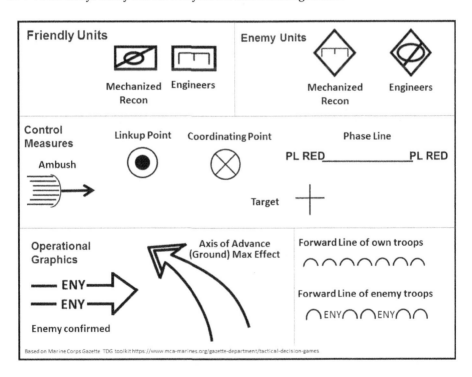

T4 | Writing: Write a description for a briefing

Look at M103.1 and Overlay below (or in the Phase 2 Map folder).

Write a description of the disposition and movement of forces.

Display the descriptions on the walls of the classroom.

Go around and read all the descriptions.

Correct any mistakes.

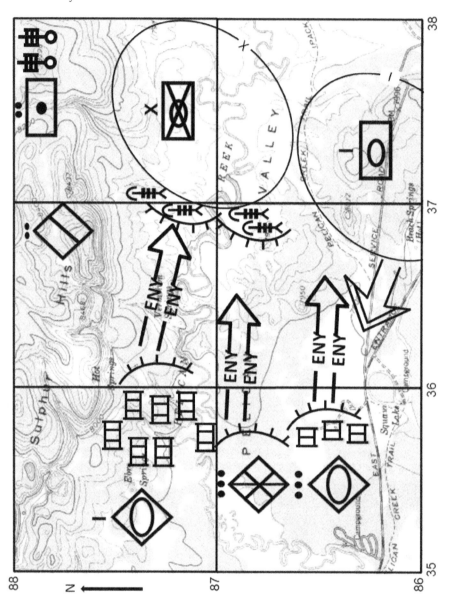

T5 | Speaking: Prepare a briefing

Use your maps. Prepare an overlay of disposition and movement of forces using the symbols from **Units 99 – 102** and **T3**. Brief the class/group on the disposition and movement of forces.

Unit 104 Survival Kits

T1 | Speaking: Talk and Report

Discuss with your partner: Do soldiers need survival kits? If yes, why?

T2 | Speaking: What is in a good survival kit?

Look at the photograph of a survival kit: P104.1. What items do you recognise?
Check with P104.2.

T3 | Listening: Listen and Answer

Listen to the man talking about 5 items in the kit.
What are they and what can they be used for? [Check with T104.1]

T4 | Speaking: What is it used for?

Discuss with your partner what each item of kit can be used for.

Language Reminder: Purpose and Use
X can be used for [signalling]/to [make a fire]
It is important to have Y so you can _____.
If you have Z, you can _____.
X is not very important/useful because _____.

Summarise your opinions about the contents of the survival kit to the class.
Is it a good kit? Why/why not? Do you all agree?

T5| Listening: Listen and Make Notes

Look at P104.3 – what can you see? Check with P104.4. Listen to a description of this
'military' survival kit. Make notes about the differences between this kit and the kit in
T2. Is this a better kit? [Check with T104.2] Write out a paragraph comparing the two
kits.

Language Reminder: Comparing
Both X and Y have a/an _____.
X is better than Y because _____.
X has a/an _____, while Y has a/an _____.
Y does not have a/an _____.
X could be made better by adding _____.
X is better/best for _____.

T6 | Speaking: Your Ideal Survival Kit

Work with a partner. Design your own personal pocket survival kit. Present your kit
to the group. Be ready to justify your choices and answer questions.

Unit 105 Survival: First Steps

Learn To Talk About Survival Priorities In English

T1 | Speaking: Talk and Report 1

Look at P105.1 - 2. What can you see?

T2 | Speaking: Talk and Report 2

What are the first steps you should take in a survival situation?

T3 | Listening: Listen to see if you agree

Listen to a talk on the steps to take in a survival situation – make notes.
Do you agree with the speaker? Check with your partner. [Check with T105.1]

T4 | Prediction: What does the acronym 'SURVIVAL' stand for?

T5 | Reading: Read the text and see if you were correct

Remember the word **SURVIVAL**.

S — Size Up the Situation: Do you need to conceal yourself? What is the rhythm or pattern of the environment you are in? What is your physical condition? What equipment do you have? Now you are ready to make your survival plan. Keep in mind your basic physical needs — water, food, and shelter.

U — Use All Your Senses, Undue Haste Makes Waste

You may make a wrong move when you react quickly without thinking or planning. Don't move just for the sake of taking action. Consider all aspects of your situation before you make a decision and a move. Plan your moves. Be ready to move out quickly without endangering yourself if the enemy is near you. Use all your senses to evaluate the situation and always be observant.

R — Remember Where You Are

You should constantly orient yourself and be aware of where you are. Always try to determine, as a minimum, how your location relates to the location of enemy units and controlled areas, friendly units and controlled areas, local water sources (especially important in the desert), and areas that will provide good cover and concealment.

V — Vanquish Fear and Panic

The greatest enemies in a combat survival and evasion situation are fear and panic which can destroy your ability to make an intelligent decision.

I — Improvise

Learn to improvise. Your imagination must take over when your kit wears out.

V — Value Living

The will to live — placing a high value on living — is vital. Stubbornness, a refusal to give in to problems and obstacles that face you, will give you the mental and physical strength to endure.

A — Act Like the Natives

The natives and animals of a region have adapted to their environment. Watch how the people go about their daily routine. When and what do they eat? When, where, and how do they get their food? When and where do they go for water? What time do they usually go to bed and get up? These actions are important to you when you are trying to avoid capture.

L — Live by Your Wits, But for Now, Learn Basic Skills

Without training in basic skills for surviving and evading on the battlespace, your chances of living through a combat survival and evasion situation are slight. Learn these basic skills now — not when you are headed for or are in the battle.

[FM3.05.70]

T6 I Vocabulary: Explain these words, collocations and phrases

1.	concealment	6.	wears out
2.	physical needs	7.	endure
3.	endangering yourself	8.	daily routine
4.	orient yourself	9.	battlespace
5.	cover and concealment	10.	chances are slight

T7 I Listen and Read: Listen to a reading of the text

Which words do you need to practice saying? Which words do you need to learn?

T8 I Listening: Listen to a talk on survival in temperate lowlands

Makes notes on what the speaker says. Do you agree.? Check with T105.2

T9 I Speaking: Group Briefings

See **Unit 105 Briefing Slides**. There are three briefings to give on survival:

Desert Survival I Tropical Survival I Cold Weather Survival

Work in groups. Prepare a briefing on survival using the slides provided.
Remember you are working as a team: help the briefer to give their best performance.
Practice your briefing. Deliver your briefing. Be ready to answer questions.

T10 I Feedback: Give feedback on your colleagues' briefings

Did you understand everything?
If not, what did you not understand?

T11 I Feedback: Your teacher will give you feedback on your briefing

Units 106 - 109 Survival Simulations Instructions

Expressing Priorities | Discussing Hypotheticals | Reaching Agreement

There are four survival simulations:

Desert | Tropical Rain Forest | Temperate Forest | Arctic/Mountain

You will work in small groups.

> **Remember: This is a speaking task to practice English as much as possible, not to solve the problem as quickly as possible.**

Follow this procedure:

T1 | Reading: Analyse the situation

Ask your teacher if you do not understand anything.

T2 | Speaking: Discuss

Discuss and agree as a group what you would do in the situation and decide on your courses of action in the first 24 hours. If there is a Day 2 supplemental in the scenario, say how you would deal with the developing situation.

What would you do? When would you do it? Why would you do it?

Remember you can do more than one thing at once.

Language Reminder: Hypotheticals

As these are **hypothetical situations** you should use this kind of language in your discussion and briefing:

I think the most important thing **would be to** [light a fire].

The **next** step **would be to** [build a shelter].

I think we **should** [light a fire].

What about [lighting a fire first to keep warm]?

After that we **should** [have something to eat].

We **would** immediately [light a fire] because it **is** [important to keep warm].

One of us **would** [climb the hill and keep a lookout].

Then we **would** _____ because _____.

After that we **would**.......because

At the same time one of us **would**_____ because _____.

T3 | Speaking: Prepare your Briefing

Structure your briefing like this:

1. Briefly recap the situation.
2. Outlines the sequence of steps you would take in the first 24 hours. Explain why you would take each step: *'We could build a fire because.......'*
3. Summarise your priorities in the first 24 hours.
4. Ask for questions [and answer them].

T4 | Speaking: Brief

Give your briefing and be ready to answer questions on your decisions.

T5 | Speaking: Questions

After listening to a briefing, ask questions using phrases like these:

Language Reminder: Questions
Could I ask a question please?
Could you explain again why you would _____?
Could you give us more details about _____?
Could you tell us more about your reasons for _____?

T6 | Speaking: Dealing with questions

When you are asked a question about your briefing, deal with questions using phrases like these:

Language Reminder: Dealing with Questions
That's a very good/ interesting question.
Thank you for asking that question.
You've obviously given this question a lot of though – what do you think?
I don't have the answer at this time.
I'm not sure I am the best person to answer that question. Perhaps X could answer it?
I'm afraid I do not know the answer to that question.

T7 | Feedback

Your teacher will give you feedback on your briefings.

Unit 106 Survival Simulation 1 Desert

Decide On Your Options And Courses Of Action

T1 | Reading: The Scenario

> **Day 1**
>
> Your unit commander on a peacekeeping mission in South Sudan is a keen ama-
> teur archaeologist and he and five colleagues (including you) have taken a car to
> visit an archaeological site near an oasis 150 kms from your base of operations.
> The site is in a remote and uninhabited region of the Sahara desert. You left at
> 0400 hours and started driving to the site. You were planning on reaching the
> site at 0900 hours, spending the day exploring the ruins and returning to the
> base at 2000 hours. Approximately 50 kms from the site your car breaks down.
> There is a leak in the fuel tank and you have run out of fuel. Someone forgot to
> load extra fuel into the car.
>
> It is now 0805 hours. You have enough water and food for the day. You have
> your personal weapons and belt kits, but no body armour or helmets. You dis-
> cover that the field radio in the car does not work and there is no mobile phone
> coverage.
>
> What should you do in the first 24 hours?

> **Day 2 Supplemental**
>
> It is 0930 the next day. In the distance you notice a large dust cloud moving to-
> wards you. This is a large 'haboob' dust storm which will reach you at about
> 1000 hours. Dust storms like this can last for 1 to 3 days. During the storms vis-
> ibility is very low and flying is restricted: all helicopters will be grounded.
>
> What should you do now?

T2 | Speaking: Discuss and prepare to present your Day 1 and Day 2 solutions

T3 | Speaking: Present your Day 1 and Day 2 solutions to the class

Listen to the other solutions. Ask questions and then give feedback.

Unit 107 Survival Simulation 2 Arctic

T1 | Reading: The Scenario

You are on Mountain/Arctic Warfare exercises with your section of 8 soldiers near Tromso in northern Norway, 350 kilometres north of the Arctic Circle. It is early autumn.

As part of the exercise you were taken by boat with your section out of a fiord to a large uninhabited island. There you had to camp for two weeks and climb all the mountain peaks on the island. On the fourth day, as you were moving your camp to the second camp location (C2) and crossing a small glacier, three of your patrol fell down a crevasse and lost their packs and the patrol radio. One of these soldiers has a broken leg and another has two broken ribs. Everyone is now safely off the glacier, in a coniferous forest, but there is now a blizzard blowing and zero visibility. The snow seems to be settling. It is 1230 hours and +1 degrees Celsius and the temperature is falling.

You made a radio check this morning and your next radio check is due at 0800 in two days time. As far as you know there are no helicopters within range and rescue would come by boat at your original landing place. You and all the other soldiers, apart from the three who fell down the crevasse, have all their equipment – tents, sleeping bags, rations, water bottles, water filters, stoves, maps, compasses etc. You are all properly dressed for the weather with warm and waterproof clothing.

What should you do in the first 24 hours?

T2 | Speaking: Discuss and prepare to present your solutions

T3 | Speaking: Present your solutions to the class

Listen to the other solutions. Ask questions and then give feedback.

Unit 108 Survival Simulation 3 Tropical Rain Forest

Decide On Your Options And Courses Of Action

T1 | Reading: The Scenario

You and your 4 man team are exploring an unmapped 150 km long tributary of the Amazon river on an inflatable boat as part of your adventure training. You were helicoptered in to the source of the river and are making your way down the river towards the confluence with the Amazon. You are approximately 45 kms along the river from the source. At 1145 hours you hit a set of rapids and your boat was upturned and washed away. You all managed to reach the shore safely and you all have your belts kits, and the clothes you are wearing. All your other gear, including the food, GPS systems and radios, was lost in the river. You take an inventory of what your have:

> Five individual belt kits which consist of: 2 x 1 litre water bottles; a small sheath knife (10 cm blade), machete, personal survival kits in a metal tin, personal medical kits, personal Katadyn water filter, and 2 days individual rations each. All of you have a lensatic compass, and maps in waterproof map cases – these are maps of the area but the river is not marked on the maps, except the part you have travelled, as you were mapping it. Everyone has a watch and a metal whistle. Two men have their own Swiss army pocket knives.

You are all dressed in long trousers, long sleeved shirts and rubber boat shoes, have broad-brimmed hats, and are wearing life jackets.

You are due at the RV 10 kms downstream of the river confluence in 15 days time. The local tribes have not been contacted and are thought to be dangerous. They have killed loggers and gold prospectors recently.

What should you do in the first 24 hours?

T2 | Speaking: Discuss and prepare to present your solutions

T3 | Speaking: Present your solutions to the class

Listen to the other solutions. Ask questions and then give feedback.

Unit 109 Survival Simulation 4 Temperate Forest

Decide On Your Options And Courses Of Action

T1 | Reading: The Scenario

You are in a party of six army personnel. You were being taken by helicopter to a meeting in Braşov in Romania. It is bad weather and your helicopter has crashed into a forested mountainside in the Făgăraş Mountains, perhaps near Moldoveanu peak (2,544 m). The pilot was not able to radio for help before the crash.

The helicopter pilot has a broken leg and is unconscious, as is the co-pilot. You removed them from the helicopter wreckage but they cannot be moved further. Two others in your party are slightly injured but they can walk with difficulty. Four of you are uninjured.

After the crash the helicopter caught fire but before that happened you had a chance to salvage equipment from the wreckage. This is the inventory of the equipment you have from the wreckage and personal equipment: A broken radio; three Swiss army knives; a first aid kit; a flare gun and six flares; eight life jackets; seven litres of water; 15m of parachute cord; some paper and 3 pencils and 10 pens; six laptops and chargers; a compass; one survival blanket; three lighters; a cosmetic mirror; three chocolate bars. Everyone has a mobile phone but there is no signal.

The helicopter fire has now burned out.

You are all wearing uniforms, overcoats and boots except for the flight crew who are wearing flight suits. It is now 4.30 pm and minus 2 degrees Celsius. It is snowing heavily and there is very low cloud cover and zero visibility. It will be dark in 45 mins. The temperature will drop to minus 15 degrees Celsius at night. You do not know exactly where you are but you think you are near Moldoveanu peak (2,544 m). You are in an area of coniferous forest with trees up to 10 – 15 m high. There is a small stream running south down the mountainside 50 m to your east. You have seen signs of bears – they are not hibernating yet. There are also wolves and lynxes in the forests.

What should you do in the first 24 hours?

T2 | Speaking: Discuss and prepare to present your solutions

T3 | Speaking: Present your solutions to the class

Listen to the other solutions. Ask questions and then give feedback.

Unit 110 Survival Quiz

T1 | Speaking: The Quiz

You are going to practice talking about what you should (and shouldn't) do in hypothetical survival situations.

One of you (or your teacher) should be the question master. This person will look at P110.1 – P110.20, and read out the situation to the class.

Example:

> **Situation**
>
> Your friend has been bitten by a snake.
>
> What should you do?
>
> What shouldn't you do?

The other students should answer individually or in small teams.

One student should say what you should or shouldn't do in the situation. Like this:

> You **should** kill the snake to identify it. You **should** wash the wound. You **shouldn't** cut the wound with a knife or try to suck the venom out.............

The other students, the ones not answering, can challenge the one answering. Like this:

> Really? Why **would** you do that?
>
> Do you really think that **would** work?
>
> What about [doing X], **wouldn't** that be better?

Score **two points** for a full and correct answer.

One point for a partially correct answer.

T2 | Grammar: Feedback

Your teacher will listen and prepare feedback on your answers:

1. Were the answers clear?
2. Were they grammatically correct?

When all the situations have been discussed the teacher will give feedback.

Unit 111 Parts of the Body and Medical Treatment 1

Learn To Talk About Parts Of The Body and Common Ailments and Treatments

T1 | Vocabulary: Parts of the Body

Do you know the parts of the body shown in P111.1 - 2? Check with P111.3 - 4.

T2 | Vocabulary: What is the difference?

cut | bruise | injury | wound | casualty | fatality

T3 | Vocabulary: Match the ailment and the definition

1.	a headache	a.	an overstretched muscle
2.	high blood pressure	b.	immune system hypersensitivity to an environmental factor e.g. dust or pollen; with sneezing, a runny nose and eyes
3.	a migraine	c.	bleeding
4.	sun/heat stroke	d.	a break in a bone
5.	hypothermia	e.	when the body core temperature is below 35.0°C; with shivering and mental confusion
6.	a fracture	f.	a pain in the head or neck
7.	a haemorrhage	g.	when blood flow stops to a part of the heart causing damage to the heart muscle, and possible death due to cardiac arrest
8.	backache	h.	a severe long-lasting headache
9.	a sprained ankle	i.	torn ligaments in an ankle
10.	a pulled muscle	j.	when the body temperature is greater than 40.6°C; with dry skin, rapid, strong pulse and dizziness
11.	an allergy	k.	elevated blood pressure in arteries
12.	a heart attack	l.	poor blood flow to the brain resulting in cell death; due to lack of blood flow or bleeding.
13.	food poisoning	m.	inflammation of the appendix
14.	diarrhoea	n.	pain in the back
15.	stroke	o.	loose or liquid bowel movements leading to dehydration
16.	appendicitis	p.	a head injury with a temporary loss of brain function.
17.	concussion	q.	Frozen skin and tissue
18.	frostbite	r.	vomiting, fever, and aches, and may include diarrhoea due to contaminated food.

T4 | Speaking: Talk and Report

Ask and answer with your partner: *Have you ever had* _____?
If the answer is 'Yes.' ask '*When did you have* _____?

Unit 112 Parts of the Body and Medical Treatment 2

Learn To Talk About Parts Of The Body and Common Ailments and Treatments

T1 | Speaking: What do you remember?

How many parts of the body do you remember from **Unit 111**?

Test your partner – point to a part of your body and ask *'What's this?'*

What ailments and treatments do you remember from **Unit 111**?

T2 | Speaking: Talk and Report

What is the standard treatment for a headache/migraine/sprained ankle?

E.g. *I think you should give _____ to someone who has a headache.*

If you have a _____, you should _____.

T3 | Vocabulary: Match the Unit 111 T3 problem with the suggested treatments below

1. Apply cold compress, bandage and rest
2. Avoid solid food until vomiting stops; prevent dehydration
3. Clean the wound and stop the bleeding
4. Do exercises to strengthen the muscles
5. Drink plenty of clean water and rehydration fluids
6. Eat healthier, quit smoking, exercise more
7. Go to hospital for scans, possible surgery and medicine
8. Have an x-ray, splint the limb or use a plaster cast
9. Perform CPR if necessary; go to hospital, take medicine to reduce blood clots
10. Remove excess clothing, reduce body temperature with water or ice packs
11. Rub the muscle to warm it and then rest it
12. Hospitalisation for an operation to remove the affected organ
13. Take anti-histamine tablets
14. Take some painkillers
15. Take some painkillers, lie down and sleep
16. Warm the victim's trunk gradually and give warm fluids if awake
17. Heating treatment on affected areas or surgery if necessary.
18. Observation and rest; CT or MRI scan.

T4 | Speaking: Giving Advice and Taking Action

Work in pairs. Each of you should choose 5 medical problems. Tell your partner one of your problems. Your partner will give you some advice and/or explain a course of action. Make a note of the advice you receive and the action taken. Repeat.

Language Reminder: Giving Advice And Explaining Action
Giving advice: *You should take some painkillers.*
Explaining a course of action: *I'm going to apply a cold compress.*

Unit 113 A Medical History

Learn To Talk About Your Medical History

T1 | Speaking: What do you remember?

How many parts of the body do you remember from **Unit 111**?

Test your partner – point to a part of your body and ask *'What's this?'*

What ailments and treatments do you remember from **Unit 112**?

T2 | Vocabulary: What is the difference?

boil | rash | spot | bruise | cut | Have you ever had a.....?

T3 | Vocabulary: A medical history

Check you know these words and then complete the text.

bad	broke	broken	convalescence	diarrhoea
diseases	fever	headaches	gastroenteritis	infectious
operation	viral	vitamin	vomiting	plaster cast

When I was a boy I [1] _____ my upper right arm playing in the school playground. My nose was [2] _____ in a pub fight and I broke my collar bone playing rugby. I've never had to wear a [3] _____ though. I used to have a lot of migraine [4] _____ but now I don't as I don't drink so much coffee. Sometimes I have a [5] _____ back, if I twist it, but if I do regular exercise I can lift things without any problems. I have hay [6] _____ – I'm allergic to grass and dust. I had the usual childhood [7] _____ – measles and mumps but I've never had a serious [8] _____ disease like TB. I don't smoke, or drink too much. I've had food poisoning (acute [9] _____) once or twice and ended up in hospital because I had [10] _____ and was [11] _____ a lot. The most serious medical problem I've ever had was when I had [12] _____ meningitis. That meant two weeks in hospital and two months [13] _____ leave. My most serious [14] _____ was to re-move my appendix. Generally, I'm fit and active, and healthy. I have a good diet and get regular exercise and go out in the sunshine for [15] _____ D when I can.

T4 | Language Analysis: Analyse the Text

T5 | Listen and Read: Listen to a reading of the text

Which words do you need to practice saying?

Which words do you need to learn?

T6 | Writing: Your Medical History

Write out your medical history notes. Include five illnesses, diseases and dates.

If you have never been ill make up an exciting life of broken bones and exotic illnesses.

T7 | Speaking: Talk and Report

Tell your partner about your medical history.

Make notes about your partner's history.

Ask checking questions: 'When exactly did you have _____?

T8 | Speaking: Reporting

Report to the class about your partner's 'medical history'.

Language Reminder
Before Now: *John has never broken a bone.*
Victoria has broken her right arm and the big toe on her left foot.
Specific time in the past: *Victoria broke her arm in 2010.*

T9 | Consolidation Tasks

Revision: Key Collocations			
1.	excess	a)	pulse
2.	bod	b)	history
3.	warm	c)	system
4.	childhood	d)	fluids
5.	regular	e)	movement
6.	solid	f)	tablets
7.	torn	g)	pulse
8.	immune	h)	cast
9.	bowel	i)	clothing
10.	strong	j)	fluids
11.	medical	k)	temperature
12.	anti-histamine	l)	exercise
13.	rehydration	m)	diseases
14.	plaster	n)	food
15.	rapid	o)	ligaments

Unit 114 Visiting the Doctor

Learn To Talk To A Doctor

T1 | Speaking: What do you remember?

How many parts of the body do you remember from **Unit 111**?

Test your partner – point to a part of your body and ask: 'What's this?'

What ailments and treatments do you remember from **Unit 112**?

T2 | Vocabulary: What is the difference?

tender | sore | painful | aching | inflamed

Have you ever had something which was.....?

T3 | Vocabulary: Doctors and treatment

Check you know these words and then complete the text.

history	illness	physical	scans	treatments
act	diagnose	diagnosis	evaluating	expertise
risks	knowledge	prescribe	information	treat

The doctor's role is to [1] _____ and [2] _____ patients. Patients trust doctors to make a correct [3] _____ , to be up to date with medical [4] _____ and be capable of deciding on the most appropriate treatment. Patients also expect the doctor to [5] _____ in the patient's best interest.

Diagnosis is a key part of a doctor's [6] _____ . This involves [7] _____ the first signs of the [8] _____ , and asking for and assessing [9] _____ from the patient. Then the doctor decides on treatment based on the diagnosis.

Doctor's should take a medical [10] _____ of the patient, do a [11] _____ examination and authorise tests such as blood work and various [12] _____ (e.g. USG) to reach the proper diagnosis.

The doctor may then [13] _____ different types of treatment such as a course of antibiotics, surgery, physiotherapy and so on.

Doctors should be able to explain and discuss the [14] _____ , benefits and uncertainties of various tests and [15] _____ so that the patient can make informed decisions about their care.

T4 | Vocabulary: What can we have? What can we feel?

cold | a cold | a temperature | tired | exhausted | stressed | a disease | a heart attack

e.g. We _feel_ cold.

T5 | Vocabulary: Check you know these words

prescription	medicine	pills	(to) prescribe	tests	x-ray	ultrasound scan

Complete the sentences.

1 I'll just [1] _____ some sleeping [2] _____ for you. You should take them two hours before going to bed with food.

2 I'd like to run some [3] _____. We'll do an [4] _____ and an [5] _____ scan.

T6 | Reading: Complete the dialogue between the doctor and patient

Good morning Mr Smith. How.....	.....get to sleep? Do you wake up in the middle of the night.
Well, I've been	.....do some blood tests and see what that tells us. I'll just call the nurse.
How.....	.....about something? Do you have problems at work?
For a couple of.....	.....been any changes in your routine? Or your diet?
Do you manage to.....	.....is normal.
It takes me a long.....	.....more than usual. No.
Are you worried.....	.....weeks now. I feel very tired when I wake up.
Nothing.....	.....having trouble sleeping.
Have there.....	.....time to get to sleep. Then I wake up two or three times in the night.
No, everything.....	.....are you feeling today?
Well, let's.....	.....long has this lasted?

T7 | Speaking: Practice the dialogue in pairs

Then change the dialogue in **T4** for a different medical problem and practice it again.

T8 | Speaking: Talk and Report

What are your annual medical check-up and and fitness tests like?

T9 | Writing: Write a paragraph

Write a paragraph about your annual medical check-up and and fitness tests.
Use the Fact File 114.1 in your Workbook to help you.

T10 | Consolidation Tasks

Unit 115 Medical Kits and TCCC (TC3)

Learn To Talk About Medical Kits And The Stages Of Tactical Casualty Combat Care

T1 | Speaking: What do you remember?

How many parts of the body do you remember from **Unit 111**?

Test your partner – point to a part of your body and ask: *'What's this?'*

What ailments and treatments do you remember from **Unit 112**?

T2 | Vocabulary: What is the difference?

chronic/intermittent/sudden/sharp/dull/continuous | pain

Which of these words collocate with *ache*?

T3 | Speaking: Talk and Report

Why do soldiers need personal medical kits?

Think of at least two reasons for a soldier to have a personal medical kit on them.

T4 | Speaking: What should be in a first aid kit?

Make a list and compare it with your partner.

T5 | Vocabulary: A first aid kit

Look at the picture of a civilian first aid kit in P115.1.

What items can you recognise?

Check with P115.2.

What things are not in the kit which should be there? Why?

Discuss with your partner and then agree with the class.

T6 | Speaking: Tactical Casualty Combat Care

What are the three stages of Tactical Casualty Combat Care?

Compare your ideas with your partner.

STAGES OF CARE

There are three distinct phases in Tactical Casualty Combat Care.

Phase 1 Care Under Fire

A soldier medic gives care under fire at the scene of the injury while he and the casualty are still under effective hostile fire. The only medical equipment available is that carried by the individual soldier or the soldier medic in his medical aid bag.

Phase 2 Tactical Field Care

When the effective hostile fire has stopped the soldier medic can give tactical field care. The term also applies to situations in which an injury has occurred but there is no hostile fire. Available medical equipment is still limited to that being carried into the field by medical personnel. The time needed to evacuate the casualty to a medical treatment facility (MTF) may vary considerably.

Phase 3 Combat Casualty Evacuation Care

Once the casualty has been picked up by an aircraft, vehicle, or boat combat casualty evacuation (CASEVAC) care can be given. There may be additional medical personnel available at this stage of casualty management.

[From: Tactical Combat Casualty Care And Wound Treatment Sub-course Md0554]

T8 | Reading: Read the text again and answer these questions

1. What equipment is available in Phase 1?
2. What equipment is available in Phase 2?
3. What equipment is available in Phase 3?
4. What are the main differences between the three phases?

T9 | Language Analysis: Analyse the Text

T10 | Listen and Read: Listen to a reading of the text

Which words do you need to practice saying? Which words do you need to learn?

T11 | Speaking: What training do soldiers receive in Tactical Casualty Combat Care?

Discuss with your partner and then brief the teacher on what training soldiers in your army receive and what training you think they *should* receive.

T12 | Consolidation Tasks

Unit 116 Medical Vocabulary for Tactical Casualty Combat Care

This unit focuses on learning important words which will be used in the next units.

T1 I Speaking: Talk and Report

Look at P116.1. What can you see?

T2 I Vocabulary: Match the words and definitions 1

airway	shock due to decreased blood pressure
haemorrhage	breathing tubes to the lungs
hypovolemic shock	bleeding from the body
shock	bandage or strap of some kind applied above a wound to stop the blood flow from the wound
tourniquet	the body's response to a severe event

T3 I Vocabulary: Match the words and definitions 2

cervical spine immobilization	an evaluation of the medical condition of a patient
penetrating injury	medicine taken to control infections by bacteria
painkillers	an injury caused when the skin is pierced.
antibiotics	stopping the neck from moving because of injury
clinical assessment	medicine taken to control pain

T4 I Vocabulary: Match the words and definitions 3

treatment rendered	injury or death caused by electricity
pulse	a body core temperature below 35.0 °C
respiration	the steps taken to solve a medical problem
hypothermia	the signal that the heart is beating
electrocution	breathing

T5 I Vocabulary: Match the words and definitions 4

traumatic	the heartbeat felt through the veins on the wrist
intravenous (IV)	an injury where the skin is torn, broken or penetrated e.g. by a knife or bullet
trunk	adjective describing a serious injury
wound	the body of a person but not head, arms or legs
radial pulse	within a vein

T6 | Vocabulary: Match the words and definitions 5

hemostasis	invasion of the body by bacteria or viruses
infection	a penetrating injury to the upper front of the trunk
blood pressure	measurement of the amount of oxygen in the blood
pulse oximetry	a process which causes bleeding to stop
chest wound	how strongly the blood moves around the body

T7 | Vocabulary: Match the words and definitions 6

splint	lack of consciousness
cardiopulmonary resuscitation	an opiate based painkiller
unconscious	a device to support or immobilize a limb i.e. an arm or a leg.
morphine	an emergency procedure of chest compression and mouth-to-mouth resuscitation

T8 | Pronunciation: Listen and repeat

Listen to the words from T2 to T7 and repeat them.

T9 | Speaking: Ask and answer:Test your partner

Take turns to ask and answer questions about the words in T2 to T7 with your partner: "*What is cardiopulmonary resuscitation?*"

T10 | Vocabulary and Grammar: choose the correct verb/word in the sentences below

1. If you have a headache you **can/can't** take painkillers.
2. High blood pressure is **good/bad** for you.
3. Morphine **is/isn't** a very strong painkiller.
4. You **should/shouldn't** use antibiotics to treat a viral infection.
5. A knife wound **is/isn't** a penetrating injury.
6. When a patient is bleeding heavily from a limb you **should/shouldn't** apply a tourniquet.
7. After a serious injury for traumatic experience a patient **will/won't** go into shock.
8. If someone has a heart attack you **should/shouldn't** attempt cardiopulmonary resuscitation.
9. A broken bone e.g. in your arm **should/shouldn't** be immobilised with a splint.
10. Loss of blood **might/won't** lead to hypovolemic shock.

T11 | Speaking: What do you remember?

How many parts of the body do you remember from **Unit 111**?
What ailments and treatments do you remember from **Unit 112**?

Unit 117 Care Under Fire

T1 I Speaking: Talk and Report

Look at P117.1. What can you see?

T2 I Speaking: Talk and Report

What is **Care Under Fire**?

What do you think are the priorities for **Care Under Fire**? Why?

T3 I Reading: Read to Check

Read the text on the next page and see if you agree with the writer.

T4 I Reading: Read and Answer

Read the text again and answer these questions.

1. Why should you keep fighting instead of helping an injured soldier?
2. If you are wounded, why should you take cover?
3. What should you do if there is no cover?
4. Are airway problems important?
5. Why is control of bleeding important?
6. What can you use instead of a litter?
7. What equipment should you try to recover? Why?

T5 I Language Analysis: Analyse the Text

T6 I Listen and Read: Listen to a reading of the text

Which words do you need to practice saying? Which words do you need to learn?

T7 I Speaking: Summarising

These are the six key points from the text.

Take it in turns to give reasons for the key points.

1. Return fire as directed or required.
   'You should return fire as directed or required because......'
2. The casualty should also return fire if able.
3. Direct the casualty to cover and apply self-aid, if able.
4. Try to keep the casualty from sustaining any additional wounds.
5. Airway management is generally best deferred until the tactical field care phase.
6. Stop any life-threatening hemorrhage with a tourniquet.

T8 I Consolidation Tasks

CARE UNDER FIRE

When you are under fire, the best offense is tactical fire superiority. It is always more important to suppress enemy fire before caring for casualties. The ongoing mission does not stop just because there is a casualty. So, all personnel should return fire and take cover. Don't stop to care for casualties.

Wounded soldiers who can fight should fight. Wounded soldiers who cannot fight and are exposed to enemy fire should take cover. If there is no cover or the wounded soldier cannot move to cover, he should lie flat and motionless (in short he should play dead). When a casualty is under cover he should apply self-aid if he can. You should all try to keep the casualty from sustaining additional wounds: the best way to do that is to win the firefight.

If the casualty is in a burning vehicle or building, move him to safety. Stop any burning. Leave airway management until the Tactical Field Care phase. Controlling haemorrhaging (major bleeding) is most important because it can quickly result in hypovolemic shock. Use a temporary tourniquet to stop the bleeding. Remember: Tourniquets hurt when applied effectively. Both the casualty and the soldier medic are in danger while applying the tourniquet. Ignore non-life-threatening bleeding until the tactical field care phase.

Penetrating neck injuries do not require cervical spine (C-spine) immobilization. Other neck injuries, such as falls over 15 feet, fast roping injuries, or motor vehicle collisions (MVC), might need C-spine immobilization unless hostile fire is a greater threat.

Use litters, ponchos, doors, dragging, or manual carries to carry casualties. Use suppressive fire, smoke, and vehicles to screen casualty movement. Leave a casualty's rucksack unless it contains items critical or sensitive items, such as maps of friendly troop disposition or radio codes. Take the casualty's weapon and ammunition, if possible, to prevent the enemy from using them against you.

[Adapted from: Tactical Combat Casualty Care And Wound Treatment Sub-course Md0554]

Unit 118 Tactical Field Care

T1 | Speaking: Talk and Report 1

Look at P118.1. What can you see?

T2 | Speaking: Talk and Report 2

What do you remember about **Care under Fire**? What is **Tactical Field Care**?

What do you think the priorities for **Tactical Field Care** are? Why?

T3 | Reading: Read the text to see if you agree with the writer

TACTICAL FIELD CARE

In the Care Under Fire phase your priority is to win the firefight and then stop the bleeding from serious wounds. There is more time to provide care and less danger from hostile fire in the Tactical Field Care phase.

Follow the **MARCH** acronym. **M** is for Massive hemorrhage: your priority is still to control life-threatening bleeding. Then **A** is for Airway: make sure the patient can breathe. If necessary, establish and maintain the patent's airway. Then **R** is for Respiration: decompress suspected tension pneumothorax, seal open chest wounds, and support breathing as required. Then **C** is for Circulation: establish Intravenous (IV) access and give fluids to treat shock. Then **H** is for Head Injury/Hypothermia: prevent or treat hypotension (low blood pressure) and hypoxia (lack of oxygen) to prevent worsening of Traumatic Brain Injury (TBI), and prevent or treat hypothermia.

TBI, shock, hypoxia, and pain medications (e.g. morphine) can cause an altered mental state. Disarm these casualties immediately as a safety measure. Remove their weapons (including knives) and grenades. You should explain to casualty: "Let me hold your weapon for you while the doc checks you out."

Do an initial assessment of airway, breathing, and circulation. If a victim of a blast or penetrating injury does not have a pulse or respiration, do not attempt cardiopulmonary resuscitation (CPR). It is too late. Only use CPR for non-traumatic disorders, like hypothermia, near drowning, or electrocution.

Close a traumatic chest wounds with a dressing. Then deal with any major bleeding sites not controlled before. Only remove the minimum of clothing required to expose and treat injuries, both because of time constraints and to protect the patient from hypothermia. Stop major bleeding as quickly as possible with a tourniquet. Dress wounds with emergency trauma dressings to prevent further contamination and help hemostasis (the stopping of bleeding). Check for exit wounds.

Gain IV access next. Any major extremity or truncal wound (in the neck, chest, abdomen, and pelvis), with or without obvious blood loss or hypotension, may need an intravenous infusion. If there is major blood loss from a wound and the casualty has no radial pulse or is not coherent, stop the bleeding by any means possible before giving fluids. Eventually, if there is no response from a casualty, you will have to pay attention to other casualties.

If the casualty can fight but is in pain, administer painkillers. If the casualty is unable to fight, give 5 mg IV morphine every 10 minutes until the pain is under control. Document the morphine given on the casualty's field medical card (FMC).

Put a splint on a fracture if possible. Do pulse, motor, and sensory (PMS) checks before and after splinting. Consider giving antibiotics for all battlefield wounds to stop infections.

Reassure the casualty and explain what you are doing. Make notes of your clinical assessments, the treatment you gave, and the changes in the casualty's status. Send the documentation with the casualty to the next level of care. Casualties are in danger of hypothermia when traveling in a CASEVAC or MEDEVAC asset. Protect the casualty by wrapping them in a protective wrap. The time to evacuation may vary from minutes to several hours.

[Adapted from: Tactical Combat Casualty Care And Wound Treatment Sub-course Md0554]

T4 | Reading: Read and Answer

Read the text again and answer these questions.

1. What does MARCH stand for?
2. When should you not do CPR?
3. When should you consider CPR?
4. Why should wounded soldiers not fighting be disarmed?
5. How much clothing should be cut away when dealing with a wound?
6. Why should wounds be dressed?
7. When might you give IV fluids?
8. Should you give morphine to a soldier who is fighting?
9. What should you do to a fractured leg?
10. Should antibiotics be given? Why/Why not?
11. Why should the medic talk to the injured soldier?
12. Why should you make notes of your care?

T5 | Language Analysis: Analyse the Text

T6 | Listen and Read: Listen to a reading of the text

Which words do you need to practice saying? Which words do you need to learn?

T7 | Writing: Write a 100 word summary of the text

T8 | Consolidation Tasks

Unit 119 Combat Casualty Evacuation Care

T1 | Speaking: Talk and Report 1

Look at P119.1. What can you see?

T2 | Speaking: Talk and Report 2

What does the **MARCH** acronym from Tactical Field Care mean?

What is **Combat Casualty Evacuation Care**?

What do you think the priorities for **Combat Casualty Evacuation Care** are? Why?

T3 | Reading: Read the text to see if you agree with the writer

---

CASUALTY EVACUATION CARE

In the Care Under Fire phase your priority is to win the firefight and then stop the bleeding from serious wounds. In the Tactical Field Care phase, you can provide more care as you have more time and there is less danger. In the **Casualty Evacuation Care phase,** the casualty will be evacuated. You should have a casualty evacuation plan for the operation you are involved in. You should have plans for primary, secondary, & tertiary options.

Any vehicle can be used to evacuate casualties including ground vehicles, aircraft, or boats. The vehicles may be organic to the unit or designated TACEVAC assets. MEDEVAC vehicles and aircraft are especially designed for casualty care. These are non-combatant assets and are designated with a Red Cross. They cannot be used when there is a high threat of hostile fire. You should use MEDEVAC assets when they are available and when the environment is permissible (i.e. the LZ is not hot). Reserve CASEVAC assets for more dangerous situations. CASEVAC assets are combat platforms with good firepower and armor. They do not have a Red Cross. You will need CASEVAC assets when you have to evacuate casualties when the threat level is high. The term Tactical Evacuation (TACEVAC) includes both types of evacuation.

Many factors will affect casualty evacuation e.g. the availability of aircraft or vehicles, the weather, the tactical situation, and the mission. Evacuation time may vary, from minutes to hours to days.

CASEVAC phase care is similar to care in the tactical field care phase. The aim is to keep the casualty alive until he reaches medical facilities. Additional medical personnel should arrive with the evacuation asset. They can assist or replace the soldier medic on the ground. The unit's medic will need to continue with the mission. Additional medical equipment can be brought in on the evacuation asset. This equipment may include electronic monitoring equipment to measure a casualty's blood pressure, pulse, and pulse oximetry (oxygen saturation of the arterial

---

blood). Oxygen should also be available during this phase. Most casualties do not need extra oxygen, but you should use it for casualties who are in shock, are unconscious, have traumatic brain injury, or a chest wound. Thermal Angel fluid warmers may be needed to warm IV fluids. Remember the danger of hypothermia: make sure the casualty is wrapped up warm enough for the evacuation.

Wounded enemy prisoners of war (EPWs) are still a potential threat so they should be restrained and watched.

[Adapted from: Tactical Combat Casualty Care And Wound Treatment Sub-course Md0554]

T4 | Reading: Read and Answer

Read the text again and answer these questions.

1. How many MEDEVAC/CASEVAC options should you have planned for?
2. What is the difference between MEDEVAC and CASEVAC?
3. What is a designated TACEVAC asset?
4. What factors can affect TACEVAC time or feasibility?
5. What kind of casualties might need help in breathing?

T5 | Language Analysis: Analyse the Text

T6 | Listen and Read: Listen to a reading of the text

Which words do you need to practice saying? Which words do you need to learn?

T7 | Writing: Write a 100 word summary of the text

T8 | Consolidation Tasks

Unit 120 TC3 Briefings

Practice Giving A Briefing On TCCC

Work in groups. There are three slides on Tactical Casualty Combat Care. See **Unit 120 Briefing Slides**. Prepare a briefing on one of the slides. Look at the materials in **Units 117** to **119** and decide what you are going to say in your briefing

T1 | Speaking: Briefing Preparation

Work in groups. Prepare your briefing. Remember you are working as a team: help the briefer to give their best performance. Practice your briefing.

T2 | Speaking: Briefing

Deliver your briefing. Be ready to answer questions. Give feedback on your colleagues' briefings.
Did you understand everything? If not, what did you not understand?
Your teacher will give you feedback on how well you gave the briefing.

Unit 121 Listening Test and Medic! Game

T1 | Listening: Listen and Make Notes

Listen to the talk about TC3.

Make notes.

Check with your partner, then the class.

Who has made the best notes?

Check your notes with the T121.1.

T2 | Speaking: Play the 'Medic!' Game

1. One of you (or your teacher) should be the Question Master.

    This person will look at the questions in the Teacher's Book

    > **Situation X**
    >
    > What would you do if a member of your patrol fractured a leg?
    >
    > Supplementary Question
    >
    > Would you call for Medevac/Casevac? Why?

2. One student (or your teacher) should be the Scorer.

3. The rest of the class should be organized into teams, or play as individuals.

4. The teacher should listen and prepare feedback on the language of the answers for the end of the game. Consider: Were the answers clear? Were they grammatically correct?

5. The teams/players take it in turns to answer the questions.

6. Play clockwise around the class.

7. Each correct answer scores 2 points. Each correct supplementary question answer scores 1 point.

8. If a team/player cannot answer the question correctly then the next team/player has the opportunity to answer it for 1 point. Each correct supplementary question answer scores 1 point.

9. If the team/player can justify a different answer from the one given e.g. which depends on the circumstances of the patrol, then the teacher will decide if they deserve points or not. The teacher's decision is final.

10. The answers should be in the form of: 'I would.....'; 'You should.....' etc.

11. The winner is the team or the player with the most points.

12. The teacher gives feedback on the English used.

Play the game again at regular intervals throughout the rest of the course.

Unit 122 Training Exercise: Island Adventure

Practice Talking About Training Activities, Logistics, Landforms, Weather Etc.

T1 | Speaking: Prepare

Work in groups. Each group will plan a briefing on a training exercise.

You are taking a group of soldiers to an island for a 10 day training exercise.

Look at the map of the island you will be going to. Each team will go to a different island.

There are six different islands: South Manitou Island; Wild Horse Island; Blakely Island; Waldron Island; Stuart Island; Matinicus Island.

See **Unit 122 Briefing Slides**.

Plan the training exercise and then brief the class on the plan.

T2 | Speaking: Discuss and prepare to present your plan

In your plan and briefing answer the following questions:

- What is the purpose of the exercise?
- What are the dates of the exercise?
- Who is going on the exercise?
- What is the weather forecast?
- How will you get to the island?
- What is the island's terrain, flora and fauna like?
- What will you do on each day of the exercise?
- What equipment do the soldiers need to take with them?
- What are your emergency procedures?

Language Reminder: Plans

This is a plan so you will use future forms, mainly will, other modal verbs, and conditionals for the what ifs.

We **will leave** at 0730 hours on. _____.

Every day we **will start** at 0430 hours.

Each/Every solder **needs to** take X, Y and Z with them.

Everyone **should be** ready **to do** Y.

If the weather **turns** bad, we **will do** X.

T3 | Speaking: Present your plan to the class

Listen to the other plans.

Ask questions and then give feedback.

Who has the most interesting training plan?

Your teacher will give you feedback on your briefing and plan.

Unit 123 Rules of Engagement 1

T1 | Speaking: Talk and Report

What are ROE?

Why are they important?

What kind of information would you find in ROE?

T2 | Grammar: Grammar Revision 1

Discuss with your partner what the different verbs marked in bold mean.

You **should** do it.

You **must** do it.

He **will** do it.

You **should** <u>not</u> do it.

You **may** do it.

He **can** do it.

It **is** true.

Which of these verbs would you expect to find in ROE? Why?

T3 | Grammar: Grammar Revision 2

Which of these verbs in **bold** are active and which are passive?

1. Privately owned property **may be used** only if publicly owned property is unavailable.

2. You **may only use** privately owned property if publicly owned property is unavailable.

3. Armed force **is** the last resort.

4. Armed force **should** only **be used** as a last resort.

5. Annex R to the OPLAN **provides** more detail,

6. More detail **is provided** in Annex R to the OPLAN

T4 | Grammar: Grammar Revision 3

Discuss: Why is the passive used in the sentences in T3?

Language Reminder

Be is the condition marker verb.

What follow **be** is the **condition** of the **subject** of the sentence.

He **is** a soldier. [Information about his condition]

Private property **may** only **be used** (by soldiers)

[Information about the private property]

T5 | Vocabulary: Read and Complete

Complete the sample ROE with a suitable verb from the box below.

are x 2	must be x 3	can be used	is	will be x 3	may not be
are not	should be x 4	should not be x 2	will	will not be	may be

All enemy military personnel and vehicles transporting enemy personnel or their equipment [1] _____ engaged subject to the following restrictions:

A. When possible, the enemy [2] _____ warned first and asked to surrender.

B. Armed force is the last resort.

C. Armed civilians [3] _____ engaged only in self-defense.

D. Civilian aircraft [4] _____ engaged, except in self-defense, without approval from division level.

E. All civilians [5] _____ treated with respect and dignity. Civilians and their property [6] _____ harmed unless necessary to save US lives. If possible, civilians [7] _____ evacuated before any US attack. Privately owned property may be used only if publicly owned property is unavailable or its use is inappropriate.

F. If civilians are in the area, artillery, mortars, AC-130s, attack helicopters, tube-launched or rocket-launched weapons, and main tank guns [8] _____ used against known or suspected targets without the permission of a ground maneuver commander (LTC or higher).

G. If civilians [9] _____ in the area, all air attacks [10] _____ controlled by FAC or FO, and close air support, white phosphorus weapons, and incendiary weapons are prohibited without approval from division.

H. If civilians [11] _____ in the area, infantry [12] _____ shoot only at known enemy locations.

I. Public works such as power stations, water treatment plants, dams, and other public utilities [13] _____ engaged without approval from division level.

J. Hospitals, churches, shrines, schools, museums, and other historical or cultural sites [14] _____ engaged only in self-defense against fire from these locations.

K. All indirect fire and air attacks [15] _____ observed.

L. Pilots [16] _____ briefed for each mission as to the location of civilians and friendly forces.

M. Booby traps [17] _____ authorized. Authority to emplace mines [18] _____ reserved for the division commander. Riot control agents [19] _____ only with approval from division level.

N. Prisoners [20] _____ treated humanely, with respect and dignity.

O. Annex R to the OPLAN provides more detail. In the event this card conflicts with the OPLAN, the OPLAN [21] _____ followed.

DISTRIBUTION: ONE FOR EACH SOLDIER DEPLOYED (ALL RANKS)

[Source: FM 7 - 20]

T6 | Reading: Read and Answer

Read the ROE again and answer these questions.

1.   Can you aim artillery over a hill to a target you cannot observe?
2.   Can a platoon leader order mines to be placed?
3.   Can you attack a church if you see the enemy have entered it?
4.   Can a company commander order a mortar barrage in an area with civilians?
5.   Can a platoon leader order an attack on a dam?
6.   If you see an armed civilian, can you engage them?
7.   Can you defend yourself?
8.   How should you treat prisoners?
9.   When can you use riot control agents?
10. How does the presence of civilians affect a firefight?

T7 | Listen and Read: Listen to a reading of the text

Which words do you need to practice saying? Which words do you need to learn?

T8 | Consolidation Tasks

Revision: Key Collocations		
1. military	a) personnel	
2. main battle	b) forces	
3. close	c) station	
4. indirect	d) target	
5. booby	e) defense	
6. division	f) force	
7. private	g) property	
8. armed	h) commander	
9. self-	i) traps	
10. suspected	j) fire	
11. air	k) air support	
12. power	l) tank	
13. public	m) utilities	
14. friendly	n) attack	

Unit 124 Rules of Engagement 2

T1 | Speaking: Talk and Report 1

What are ROE?

Why are they important?

What kind of information would you find in ROE?

T2 | Speaking: Talk and Report 2

A useful acronym for remembering some of the basics of the ROE is RAMP. What do you think RAMP stands for?

R: _____

A: _____

M: _____

P: _____

T3 | Listening: Listen and Complete

Listen to the talk about ROE and RAMP and complete the text with a suitable word.

> R—[1] _____ Fire with Aimed Fire. [2] _____ force with force. You always have the right to repel hostile acts with necessary force.
>
> A—[3] _____ Attack. Use force if, but only if, you see clear indicators of hostile intent.
>
> M—[4] _____ the amount of Force that you use, if time and circumstances permit. Use only the amount of force necessary to protect lives and accomplish the mission.
>
> P—[5] _____ with deadly force only human life, and property designated by your commander. Stop short of deadly force when protecting other property.

T4 | Speaking: Talk and Report

The situation: You are at war with the Zanadu Liberation Front, a rebel insurgency operating in the east of your country.

What ROE do you want for your patrols in insurgent held areas?

T5 | Writing: Write out your ROE from T4

T6 | Consolidation Tasks

Unit 125 Talking About Position 1

T1 | Speaking: Talk and Report

Look at P125.1 - 2.

What can you see?

Cover up T3 before doing T2

T2 | Vocabulary: Collocations with position

How many words do you know which collocate with position?

    e.g. a bad position

T3 | Vocabulary: Match the words and the definition

1.	in position	(a)	a position hardened ready for attack
2.	fortified position	(b)	go into position
3.	concealed position	(c)	to go around an enemy position
4.	move into position	(d)	preposition + position
5.	defensive position	(e)	a position held by the enemy
6.	prepared position	(f)	remain in position
7.	firing position	(g)	a position you will fight from
8.	take up position	(h)	a hidden position
9.	attack a position	(i)	your position now
10.	enemy position	(j)	a position you have made ready
11.	fighting position	(k)	assault a position
12.	current position	(l)	a secondary position
13.	bypass an enemy position	(m)	go into position
14.	alternate position	(n)	a position which you will fire from
15.	hold in position	(o)	a position you will defend

Agree on the correct translation with your partner.

T4 | Vocabulary: Complete the sentences with words from T2

1. Make sure you are _____ position by 1600.

2. _____ into position just after dark.

3. _____ up your positions.

4. We will need to _____ the enemy's fortified/prepared position.

5. You should _____ in position until relieved.

6. I want you to _____ these positions here, here and here at 0430.

7. Can you see the _____ positions?

T5 | Vocabulary: Complete the sentences with words from T2

1. This hill is a strong _____ position.

2. I want you to dig _____ positions in this area.

3. Where are you? What is your _____ position?

4. If we have to withdraw, we will move to these _____ positions.

5. We need to dig trenches to connect the _____ positions.

6. Soldiers who attack _____ positions should expect to encounter planned enemy fires.

7. A soldier must be able to use hasty _____ positions when attacked.

T6 | Speaking: Map Task

Look at your maps and select 10 suitable places for different kinds of positions from T3. Note the grid references. Then tell your partner what you want him/her to do: '*I want you to dig firing positions at GRID 349275*'. Your partner should note the positions on the map and then confirm with you what you want him/her to do. Change roles.

Unit 126 Talking About Position 2

Learn To Describe Position

T1 | Speaking: Talk and Report

Which collocations of 'position' do you remember from **Unit 125**?

T2 | Listening: Listen to a talk about defensive positions

Make notes on the key points. Check your notes with your partner.

T3 | Listening: Listen to a talk about attacking fortified positions

Make notes on the key points. Check your notes with your partner.

T4 | Listening: Transcript Tasks: Complete the texts and listen to check

Task 1: Defending Position Listening

avenue	buys	destroy	fix	key	maneuver	position	possession

A unit defends from a battle [1] _____ in order to do one of four things. One. To [2] _____ an enemy force in the engagement area. Two. To block an enemy [3] _____ of approach. Three. To control [4] _____ or decisive terrain. It is important to deny the enemy the [5] _____ of this terrain, so it must be defended. Four. To [6] _____ the enemy force in position to allow another friendly unit to [7] _____. For example to flank and then attack the fixed enemy force. Fixing the enemy in position [8] _____ other units time to maneuver.

Task 2: Attacking fortified positions

alternate	counter	fires	fortifying	internal
obstacles	positions	reinforce	spoiling	trenches

Fortifications are works emplaced to defend and [1] _____ a position. If enemy defenders have time they will build bunkers and [2] _____, concealed [3] _____, emplace protective [4] _____, and position mutually supporting fortifications when [5] _____ their positions. Soldiers who attack prepared positions should expect to encounter a range of planned enemy [6] _____.... These will include [7] _____ attacks, [8] _____ repositioning, [9] _____ attacks, and withdrawing to [10] _____ defensive positions.

T5 | Speaking: Talk and Report

Which do you prefer? Attacking or Defending? Why? Explain 'the defender's advantage' to your teacher.

Revision: Key Collocations	
1. battle	force
2. prepared	position
3. enemy	in position
4. friendly	defenders
5. concealed	attacks
6. held	of approach
7. fire	unit
8. enemy	position
9. avenue	by
10. spoiling	fire
11. hold	from

Unit 127 Talking about a Base

T1 | Speaking: Talk and Report 1

What kinds of buildings can you find on an army base? Make a list.

T2 | Vocabulary: Check the meaning of these words

PX/NAAFI	officers' mess	quartermaster stores
stockade	control tower	communications centre
barracks	guardhouse	dining facility
airstrip	obstacle course	armory/armoury
runway	medical centre	firing range
hanger	cookhouse	the base mission operations center

T3 | Listening: Listen to this description of an Army base

Label the buildings on the plan below. Check with P127.1

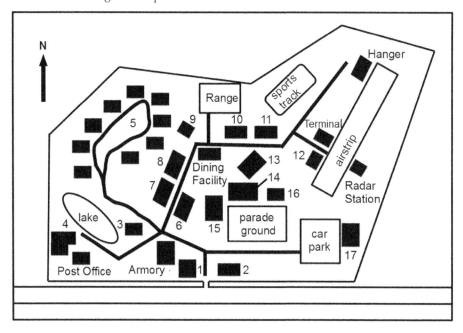

T4 | Listening: Listen Again

What is missing from the plan? Listen again and draw in the missing parts.
Check P127.2

T5 | Listening: Listen Again

What language is used to describe the position of the buildings? Write down the phrases. Check with T127.1.

T6 | Speaking: Talk and Report 2

Discuss the base in T3

Is this a good layout for a base?

Are there any weaknesses?

Remember to think about base security.

Discuss with your partner:

Report to the class.

Language Reminder: Talking About Problems
The main weakness is _____
A big problem is _____
The most serious problem is the position of the X.
The position of the X is a problem because...
The X shouldn't be there because _____. It should be _____.
The X should be _____

T7 | Speaking: Draw and Describe

Draw a plan of an army base. Do not show it to your partner.

Then on a second piece of paper draw the perimeter outline of your base and the roads and give it to your partner. Then describe your base to your partner, who will draw in all the details. Then compare your plans. Why is your plan better?

Language Reminder: Explaining Position
The main entrance is _____.
In the north/south/east/west is _____.
Next to the X is a Y
Opposite the X is a Y.
To the left of the X is a Y.
X is at the north end of _____.

T8 | Speaking: Giving Directions

Practice giving directions from X to Y on your base (see Unit 46).

T9 | Writing: Write a description of your base plan from T7

T10 | Consolidation Tasks

Unit 128 Fundamentals of Base Security 1

Learn To Talk About The Fundamentals Of Base Security

T1 | Speaking: Talk and Report 1

Look at P128.1. What can you see?

T2 | Speaking: Talk and Report 2

What are the eight fundamentals of base security?

Discuss your ideas with your partner and then check with the class.

T3 | Speaking: Talk and Report 3

Look at P128.2. Were you correct ? Do you agree?

T4 | Speaking: Talk and Report 4

1. What advantages do defenders have?
2. How can they use these advantages to best effect?
3. Which is 'better'? Attack or defence?

T5 | Vocabulary: Read and Complete

Complete the text with a suitable word.

cover	deceive	defensive	dispositions	fields
indirect	numerically	operations	positions	terrain

Use of the Defenders' Advantages.

Defenders' advantages may permit a [1] _____ inferior force to defeat a much larger one. Some of these advantages are:

- The ability to fight from [2] _____ ;
- More detailed knowledge of local [3] _____ and environment;
- The ability to prepare [4] _____ , routes between them, obstacles, and [5] _____ o f fire in advance;
- The ability to plan communications, control measures, [6] _____ fires, and logistic support to fit any predictable situation;
- The ability to [7] _____ enemy forces about friendly [8] _____ capabilities, [9] _____ , and execution of [10] _____ .

T6 | Speaking: Talk and Report 3

What kind of physical perimeter defence measures does your army use around a base? Discuss and check with the class.

Check with P128.3. Are these the same as in your army?

Unit 129 Fundamentals of Base Security 2

T1 | Speaking: Talk and Report 1

What are the eight fundamentals of base security?

T2 | Speaking: Talk and Report 2

Discuss these questions with your partner.

1. Why do you need to understand the enemy?
2. Why do you need to see the battlespace?
3. Why must the base commander concentrate his forces at critical times and places?
4. Why should the base commander conduct counter reconnaissance and counter attacks?
5. Why is it important to coordinate Critical Defense Assets?
6. Why is it necessary to balance base security with political and legal constraints?
7. Why should ROEs be complied with?

T3 | Reading: Read the text below to check your answers from T2

Intelligence

In all aspects of war it is vital to understand the enemy. Defenders must be familiar with the capabilities and limitations of enemy forces, weapons, equipment, and tactics. The base commander also must have access to the latest intelligence concerning probable enemy intent. Commanders need to be able to see the battlespace for what it really is and intelligence operations are key to assembling an accurate picture of the battlespace. Commanders need a continuous, integrated, and comprehensive analysis of the effects of enemy capabilities, terrain, and weather on operations. This analysis is called the intelligence preparation of the battlespace. This analysis helps the commander anticipate battlespace events and then commanders can develop their priority intelligence requirements (PIR) and information requirements based on those battlespace events. Intelligence officers should prepare intelligence and multidiscipline counter-intelligence (CI) estimates and they should be continuously updated, and integrated into the base commander's staff decision making process.

Concentrating Combat Firepower

For effective defence it is extremely important to be able to concentrate combat power at critical times and places. Defense of a base is normally conducted along interior lines, permitting the timely and secure movement of forces to engage the most critical threats. The commander must mass enough combat power at points of decision by economizing in some areas, employing a reserve, and maneuvering to gain local superiority at critical points.

Counter-reconnaissance and Counter Attacks

A good commander will conduct counter-reconnaissance and counter-attacks. Fixed bases with well-established perimeters usually have limited depth. Counter-reconnaissance and counter-attack add depth to the battle outside the perimeter, allowing the base to continue its primary mission with minimal interference. By taking the battle to the enemy you relieve pressure on the base itself.

Coordination: It is crucial to coordinate critical defense assets. Synchronization of indirect fires, air and missile defense resources, tactical aircraft, engineers, dismounted troops, armored vehicles, naval surface fire support, and helicopters can produce a combined arms effect. By synchronizing forces and fires a smaller force can be capable of defeating a larger enemy force. By making enemy movement difficult or impossible and by causing a reaction enemy forces may become more vulnerable to other friendly capabilities.

Legal Issues

A commander needs to balance base security with political and legal constraints. Base security may have to be designed around numerous political constraints which restrict how and when force can be used; in peacekeeping there will be clear guidance in the mandate of the operation. Base commanders and all their subordinates must also comply with ROE; this is a legal requirement. They should ensure that inconsistencies among Service component ROE are reconciled so that everyone is on the same page.

[Adapted from Joint Pub 3-10.1 Joint Tactics, Techniques, and Procedures for Base Defense]

T4 | Language Analysis: Analyse the Text

T5 | Listen and Read: Listen to a reading of the text

Which words do you need to practice saying? Which words do you need to learn?

T6 | Vocabulary: Complete the collocations from the text

1. latest _____
2. enemy _____
3. continuously _____
4. decision-making _____
5. effective _____
6. critical _____
7. critical _____
8. limited _____
9. minimal _____
10. relieve _____
11. combined _____
12. legal _____
13. political _____
14. clear _____
15. legal _____
16. interior _____

T7 | Consolidation Tasks

Unit 130 Fundamentals of Base Security 3

T1 | Speaking: Talk and Report 1

Look at P130.1. What can you see?

Cover up T4 before doing T2

T2 | Speaking: What do you remember from Unit 128 and 129?

What are the eight fundamentals of base security?

T3 | Speaking: Talk and Report 2

What are the essential actions of base defence forces? Make a list.

T4 | Vocabulary: Read and complete the text

Complete the text with a suitable word.

delay	deny	destroy	detect	warn

Essential actions of the defense force are:

[1] _____ Enemy attempts to reconnoiter or attack the base or interfere with the performance of base functions must be detected at the earliest stage.

[2] _____ The base must be warned that an attack is imminent or under way.

[3] _____ Defense forces must prevent the enemy from access to the base and from degrading the base's primary function.

[4] _____ If possible, defense forces must eliminate the attacking enemy's capability to threaten the base.

[5] _____ If base forces lack the combat power to defeat the attacking enemy, defense forces must disrupt the attack and attempt to create the conditions for response forces or tactical combat forces to react and destroy the enemy force or to remove or deny base resources to the enemy.

T5 | Speaking: Talk and Report 4

Check you understand these terms with a partner.

Then discuss why these are important when talking about base defence.

1. defense in depth
2. OPs
3. mobile reserve
4. security area
5. boundary areas
6. entrances
7. patrols
8. evacuation
9. area of operations
10. medical facilities
11. avenues of approach
12. fire support planning
13. anti-armour weapons
14. aviation support
15. security measures
16. counter-attack plans
17. obstacles and mines
18. indirect fire systems
19. working and living areas
20. primary defence position
21. air and missile defense measures
22. area damage control measures
23. OPSEC measures and deception
24. intrusion detection
25. communication systems

Then check your ideas with the class.

T6 | Writing: Write 10 sentences

Write 10 sentences about base security based on **Units 128 - 130**.

T7 | Revision: Picture Description

Look at P130.2 – P130.9 and discuss with a partner what you can see.

Unit 131 Fundamentals of Base Security 4

T1 | Speaking: Talk and Report 1

Look at P131.1. What can you see?

T2 | Reading: Read and Answer

1. Why is patrolling important for base security?
2. What two kinds of patrol are there?
3. What are the differences between mounted and unmounted patrols?
4. How should a patrol leader prepare for a patrol?

TACTICAL SECURITY: Patrols

Patrolling is necessary outside the physical base but within the AO to provide additional base security. Patrolling urban areas involves different risks and considerations than patrolling open or cleared uninhabited areas. The two categories of patrol are reconnaissance and combat. A patrol will be tasked to collect information, confirm or deny accuracy of previously gained information, provide security, and harass, destroy, or capture the enemy.

Patrols can be conducted dismounted or mounted.

a. **Dismounted Patrols.** A patrol may be a fire team, squad, platoon, or company. Patrol members must be able to interact with local inhabitants but still should be ready to conduct combat operations. Multiple units maintain mutual support for each other as they move and operate.

b. **Mounted Patrols.** Mounted patrols are especially useful in an economy of force mission where the unit has a large sector to cover and few personnel to patrol. Mounted patrols can be used to cover gaps between units in the defense, flank security and coordination, patrol forward of the base perimeter to provide early warning, and assist in reconnaissance when a large sector must be covered in a relatively short time.

Organization and Preparation. The leaders of the patrol must analyze the mission, determine what elements are needed, and decide how to accomplish the mission. The patrol leader must consider route selection, link-up procedures, resupply, signal plan, departure from and re-entry to base defense positions, and other friendly units in the area. Recognition signals must be firmly established to provide early and immediate identification by friendly forces. A map, ground, or aerial reconnaissance by the leader will help balance the size of the area, the time constraints of the mission, and the patrol's security requirements.

[Adapted from Joint Pub 3-10.1 Joint Tactics, Techniques, and Procedures for Base Defense]

T3 | Language Analysis: Analyse the Text

T4 | Listen and Read: Listen to a reading of the text

Which words do you need to practice saying?

Which words do you need to learn?

T5 | Vocabulary: Complete the collocations from the text

1. physical _____
2. base _____
3. urban _____
4. uninhabited _____
5. collect _____
6. combat _____
7. mutual _____
8. flank _____

9. base _____
10. early _____
11. route _____
12. link-up _____
13. signal _____
14. recognition _____
15. security _____

T6| Consolidation Tasks

Revision: Key Collocations	
1. defender's	a) security
2. control	b) forces
3. enemy	c) intent
4. enemy	d) power
5. combat	e) attack
6. counter-attack	f) advantageous
7. legal	g) measures
8. indirect	h) forces
9. defense	i) requirements
10. base	j) security
11. flank	k) fire
12. large-scale	l) sector
13. friendly	m) units
14. time	n) constraints

Check with Units 128-131.

Unit 132 Guard Duty

T1 | Speaking: Talk and Report 1

Look at P132.1 and P132.2. What can you see?

T2 | Grammar and Vocabulary: Complete the phrases

_____ duty/guard/alert | all passes must be _____ | _____ roster

T3 | Grammar: Complete the sentences with the correct preposition

at x 4	in x 3	down	up	on	to

1. I will meet you _____ the entrance.
2. Stand _____ the barrier.
3. I am _____ duty from 1800.
4. Who is _____ charge here?
5. You must stop _____ the barrier.
6. Slow _____ as you approach the entrance.
7. Keep alert _____ all times.
8. Lift the barrier _____ to let the vehicles _____ and out.
9. The guard house is over there next _____ that tree.
10. There is concertina wire behind and _____ front of the wall.

T4 | Speaking: Talk and Report 2

What physical perimeter defence measures do you remember from Unit 128? Check with P128.3.

T5 | Speaking: Prepare a plan

Work with a partner. Draw a plan of an entrance to a base that you are familiar with. Do not label the features. Mark where the personnel stand and decide what they their duties are. Prepare to explain to another pair the layout and features of the base entrance, and the duties of the personnel.

T6 | Speaking: Pairwork chain

1. Explain to another pair the layout and features etc. of your base entrance in T5. Answer any questions they have.
2. Listen to their explanation and ask questions.
3. Exchange paper plans.
4. Pair up with another pair and explain to this pair the layout and features etc. of the base you now have.

T7 | Speaking: Talk and Report 3

Think about the standard operating procedure when a vehicle approaches base entrance. What happens? List the steps and then check as a class.

T8 | Speaking: Role-Play Preparation

Think about the steps in T6. What do people say at each step?

e.g. *'Can I see your identification please?'*

Make a list.

T9 | Speaking: Role-play

Work in groups.

Arrange the furniture in the class to make an entrance to a base.

Decide who will play which role.

A vehicle arrives at the entrance to the base.

Check the occupants and the vehicle and let them into the base.

Practise your role-play and then present it to the class.

Give feedback on the other role-plays.

T10 | Revision: Picture Description

Look at P132.3 and discuss with a partner what you can see.

Unit 133 FOB Simulation

Practice Talking About Bases, Security, Patrolling Etc.

T1 | Speaking: FOB Simulation Preparation

Work in groups.

Look at your maps and decided on a good location for a Forward Operating Base.

Decide where the enemy forces will be and in what strength.

Decide on the composition of your forces.

Plan your FOB.

Prepare a detailed plan of the base to show the class.

Include all aspects of base design, and include information about base security, base defense forces, response forces and threats. - see P133.1

Decide who is going to present on which aspects of the base.

Practice your briefing.

Remember: The group are responsible for the success of the briefing: help and coach your briefer(s).

T2 | Speaking: Present your Forward Operating Base to the class

Give a briefing about your FOB.

Follow this sequence and include these points:

1. Welcome to the base.
2. Location and purpose of the FOB.
3. The layout of the base.
4. Overview of area of operations, including enemy dispositions
5. Questions?

Be ready to answer questions.

T3 | Feedback: Give feedback on your colleagues' briefings

Did you understand everything?
If not, what did you not understand?

T4 | Feedback: Your teacher will give you feedback on your briefing

Unit 134 Observation Posts

T1 | Speaking: Talk and Report 1

Look at P134.1 and P134.2. What can you see?

T2 | Speaking: Talk and Report 2

What are observation posts for?

T3 | Reading: Using an Observation Post

Read the **OP Guidelines** text on the next page.

How many mistakes are there? Correct the mistakes.

T4 | Speaking: Talk and Report 3

Look at the table of **Information for OPs** on the next page.

Which of these instructions/information on the next page should a squad leader give to the soldiers manning an OP? Why?

T5 | Speaking: Talk and Report 4

What of this equipment should an OP have? Why?

binoculars	maps	a compass	paper and pencil
trip flares	a field phone	a watch	night vision devices

T6 | Listening: Listen to the instructor explaining what should happen at the OP

Make notes on the points the instructor makes. Check your notes with your partner and class. Check with T114.1.

T7 | Vocabulary: Visual Terrain Search

Look at P134.3 and P134.4 and complete the text with these words:

entire	obvious	overall	overlapping
position	sections	strips	suspicious

> The observer makes an [1] _____ search of the entire area for [2] _____ targets, unnatural colors, outlines, or movement. To do this quickly, he raises his eyes from just in front of his [3] _____ to the greatest range he wants to observe. If the sector is wide, he observes it in [4] _____. Then he observes [5] _____ 50-meter wide [6] _____ , alternating. from left to right and right to left until he has observed the [7] _____ area. When he sees a [8] _____ spot, he searches it well.

T8 | Consolidation Tasks

OP Guidelines

OPs are used to watch and listen for enemy activity and provide security and intelligence for the platoon. OPs shouldn't be sited to allow observation of the designated area. They shouldn't be sited to take advantage of natural cover and concealment to provide protection for the soldiers manning it and OPs should never be located within small-arms range of the platoon positions. When selecting observation posts, you should chose the most prominent position. Avoid obvious terrain such as hilltops and use easily identifiable terrain features such as water towers, church steeples, tallest buildings, lone buildings or trees, or isolated groves. A selected observation post should be observed for 10 to 15 minutes to ensure it is not occupied. Do not select a covered and concealed route to and from the OP: use routes or positions that skyline soldiers. If the post is located on a hill, crawl to a position where the skyline is broken. If a tree is used, the position should have a background so as not to be silhouetted against the sky while climbing or observing. At least two soldiers must man each OP. A fire team may man the OP if it will remain in place or not be relieved for long periods. All soldiers should prepare fighting positions at the OP for protection and concealment. Additionally, each soldier must have a prepared position to return to in the platoon position. An observation post should always be manned for more than 24 hours. As a guide, OPs should be relieved every two to four hours. When leaving the observation post, the same route from that of the approach should be used. If a radio is used, its antenna should be located to provide clear communication to the controlling commander but masked from enemy observation and direction-finding equipment. Upon departure, scouts shouldn't remove the antennae from the observation post so as not to give away the position.

[Source: MCWP3-11.3]

Information for OPs	
challenge and password	"You need a challenge and password because...."
running password*	
when to engage and when not to engage the enemy	
conditions when the OP can withdraw	
when to expect relief	
contingency plans for loss of communications	

*This code word alerts a unit that friendly soldiers are approaching in a less than organized manner and possibly under pressure. This may be used to get soldiers quickly through a compromised passage of friendly lines. The running password is followed by the number of soldiers approaching ("Moosebreath five"). This prevents the enemy from joining a group in an attempt to penetrate a friendly unit.

Unit 135 Overwatch 1

Learn To Talk About Overwatch

T1 | Speaking: Talk and Report 1

Look at P135.1 - 4. What can you see?

T2 | Speaking: Talk and Report 2

What are the differences?

1. Travelling
2. Travelling overwatch
3. Bounding overwatch

T3 | Listening: Listen and Make Notes

Listen to the soldier talking about the differences between travelling, and travelling
and bounding overwatch. Complete this table. Check with your partner.

[Check T135.1]

MOVEMENT TECHNIQUE	WHEN NORMALLY USED	CHARACTERISTICS			
		CONTROL	DISPERSION	SPEED	SECURITY
TRAVELLING					
TRAVELLING OVERWATCH					
BOUNDING OVERWATCH					

T4 | Vocabulary: Complete the Texts

alternate	contact	control	crossed	discipline
distance	element	extends	formation	forward
near	overwatch	overwatches	positions	possible
required	rushes	signals	suppress	trailing

Travelling Overwatch

Travelling Overwatch is used when contact is [1] _____ but speed is
[2] _____ . The platoon leader moves where he can best
[3] _____ the platoon. The platoon sergeant travels with the
[4] _____ squad, though he is free to move through the
[5] _____ to enforce security, noise and light [6] _____ and
distances. The lead squads use travelling overwatch, and the trailing squad use
travelling. The [7] _____ between the lead squad and the platoon HQ
element [8] _____ from the normal 20m out to 50 – 100m.

Bounding Overwatch

Bounding overwatch is used when [1] _____ is expected, when the unit leader feels the enemy is [2] _____, or when a large open danger area must be [3] _____. Platoons conducting bounding overwatch using successive or [4] _____ bounds. One squad (the trail fire team) bounds [5] _____ to a chosen position, then it becomes the overwatching [6] _____ unless contact is made en route. The bounding squad can use either travelling overwatch, or individual techniques (low and high crawl, and short [7] _____ by the fire team or pairs). While this squad moves for-ward another squad [8] _____ from covered [9] _____ from which it can see and [10] _____ likely enemy positions. The unit leader usually stays with this overwatch team. The trail fire team [11] _____ the unit leader when his team completes its bound and is prepared to [12] _____ the movement of the other team.

T5 | Drawing: Draw a diagram to explain travelling and bounding overwatch

Explain your diagram to another student and then to your teacher.

Unit 136 Overwatch 2

T1 I Speaking: Talk and Report 1

What are the differences?

travelling I travelling overwatch I bounding overwatch

T2 I Grammar and Vocabulary: Complete the Orders

Look at P136.1. Complete these orders with these words:

await	up x 2	left	orders	position x 3	mirror
move	set	clear	signal	overwatch x2	

First squad, [1] _____ from this [2] _____. Second squad, [3] _____ through those trees to the left and [4] _____ that small hill one hundred meters to our front and [5] _____ up an [6] _____ on the hill. [17] _____ with your [8] _____ when in position. I will move [9] _____ with the first and third squad, and give you your next [10] _____. Third squad , move [11] _____ behind first squad and [12] _____ orders. Platoon sergeant, [13] _____ your machine guns and antitank weapon to the right of the first squad. I will [14] _____ mine to the [15] _____ of the first squad.

T3 I Speaking: Talk and Report

How would you cross a large open area on patrol?

T4 I Listening: Listen and complete the notes

Listen to the solder talking about crossing large open areas.

Complete the diagram below. Check with P136.2

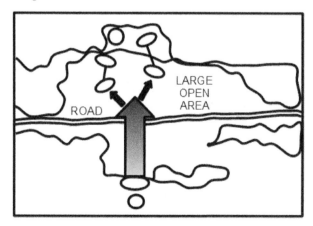

T5 I Consolidation Tasks

Unit 137 Organising Convoys 1

Learn To Talk About Convoys

T1 | Speaking: Talk and Report 1

Look at P137.1 and P137.2. What can you see?

T2 | Speaking: Talk and Report 2

When and why would you use convoys?

T3 | Reading: Read and Answer

Read and answer the questions about US Army convoy organisation:

Convoy Elements. Vehicles in a convoy are organized into groups to facilitate command and control. A convoy may be as small as a 6-vehicle march unit or as large as a 300-vehicle column. Whenever possible, convoys are set up along organizational lines, such as squad, platoon, company, battalion, and brigade. Convoy elements include march units, serials, and columns

(1) *March units*. A march unit is the smallest element of a convoy. As the smallest subdivision of a column, march units may have up to 25 vehicles assigned. A march unit usually represents a squad- to platoon-size element. Each march unit has a march unit commander.

(2) *Serials*. A serial is a group of two to five march units. It represents approximately a company- to battalion-size element. Each serial has a serial commander.

(3) *Columns*. A column is a group of two to five serials. It represents approximately a battalion- to brigade-size element. Each column has a column commander.

For example, a medium truck company commander can organize his convoy as a serial by dividing the 60 task vehicles by platoons into three march units of 20 vehicles each. The company commander would then serve as the convoy commander and the platoon leaders would serve as march unit commanders. Remaining vehicles would be added to each march unit for command and control and convoy support.   [Source: FM 55-30]

---

1.   What is the minimum size of a convoy?
2.   Why are there three different convoy elements?
3.   Why do these elements have separate commanders?

T4 | Listening: What is the composition of the convoys?

Listen about three convoys.

Make notes on the composition of the convoys.

T5 | Consolidation Tasks

Unit 138 Organising Convoys 2

T1 I Speaking: Talk and Report 1

Look at P138.1 - 2. What can you see?

T2 I Vocabulary: Convoy Control Personnel

What do these people do on convoys?

Guide I Pacesetter I Trail Maintenance Officer I Trail Officer

T3 I Vocabulary: Complete the text below with the people from T2

Convoy Control Personnel.

Control is exercised by the column commander, serial commanders, and march unit commanders. The advance party officer, trail party officer, pacesetter, and escorts assist the convoy commander in controlling the movement.

(1) *Column, serial, and march unit commanders* plan and control the motor movement and enforce march discipline. They may be either officers or non-commissioned officers.

(2) The ___A_____ should be an experienced officer or NCO who rides in the first vehicle of each element in the convoy. The ___A_____ maintains or adjusts the rate of march necessary to meet the schedule. In so doing, the ___A_____ will direct that the convoy speed-up to compensate for lost time due to terrain, weather, traffic conditions, or other obstacles. The ___A's_____ job is critical as he must ensure the convoy averages the march rate over the length of the route.

(3) The _____B_____ is positioned at the rear of the column. He checks and observes vehicles, march units, or serials at the SP. He ensures that approaching traffic from the rear is warned when the column halts. He also picks up guides and markers left by preceding elements of the march column. He investigates accidents on-the-spot, directs evacuation of injured personnel, and effects disposition of disabled equipment.

(4) A _____C_____ rides at the rear of the column with maintenance and recovery personnel and equipment and supervises en route maintenance operations. In a small column, the _____B_____ officer and the _____C_____ may be the same person.

(5) _____Ds_____ are used to ensure the convoy follows the prescribed route. They become very important when operating in an area where road signs are poor or non-existent. On controlled routes, the area commander may furnish _____Ds_____ are to direct units or vehicles moving over these routes. Highway regulation authorities will use movement regulation teams and military police to assist moving units. Although these teams do not normally escort convoys, they assist convoy commanders in locating supported units, preventing conflict with

other convoys, and providing other information on the route. On routes that are not controlled, the moving unit is usually responsible for providing its own _____Ds_____.

[Adapted from: FM55-30]

T4 | Vocabulary: Convoy Sections

Complete the text below with these words. Listen to check.

checkpoints	clear	discipline	first	last	majority	security
pacesetter x 2	rear	multiple	route	march x 2	subdivided	

Convoy Sections

All columns, serials, and march units, regardless of size, have three parts: a head, a main body, and a trail Each of these parts has a specific function.

Head. The head is the [1] _____ vehicle of each column, serial, and march unit. Each head should have its own [2] _____. The [3] _____ rides in this vehicle and sets the pace needed to meet the scheduled itinerary along the route. The officer or non-commissioned officer at the head ensures that the column follows the proper [4] _____. He may also be required to report arrival at certain [5] _____ along the route. With the head performing these duties, the convoy commander has the flexibility to move up and down the column to enforce [6] _____ discipline.

Main body. The main body follows immediately after the head and consists of the [7] _____ of the vehicles moving as part of the convoy. This is the part of the convoy that may be [8] _____ into serials and [9] _____ units for ease of control.

Trail. The trail is the [10] _____ sector of each march column, serial, and march unit. The trail officer/NCO is responsible for recovery, maintenance, and medical support. The recovery vehicle, maintenance vehicles, and medical support vehicles/teams are located in the trail. The trail officer/NCO assists the convoy commander in maintaining march [11] _____. He may also be required to report [12] _____ times at checkpoints along the route. In convoys consisting of [13] _____ march units and serials, the convoy commander may direct minimum support in the trail of each serial or march unit and a larger trail party at the [14] _____ of the column. As the trail party may be left behind to conduct repairs or recovery, the convoy commander should provide trail [15] _____ and communications.

[Adapted from: FM55-30]

T5 | Listening: Convoy Security

Listen and make notes about convoy security. There are three parts to the listening Use these headings to help you.

Part 1: Methods of control
Part 2: Advance Security Elements, Main Body and Rearguard
Part 3: Screening and OPSEC

T6 | Consolidation Tasks

Unit 139 Convoy Driving

Present About Driving In Difficult Conditions

There are three briefings to give on driving and vehicle maintenance in difficult conditions

1. Desert Operations
2. Jungle and Forest Operations
3. Operations in Snow, Ice, and Extreme Cold

T1 | Speaking: Group Briefing Preparation

Work in groups.

Prepare a briefing using **Unit 139 Briefing Slides**.

Decide who will speak about each slide.

Practice your briefing.

T2 | Speaking: Briefing

Deliver your briefing.

Be ready to answer questions.

T3 | Speaking: Questions

Ask questions about your colleagues' briefings.

T4 | Feedback: Give feedback on your colleagues' briefings

Did you understand everything?
If not, what did you not understand?

T5 | Feedback: Your teacher will give you feedback on your briefing

Unit 140 The Convoy Briefing 1

Cover up T2 and T3 before doing T1

T1 | Speaking: Talk and Report

What information would you expect in a convoy briefing?

Make a list and share it with the class.

T2 | Vocabulary: The Convoy Briefing 1

These are the suggested elements of a convoy briefing.

Which heading would the items on your list from **T1** go under?

1. Situation	2. Mission
3. Execution	4. Execution: Emergency measures
5. Administration and Logistics	6. Command and Signal
7. Other prearranged signals	8. Radio frequencies and call signs
9. Safety	10. Environmental protection

T3 | Vocabulary: The Convoy Briefing 2

Decide where each item below would come in the briefing.

The numbers indicate how many items there are in each section. For example, there are three items (3) in the situation part of the briefing.

Situation (3)	Accidents.
	Action of convoy personnel if ambushed.
	Action of security force commander.
	Action of security forces during ambush.
	Ambush.
Mission (3)	Arm and hand signals.
	Billeting arrangements.
	Breakdowns.
	Catch-up speed.
Execution (6)	Control of personnel.
	Control personnel.
	Convoy speed.
	Defensive driving.
	Destination.
	Enemy situation.
	Fire support elements.
	Friendly forces.

Execution: Emergency measures (8)	General organization of the convoy.
	Hazards of route and weather conditions.
	Location of convoy commander.
	Medical evacuation support.
	Medical support.
	Messing arrangements.
	Obstacles
	Origin.
	Refueling and servicing of vehicles, complying with spill prevention guidelines.
Administration and Logistics (4)	Reserve security elements.
	Routes.
	Security force commander.
	Separation from convoy.
	Serial commander's responsibility.
Command and Signal (5)	Spill prevention.
	Succession of command.
	Support units.
	Time schedule.
	Transporting HAZMAT.
	Type of cargo.
	Vehicle distance.
Other prearranged signals. (0)	
Radio frequencies and call signs for: (5)	
Safety (2)	
Environmental protection (2)	
	[Source: FM 55-30]

T4 | Listening: Listen to check

T5 | Speaking: Talk and Report: Why is this information important?

Unit 141 The Convoy Briefing 2

Learn To Make Notes While Listening To A Briefing About A Convoy

T1 | Speaking: Talk and Report 1

Look at P141.1 - 2. What can you see?

T2 | Listening: Listen to a Convoy Briefing

Make notes about the convoy and mark the route on the map below.

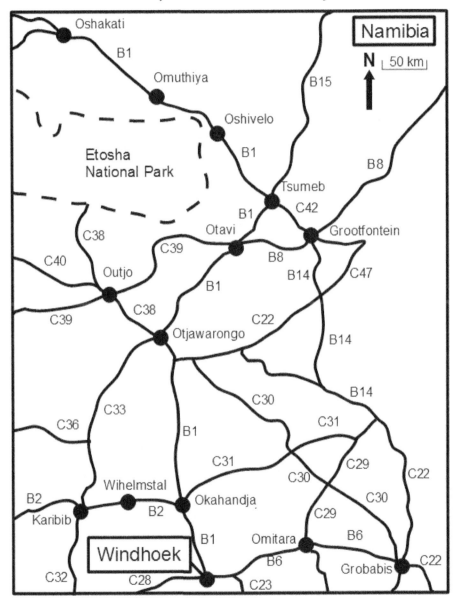

Check your route with P141.3 after listening.

T3 | Speaking: Talk and Report 2: Evaluate the Convoy Briefing

Unit 142 The Convoy Briefing 3

T1 | Speaking: Prepare a Convoy Briefing

Work in groups.

Use your maps.

Prepare a convoy briefing.

Use the Sample Convoy Briefing from Unit 141 to help you.

You decide on the type of convoy, composition, route etc.

Language Reminder: Futures

The convoy will take place in the future so use:

Future fact forms: *The convoy departs at 1500.*

Will for certainty about the future: *The convoy will drive up Route Bravo to _____.*

Hypothetical forms to talk about emergency measures etc.: *If the convoy is ambushed, you should _____.*

Practice and get ready to brief the class

T2 | Speaking: The Convoy Briefing

Brief the class on your convoy.

The other students will make notes about the convoy.

Be ready to answer questions.

T3 | Speaking: Questions

Ask questions about your colleagues' briefings.

T4 | Feedback: Give feedback on your colleagues' briefings

Did you understand everything?

If not, what did you not understand?

T5 | Reading: Review of notes

When all the briefings have finished, put your briefing notes on display on the walls around the room.

Each student can go and read the briefing notes and see if their own notes they made while listening to the briefing are accurate (or not).

T6 | Feedback: Your teacher will give you feedback on your briefing

Unit 143 IEDS and UXO 1

Learn To Talk IEDs And UXO

T1 | Speaking: Talk and Report 1

Look at P143.1 - 3. What can you see?

T2 | Speaking: Talk and Report 2

1. What are IEDS?
2. Why are IEDS used?

T3 | Reading: Read and Answer 1

Read the first part of the text and answer the questions.

1. Why are IEDS used?   2. How are they detonated?

Improvised explosive devices (IEDs), car bombs, unexploded ordnance (UXO), and suicide bombers pose deadly and pervasive threats to soldiers and civilians in operational areas all over the world. IEDs are non-standard explosive devices used to target soldiers, civilians, NGOs, and government agencies. IEDs range from crude home-made explosives to extremely intricate remote-controlled devices. The devices are used to instil fear and increase casualties. Timed Explosive Devices are detonated by remote control such as by the ring of a cell phone, by other electronic means, or by the combination of wire and either a power source or timed fuse. Impact Detonated Devices detonate after being dropped, thrown, or impacted in some manner. Vehicle Bombs may include explosive-laden vehicles detonated with electronic command wire or wireless remote control, or with timed devices. They might be employed with or without drivers.

T4 | Reading: Read and Answer 2

Read the second part of the text and answer the questions.

1. What is the 5 C's technique?   2. Why is it used?

Using the five C's technique helps to simplify both awareness and reaction to a suspected IED. The first step soldiers should take when encountering a suspected IED is to **confirm** that it is an IED by using 5- and 25-meter searches of their positions to look for telltale signs such as wires, protruding ordnance, or fleeing personnel. If an IED is confirmed, the next step is to **clear** the area. The safe distance is determined by several factors: the tactical situation, the avoidance of predictability, and the need to control movement up to several hundred meters away. Everyone within the danger zone should be evacuated. While the area around the IED is being cleared, a IED/UXO report should be **called in**. After the area has been cleared and the IED has been called in, soldiers should establish fighting positions in a **cordon** around the area to prevent vehicle and foot traffic from approaching the IED. They should assure the area is safe by checking for secondary IEDs. The entire perimeter of the affected area should be secured and dominated by all available personnel. Available obstacles should be used to block vehicle approach routes. Scan near and far for enemy observers who might try to detonate the IED. Since the distance of all personnel from the IED directly affects their safety, soldiers should **control** the site to prevent people from straying too close until the IED is cleared and the EOD officer gives the "all clear."

T5 | Reading: Read and Answer 3

Read the third part of the text and answer the question: What are the different kinds of UXO?

Unexploded ordinance (UXO) are made up of both enemy and friendly force ordnance that have failed to detonate. This includes: projectiles such as HE, chemical, illumination rounds, mortar rounds, rockets such as self-propelled projectiles, guided missiles and rifle grenades, similar to mortars but fired from rifles. Thrown ordnance including fragmentation, smoke, illumination, chemical, and incendiary hand grenades. Placed ordnance includes AP mines and AT mines. Dropped ordnance includes bombs, dispensers, which look similar to bombs but may have holes or ports in them, and very sensitive submunitions such as small bombs, grenades, or mines.

T6 | Reading: Read and Answer 4

Read the last part of the text and answer the question: Why are booby traps used?

Booby traps are typically hidden or disguised explosive devices rigged on common items to go off unexpectedly. They may also be employed as anti-handling devices on UXO, emplaced mines, or as improvised explosive devices (IED).

[Note: All Texts: Source: FM 3-21.8]

T7 | Listen and Read: Listen to a reading of the texts from T3 - T6

Which words do you need to practice saying? Which words do you need to learn?

T8 | Listening: Listen and Make Notes

Listen to a briefing about IEDS and make notes. Check with T143.1.

T9 | Consolidation Tasks

Unit 144 IEDS and UXO 2

Learn To Call In A 10-Line UXO/IED Report

T1 | Speaking: Talk and Report 1

Look at P144.1 and P144.2. What can you see?

T2 | Speaking: Talk and Report 2

What should you do if you find a suspected IED?

T3 | Vocabulary: UXO/IED REPORT

Make sure you understand the UXO/IED REPORT.

[Note: some armies use a 9-line report format]

10 LINE UXO/IED REPORT		UNIT			
1	DTG of discovery				
2	Reporting unit or activity	Call sign:		Location:	
3	Type of ordinance				
	UXO	DROPPED	PROJECTED	PLACED	THROWN
	IED	DESCRIPTION:			
4	LOCATION OF UXO/IED				
5	LOCATION OF RP AND SAFE ROUTE				
6	CONTACT METHOD	Radio Frequency	Call Sign	Point Of Contact	Phone Number
7	TACTICAL SITUATION	NO ENEMY	POSSIBLE ENEMY	ENEMY PRESENT	
8	COLLATERAL DAMAGE	[Hazards/resources threatened/impact on mission]			
9	Protective MEASURES	[measures taken e.g. marked device; established security cordon]			
10	RECOMMENDED PRIORITY for EOD to respond	No Threat	Minor	Immediate	Indirect

[Form: Courtesy of MAF]

T4 | Speaking: Radio call

Work in pairs. Use your maps. Prepare a radio call about an IED or UXO using the 10 Liner format. Demonstrate your call to the class.

Study Page: Collocations of Explosives

Match the words with 'explosives' to make collocations

e.g. high + explosives

Collocations: **Explosives**

crude   trained

hazardous

home-made   high

low

vehicles

use

detect   **explosives**

high-yield   with   plastic

to   lethal

conceal   loaded

vehicle-delivered   dogs

---

verb + noun: _____

_____

adjective + noun + noun: _____

noun + noun: _____

adjective + noun: _high explosives_ _____

_____

_____

_____

noun + verb + preposition + noun: _____

noun + verb + to + verb + noun: _____

Unit 145 Checkpoints and Roadblocks 1

T1 | Speaking: Talk and Report 1

Look at P145.1 and P145.2. What can you see?

T2 | Speaking: Talk and Report 2

1. Why are checkpoints and roadblocks useful?
2. When and where should they be used?
3. What different kinds of checkpoint and roadblock are there?

T3 | Reading: Read the text below to check your answers to the questions in T2

Roadblocks and Check Points (CPs) are a means of controlling movement on roads, tracks, and footpaths. A roadblock is used to block or close a route to vehicle or pedestrian traffic. Checkpoints may have a more limited and specific purpose, usually apparent from their title, as vehicle CP, personnel CP etc. For simplicity, they are all referred to as roadblocks. Roadblocks are set up for one or more of the following reasons:

1. To maintain a broad check on road movement to increase security and the assurance of the local population.

2. To frustrate the movement of arms or explosives.

3. To enforce movement control of people and material.

4. To gather information and related data on suspected persons, vehicles, and movement.

There are four types of roadblocks, as follows:

Deliberate. Permanent or semi-permanent roadblocks placed on a main road, perhaps near a border, on the outskirts of a city, or on the edge of a controlled area. View deliberate roadblocks as a deterrent to movement. They are unlikely to be productive sources of information/contraband material once their positions and activities are observed.

Hasty. These roadblocks are easy to set up and dismantle. Ground troops, already on patrol, or a rapid reaction force deployed by helicopter can deploy the roadblock. Two vehicles placed diagonally across a road with a search area in between is a simple roadblock. In a rural area, helicopters can place hasty roadblocks, in which case, forces can improve obstacles, such as narrow bridges or level crossing gates, with a single coil of barbed wire.

Triggered. This is a variation of the hasty roadblock, usually used under circumstances where it is often easy for anyone to take avoiding action on sighting a block in operation. This roadblock is particularly effective in defeating the use of convoys and 'scout cars' by hostile groups. Allowing a suspected 'scout car' to pass through the roadblock triggers the roadblock to catch the target vehicle. Units operating the roadblock must occupy covered and concealed positions and wait for selected targets. Additionally, they can stop and search personnel out of sight of anyone approaching on the road. As with hasty roadblocks, a covert protection force and a helicopter borne reaction force are required. Foot and vehicle insertion, from a carefully sited patrol base, are most common.

Reactionary. This is a version of the hasty roadblock, but is used in reaction to an incident or attack in another area. Ground or helicopter based, this roadblock is useful in interdicting hostile activity following the occurrence.

[Adapted from FM 3-07.31/MCWP]

T4 I Reading: Read the text again and answer these questions

1. Which roadblocks can involve helicopters?
2. Which roadblocks require a covert protection force?
3. Which roadblocks require most equipment?
4. Which roadblocks are used in response to something happening?

T5 I Language Analysis: Analyse the Text

T6 I Listen and Read: Listen to a reading of the text

Which words do you need to practice saying? Which words do you need to learn?

T7I Vocabulary: Explain these terms

pedestrian traffic	broad check	concealed positioning
frustrate	semi-permanent	interdicting
dismantle	avoiding action	covert protection force

T8 I Listening: Listen to the description and complete the diagram key A – F

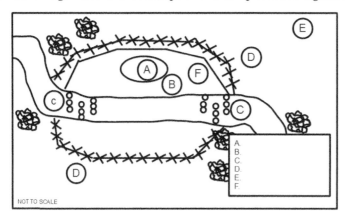

Check with
P145.3

A.
B.
C.
D.
E.
F.

NOT TO SCALE

T9 I Consolidation Tasks

Unit 146 Checkpoints and Roadblocks 2

T1 | Speaking: Talk and Report 1

Look at P146.1 - 3. What can you see?

T2 | Speaking: Talk and Report 2

1. From **Unit 145**, what four types of roadblocks are there?
2. What are their features?

T3 | Vocabulary: Manning a Roadblock

Check you know the meaning of these words. Then complete the text below.

presence	minimum	signaler	sentry	special	overwatch
man	covering	sergeant	search	element	volume

> The number of troops required will depend upon the number of roads and expected [1] _____ of traffic. If searching women, forces must have women searchers, and provide [2] _____ accommodation. The military commander should have, where possible, the rank of [3] _____ or above. Keep a police [4] _____ at a military roadblock, whenever possible, especially when military powers of [5] _____ , arrest, or control of movement is limited. Interpreters are also useful. Normally, [6] _____ a control point with at least a platoon, but relate the strength required to the number of roads controlled and the anticipated traffic. At a [7] _____ , man the roadblock with the following:
>
> **Control point headquarters**. Commander, [8] _____ , and runner.
>
> **Barrier Sentries**. One non-commissioned officer (NCO) for each road or lane of traffic blocked, and one [9] _____ for each barrier.
>
> **Covering party**. Two military personnel [10] _____ each set of barrier sentries.
>
> **Assault Force.** A designated unit is critical in the event an [11] _____ breaks through a roadblock or CP.
>
> **Overwatch.** Where possible, man an [12] _____ on a nearby rooftop.
>
> [Adapted from US Army FM 3-07.31/MCWP]

T4 | Language Analysis: Analyse the Text

T5 | Listening: Listen and Make Notes

Make notes about what the speaker says about manning a checkpoint.

*

T6 | Listening: Transcript Task

Complete the transcript with the words given below, then listen again to check.

all	bypassing	comprising	reaction	element x 2	flow
guard	personnel	positions	provide	concealed	secure
react	security	holding	leader x 2	situations	observes

So, number one. The Headquarters element. The headquarters element consists of the platoon [1] _____ , PSG, or section [2] _____ ; an RTO; and medical [3] _____. Two, the Security force consists of a security [4] _____ and a checkpoint [5] _____ force. The checkpoint security element mans overwatch positions and/or perimeter security [6] _____. Security element personnel maintain overwatch of activities in the search area and provide [7] _____ for personnel operating the checkpoint. Overwatch positions also [8] _____ security for sentry teams and the [9] _____ area. The checkpoint reaction force is a [10] _____ element whose purpose is to prevent traffic from avoiding or [11] _____ the checkpoint. This force can be part of the perimeter security and can [12] _____ to surprise attacks against the checkpoint or to other emergency [13] _____ . Element three – the Search teams. The search team, [14] _____ two to three soldiers, searches vehicles and personnel. The team is organized into a [15] _____ security element and a search element. The guard [16] _____ provides security during the searches; at least one member of the guard element guards or [17] _____ the individuals or vehicles being searched at [18] _____ times while the searcher conducts the search. Team Four is the Sentry team. Sentry teams [19] _____ the entrance and exit of the checkpoint and the holding area. They control the [20] _____ of traffic through the checkpoint.

T7 | Vocabulary: Complete the collocations and listen to check

1. assault _____
2. covering _____
3. barrier _____
4. control _____
5. man a _____

T8 | Speaking: Talk and Report 3

What do these elements do at a checkpoint? Brainstorm ideas before doing **Task 9**.

C2 Element | Security Element | Search Element | Assault Element

Complete the table to match who does what at checkpoints.

Who	Does what?
Command and Control	Able to reinforce as necessary
	Able to reinforce position as necessary
	Co-ordinates linkups as required
	Co-ordinates local patrols
	Co-ordinates RIP as required
	Co-ordinates the role of civil authorities
	Conducts personnel searches: male and female
	Conducts vehicle searches: passenger and cargo
	Destroys escaping personnel and vehicles
Security Element	Detains personnel as directed
	Directs cleared vehicles out of the CP
	Exercises C2
	Guides vehicles to the search area
	Halts vehicles at the checkpoint
Search Element	If available, uses a vehicle for patrolling, moving elements etc.
	Integrates reserve /QRF
	Maintains a log of all activities
	Maintains communications with HQ
	Monitors traffic flow up to and through the checkpoints
	Observes and reports suspicious activity
Assault Element	Prevents ambush
	Provides early warning to CP

Task 10 | Reading: Do's and Don'ts

Decide which are do's and which are don'ts.

Do's	Do's or Don'ts?
	All vehicle occupants are required to exit vehicle
	Allow driver to observe the search
	Ask politely to follow your instructions
	Be courteous when searching
	Be disrespectful or give any hint of dislike
	Become careless or sloppy in appearance
	Become involved in a heated argument
	Frisk women or ask them to put their hands up
	Have the driver open all the doors and compartments before the soldier searches the vehicle
Don'ts	Maintain a high standard of dress, military bearing, and stay in uniform
	Put your head or arm in the vehicle without permission
	Shout or show impatience
	Speak naturally and no louder than necessary
	Speak to the driver; driver speaks to occupants
	Stay calm and make a special effort to be polite
	Use force unless as directed by ROE
	Use scanners and metal detectors when possible

T11 | Consolidation Tasks

Unit 147 Checkpoints and Roadblocks 3

Learn to talk about checkpoint equipment and layout and construction

T1 | Speaking: Talk and Report 1

Look at P147.1 and P147.2. What can you see?

T2 | Speaking: What do you remember?

1. What four types of roadblocks are there?
2. What are their features?
3. What personnel are required for CPs or roadblocks?
4. What are their roles?

T3 | Vocabulary: Ten Key Words for Checkpoints

Check you know the meaning of these terms. What are they used for?

Agree on the correct translation with your partner.

lightweight barrier	mine detector	traffic signs	tire puncture chains
telescopic mirror	traffic cones	portable lamps	concertina wire
flashlight/torch	knife rest	measuring tape	metal cutting tools

T4 | Listen: Listen and Make Notes

Listen to the instructor explaining the use of the equipment in **T3**.

What two mistakes does he make?

T5 | Speaking: Talk and Report

Why are security and concealment important for roadblock ops?

T6 | Reading: Read the text on the next page to see if you agree with the writer

T7 | Reading: Read the text again and answer these questions

1. How many areas are there in the search and admin area?
2. Why should these areas be separate?
3. How visible should a roadblock be? Why?
4. What is the role of security?
5. What elements of security are there?

T8| Language Analysis: Analyse the Text

T9 | Listen and Read: Listen to a reading of the text

Which words do you need to practice saying? Which words do you need to learn?

Construction and Layout

A simple construction is two parallel lines, each with a gap across the road approximately 50 meters apart. This enclosure is then used as a search and administrative area. The search area there could have a vehicle waiting area and a vehicle search area, separate male and female search areas, a holding area for detaining persons before their being handed over to the local authorities, roadblock headquarters, and an administrative area.

Tactical guidelines for setting up a deliberate roadblock are as follows:

Concealment. Site the roadblock tactically where people cannot see it from more than a short distance away. Sharp bends or dips in the road provide good positions if the requirements of road safety are met. Leave no room for an approaching vehicle to take avoiding action by turning, leaving the road, or reversing.

Security. Assign enough troops to protect the roadblock, particularly during the initial occupation. Site sentries to act as backstops on both sides, well clear of the search area, to watch approaching traffic and prevent evasion. Where the threat of an attack on a roadblock is likely, then the block must have a back up force.

[Adapted from US Army FM 3-07.31/MCWP]

T10 | Vocabulary: Explain these words, collocations and phrases

1. parallel
2. enclosure
3. holding area
4. dips
5. avoiding action
6. backstops
7. evasion
8. approximately
9. tactical guidelines
10. sharp bends
11. initial occupation
12. site the roadblock tactically
13. approaching vehicle
14. reversing
15. road safety

T11 | Consolidation Tasks

Unit 148 Checkpoints and Roadblocks 4

T1 | Speaking: Talk and Report 1

What do you remember about checkpoints and roadblocks from **Units 145 – 147**?
Test your partner. e.g. *'What is a backstop?'*

T2 | Speaking: Talk and Report 2

Look at P148.1. What would you do if you found someone dressed like this near your
checkpoint?

T3 | Listening: Listen for the mistakes

Look at the diagram of the Mobile Checkpoint.

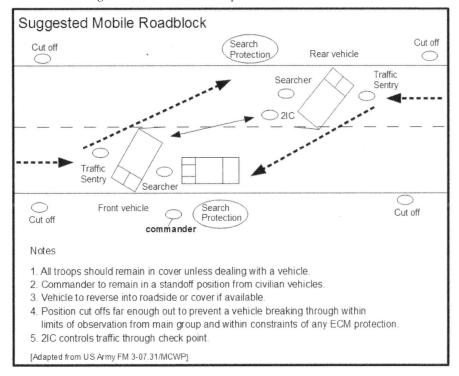

Listen to a description of the checkpoint. What mistakes are made?

T4 | Listening: Listen again and tick the prepositions you hear

of	√	under		out		to		by	
on		of		in		between		above	

T5 I Grammar: Complete the text below with the correct prepositions

This roadblock consists [1] _____ two vehicles. The front and rear vehicles block traffic [2] _____ one lane each. Search Protection is placed [3] _____ of sight [4] _____ both sides [5] _____ the road. The 2IC runs the checkpoint [6] _____ the road while the commander waits [7] _____ a standoff position. Vehicles can be stopped [8] _____ both directions. The two traffic sentries direct traffic [9] _____ the search areas. There are two Searchers waiting [10] _____ the search areas. There are four Cut Offs – two [11] _____ either side [12] _____ the roadblock – [13] _____ the road before vehicles reach the roadblock.

T6 I Writing: Write a description

Write out a description of the Urban and Rural Checkpoints (below).

Check your partner's description, then give them to your teacher to check.

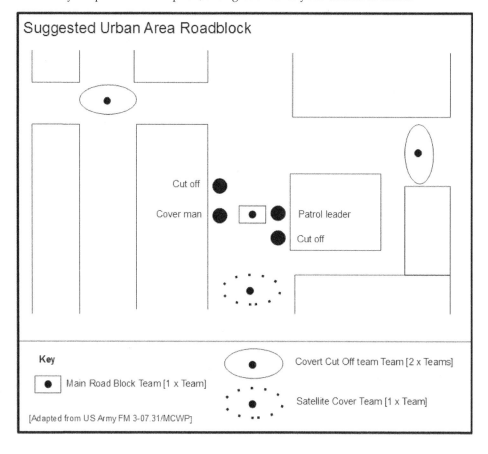

Suggested Urban Area Roadblock

Cut off

Cover man

Patrol leader

Cut off

Key

Main Road Block Team [1 x Team]

Covert Cut Off team Team [2 x Teams]

Satellite Cover Team [1 x Team]

[Adapted from US Army FM 3-07.31/MCWP]

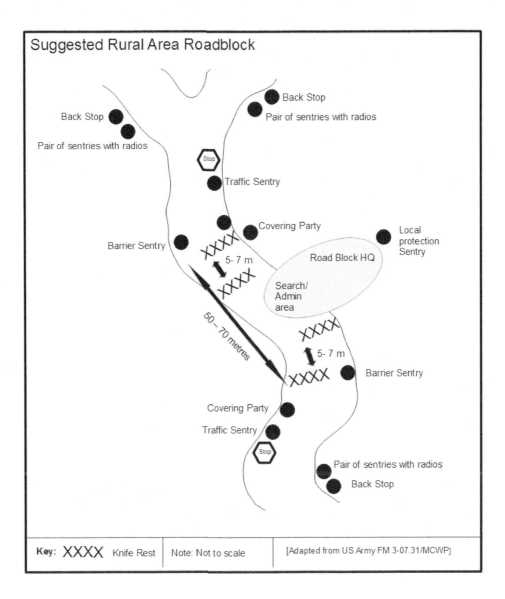

Suggested Rural Area Roadblock

Back Stop
Pair of sentries with radios

Back Stop
Pair of sentries with radios

Stop

Traffic Sentry

Covering Party

Local protection Sentry

Barrier Sentry

5- 7 m

Road Block HQ

50 – 70 metres

Search/ Admin area

5- 7 m

Barrier Sentry

Covering Party

Traffic Sentry

Stop

Pair of sentries with radios

Back Stop

Key: XXXX Knife Rest | Note: Not to scale | [Adapted from US Army FM 3-07.31/MCWP]

T7 | Vocabulary: Practice

Look at the diagrams of the three checkpoints. Write out ten sentences comparing each one with the others. Then compare your examples with your partner/group. Correct the sentences if necessary. Then do a class check.

Language Reminder: Comparisons, Similarities and Differences
Both the _____ have [X];
All of them have [X].
Two of them have [X] and one has [Y].

Unit 149 Checkpoint and Roadblocks 5

Brief About A Checkpoint

T1 I Speaking: Group work

Work in three groups and lay out a model of **one** of the three plans of checkpoints from **Unit 148**. Use whatever you have available to make the model e.g. sticks, ribbons, Lego blocks, pens and pencils, toy cars etc. Use model soldiers if you have them.

T2 I Speaking: Preparation for the Briefing

Prepare to explain the set-up of the checkpoint to the other groups.

Structure your briefing like this:

Welcome your colleagues to your briefing.

Tell them what you are going to do and how long it will take.

Explain when you will deal with questions.

Tell your colleagues the type of checkpoint and what it is for.

Point out the all the features of the checkpoint:

The physical features e.g. barriers: *This is a/the ………*

The vehicles: *This is a/the ……………*

The personnel: *This is a/the ………….*

Then explain the purpose of each feature in detail.

Conclude and ask for questions.

Language Reminder: is used for/to

[X] is used for [Y]: Sentries are used for security.

[X] provides [Y]: Sentries provide security.

[X] is/are needed to do [Y]: Sentries are needed to secure an area.

[X] is used to do [Y]: Sentries are used to secure an area.

T3 I Speaking: Briefing

Presenters: Present your checkpoint model to the other groups.

Be ready to answer questions.

Audience: Watch the briefing, ask questions

T4 I Feedback: Give feedback on your colleagues' briefings

Did you understand everything?

If not, what did you not understand?

T5 I Feedback: Your teacher will give you feedback on your briefing

Unit 150 Running a Checkpoint: Body Searches

T1 | Speaking: Talk and Report 1

Look at P150.1 and P150.2. What can you see?

Body Searches. You want to search someone. What do you say to them?

T2 | Vocabulary: Stops and Searches. Total Check or Spot Check? Complete the text.

A [1] _____ occurs when everyone passing the CP is searched. This form of checking is hard on resources (both time and personnel) and is often performed only when the CP is located on borders, frontiers, etc. (e.g., national frontiers or cease fire lines).

A [2] _____ refers to a certain number of persons/vehicles being searched. The remainder can pass freely, be briefly questioned, or will have to show their identity cards. Over a period, [3] _____ should prove effective in curtailing illegal movement of people or material in the AO. This method conserves resources compared with the [4] _____ method.

[Adapted from US Army FM 3-07.31/MCWP]

T3 | Grammar: Body Searches

Reorder the words in these requests and instructions.

1. to agree you searched be do ?
2. bag this your is?
3. here please over come
4. please empty your pockets
5. out car/vehicle get of please the
6. please this like stand
7. stand there over please
8. take please coat/jacket off your
9. need we you search to
10. name is what your?
11. this bag is whose?
12. out put feet and your your apart arms

Now, put these requests and instructions into the sequence you would say them.

T4 | Pronunciation: Practice saying the requests and instructions from T3

T5 | Vocabulary: Read and complete the instructions

Complete the text on the next page with these words.

conduct	do not (x 3)	watch	search	pay attention (x 3)
position	establish	use	significant	do not show emotion

Searches: Do's and Don'ts: Quick Body Searches

[1] _____ stand directly in front or behind the subject to avoid confrontation.

[2] _____ become distracted. Avoid eye contact with the subject.

[3] _____ for non-verbal communications, e.g., increased nervousness or silent gestures to others.

[4] _____ cross the line of fire of the cover man.

[5] _____ the subject with legs slightly apart and arms extended parallel to the ground. Do not spread-eagle the subject as this may interfere with the collection of forensic evidence.

[6] _____ the search quickly and systematically from head to toe, down one side and up the other, covering all body parts, front, and back. [7] _____ to pockets and waistbands. [8] _____ when searching the small of the back, armpits, crotch areas and closed hands. [9] _____ a stroking squeezing movement when searching. When searching limbs, both hands are used with thumbs and index fingers touching. This method increases the chances of detecting foreign object through the clothing.

[10] _____ and be respectful of any baggage or removed clothing.

The use of metal detectors or X-ray machines can be a force multiplier especially when searching large groups.

Detailed Body Search Considerations

[12] _____ the identity of the subject and the ownership of baggage and other articles. Invite the subject to empty all pockets and remove all items. If it is necessary to remove clothing, the subject may do so voluntarily (should be recorded) or powers exist to require the removal of certain items in or out of the public eye. Typically, the outer coat, jacket, and gloves may be removed in public. In private, there may be grounds to remove other clothing. Note that only outer clothing may be removed. [13] _____ to every detail i.e. clothing seams, waistbands, belts, collars, lapels, padding, shirt, and trouser cuffs. Socks and shoes provide easily missed hiding places. Medical dressings are always suspected and medical personnel should examine dressings if necessary. Clothing nametags, manufactures labels, and laundry tags can be valuable. [14] _____ upon finding illegal or prohibited items. [15] _____ articles should not be separated from others but all should be out of reach of the subject. [Adapted from US Army FM 3-07.31/MCWP]

T6 | Speaking: Role play body searches

T7 | Speaking: Talk and Report

What do you do if someone does <u>not</u> want to be searched?

T8 | Consolidation Tasks

Unit 151 Running a Checkpoint: Vehicle Searches

T1 | Speaking: Talk and Report 1

Look at P151.1 and P151.2. What can you see?

T2 | Speaking: Talk and Report 2

Can you remember the instructions and requests you can use when doing a body search?

T3 | Grammar: Vehicle Searches

Reorder the words in these requests and instructions.

1. searched be please there drive over to

2. out please car/vehicle get the of

3. where please can keep them your I see hands

4. please bonnet/hood the open

5. open please boot/trunk the

6. there stand/wait over please

7. away please step vehicle from the

8. please the turn engine off

Now, put these requests and instructions in the sequence you would say them.

T4 | Pronunciation: Practice saying the requests and instructions from T3

T5 | Vocabulary: Read and Complete

Complete the text about vehicle searches below with these words.

aroused	examination	exit	intensity
selected	suspicion	thorough	threat

Search techniques are divided into three categories. The categories vary according to the [1] _____ of the search. There is no clear boundary between the categories and the extent of the investigation as each stage depends on the [2] _____ aroused. Categories include:

Initial check. The initial check is the first part of the searching process carried out on all vehicles and used to select vehicles for a more detailed [3] _____. This check is normally carried out without the occupants dismounting, although search personnel may ask the driver to open the trunk and hood. Search personnel at the entrance to barracks and other installations should know the [4] _____ from large vehicle mounted bombs. Up to three personnel are required for the search, and the search normally takes about 3 minutes per vehicle.

Primary search. The primary search is done on the vehicles [5] _____ for a more detailed examination, due to either intelligence or suspicion [6] _____ during the initial check. During the primary search, if any of the search unit becomes suspicious for any reason, a more detailed search may be conducted.

Secondary search. The secondary search is a [7] _____ search of highly suspect vehicles. It is recommended that search unit members work in pairs, examining the relevant section of the vehicle. For a more detailed search, have the occupants [8] _____ the vehicle, and then search them.

[Adapted from US Army FM 3-07.31/MCWP]

T6 | Speaking: Talk and Report

What do these people do during a vehicle check?

Patrol Leader | Stopper | Searcher | Cover man

T7 | Reading: Read the text and see if you were right

The Road Party

The patrol leader remains off the road, uses the radio to run a check of vehicle registration numbers, and selects vehicles to be searched. The patrol leader must have an alternate signal, e.g., a whistle, to trigger the cut offs.

The stopper stops vehicles, speaks to the occupants, and completes the appropriate forms. The searcher, once tasked with searching a vehicle, removes personal web gear and weapon and leaves it with the cover-man. The searcher then targets areas of the vehicle to search and searches the occupants.

The cover-man covers the vehicle occupants, from a concealed position, and protects the searcher's equipment. The road party should not close in to a small space, but stay spread out in case a problem should arise.

[Adapted from US Army FM 3-07.31/MCWP]

T8 | Reading: Read and Answer

Read the text again and answer these questions.

1. Why does the patrol leader remain off the road?
2. Why does the searcher remove their web gear and leave their weapon with the cover man?
3. Why should the cover man be in a concealed position?

T9 | Speaking: Where to search?

Look at P151.3 – 5 or the **Unit 151 Slides** and discuss the most important places to search.

T10 | Speaking: Vehicle Searches Practice: see P151.6

T11 | Consolidation Tasks

Unit 152 Running a Checkpoint: Role Play

Practice Setting Up And Running Vehicle checks At A Checkpoint

T1 | Speaking: Preparation and Practice

Work in three groups.

Your teacher will assign you a checkpoint to run.

Your task is to prepare to run a checkpoint according to the plan.

You will need a number of vehicles and a quiet road/car park area.

In each group, decide who is the Checkpoint Commander.

The Checkpoint Commander will decide who will do what at the checkpoint, according to the diagram. Make sure everyone knows what to do.

Record this information about the search as shown below. Use the Person and Vehicle Search Report Form on the next page.

Records and Reports

For all categories of search, apart from initial searches, a record should be maintained containing:

- Details of the person.
- The reason for the search.
- The date and time group.
- The location.
- Details of anything significant.
- Details of damage or injury to person or property.
- If done in conjunction with an investigation, do not identify search team members. Call signs or other identification should be used.

[Adapted from US Army FM 3-07.31/MCWP]

Do a practice run through.

Another group will provide the occupants of the car which you will be searching. You will provide the occupants of the car for another group.

T2 | Speaking: Demonstration

When you are ready, **go outside** and demonstrate the running of your checkpoint complete with initial, primary and secondary searches and body searches.

T3 | Feedback: Give feedback on your demonstration

T4 | Feedback: Your teacher will give you feedback on the language you used

Person and Vehicle Search Report Form

1.	**Time**		**2. Grid Location**

3.	**Forces who conducted search**

4.	**Information about Person Searched**

Name:	Place Of Birth:
ID Number:	Name of Father:

Current Address:

Description of Person Searched

Age:	Build:
Height:	Hair:

Face:

Distinguishing Marks (e.g. scars, tattoos, burns...):

Clothing (Start at head):

5.	**Vehicle Search: Vehicle Description**

Type of vehicle:	Make and Model:
Registration Number:	Colour:

Identifying Features:

Type and quality of cargo:

Weapons, contraband, prohibited items found in search:

6.	**Vehicle Search: Passengers**

No. of passengers per vehicle, ages, gender:

Condition of passengers (health, dress, attitude etc.):

Point of origin and destination:

Stated reason for passenger travel:

Any passenger reports of sightings of weapons, military vehicles, warring parties:

Anything unusual observed/reported by passengers:

7.	**Other Important Information:**

Unit 153 Patrols 1

T1 | Speaking: Talk and Report

Look at P153.1 - 3. What can you see?

T2 | Speaking: Talk and Report

1. Why do soldiers need to patrol?
2. What is the difference between a reconnaissance and a combat patrol?
3. What kinds of combat patrols are there?

T3 | Reading: Read to check your answers from T2

Reconnaissance Patrols

Reconnaissance patrols gather information about the enemy, terrain or resources. Relying on stealth rather than combat strength, they gather this information and fight only when necessary to complete the mission or to defend themselves. The distance covered by reconnaissance patrols varies based on the terrain and mission. A squad is ideally suited for reconnaissance patrol missions because of its relative small size and its experience of working together.

Combat Patrols

A combat patrol is a fighting patrol assigned missions that require engagement with the enemy in combat. Larger and more heavily armed than reconnaissance patrols, combat patrols have a mission to capture enemy documents, provide security, and capture or destroy enemy equipment and installations. Such action is ordinarily followed by a return to friendly positions. Regardless of the mission, the patrol reports any information concerning the enemy and terrain acquired during the accomplishment of the assigned mission. There are four types of combat patrols: raid, contact, ambush, and security (normally conducted by a Marine rifle platoon). A rifle platoon reinforced with crew-served weapons is normally considered the minimum size for contact, economy of force or ambush patrols. In some situations, such as the capture of a small enemy outpost, a rifle platoon could conduct a raid. However, a raid is a complex mission and, due to the organization of a raid force (command, reconnaissance, assault, support, security, and reserve elements), a rifle company is normally the smallest force assigned to a raid.

[From the US Marine Corps Scouting and Patrolling Manual MCWP 3 – 11.3, 2000]

T4 | Reading: Read again to answer the questions

1. Why is a squad a good unit for recon?
2. What kind of missions do combat patrols have?
3. Why is a company needed for a raid?

T5 | Language Analysis: Analyse the Text

T6 | Listening: Listen and Make Notes 1

Listen to Part 1 of a talk on patrolling and make notes.

Check your notes with your partner; then check with the class.

T7 | Listening: Listen and Make Notes 2

Listen to Part 2 of the talk on patrolling and make notes.

Check your notes with your partner; then check with the class.

T8 | Vocabulary: Complete the phrases from the listening. Check with T153.1

1. gathering _____
2. current _____
3. enemy _____
4. adjacent _____
5. assigned _____
6. defensive _____
7. concealed _____
8. kill _____
9. establish _____
10. surprise _____
11. critical _____
12. poor _____
13. decisive _____
14. enemy _____
15. resupply _____

T9 | Speaking: Talk and Report

What equipment do you normally take on patrols? Why?

Language Reminder: take to do/ so I can
I take X to do Y.
I take a map and compass to navigate.
I take X so I can Y
I take a water bottle so I can drink/have a drink.

T10 | Consolidation Tasks

Unit 154 Patrols 2

T1 | Speaking: Talk and Report 1

Look at P154.1 - 2. What can you see?

T2 | Speaking: Talk and Report 2

1. What are the advantages and disadvantages of foot patrols?
2. What are the advantages and disadvantages of motorized patrols?
3. What are the advantages and disadvantages of waterborne patrols?
4. When should helicoptorborne patrols be used?

T3 | Reading: Read to check your answers from T2

Foot Patrols

Movement by foot is the most common means; however, there are inherent disadvantages. Foot patrols travel slowly and carry limited quantity and types of equipment and supplies. Range and area coverage is relatively restricted. Foot patrols also have apparent advantages in that they have fewer restrictions as to terrain that can be covered; are more difficult for the enemy to detect; provide thorough coverage within limits of range; and are generally not inhibited by weather.

Motorized Patrols

Where terrain and road networks permit, a motorized patrol overcomes the inherent disadvantages of the foot patrol. Mechanized forces require patrolling units that can keep pace with them. However, motorized patrols are restricted to certain types of terrain, and tend to bypass areas that may be advantageous to and occupied by enemy infantry.

Waterborne Patrols

Waterborne patrols move over seas, lakes, rivers and streams, canals, and other inland waterways. The water is either used as a medium of entry to an objective area or is the actual patrol route. Waterborne patrols are limited by the location of water routes in the terrain and tend to bypass areas that may be advantageous to and occupied by the enemy.

Helicopterborne Patrols

Where terrain is extremely difficult or the enemy situation precludes the use of vehicle or motorized patrols, helicopterborne patrols are a method or means to conduct a patrol.

[From the US Marine Corps Scouting and Patrolling Manual MCWP 3 – 11.3, 2000]

T4 | Language Analysis: Analyse the Text

T5 | Listening: Listen and Make Notes 1

Listen to Part 1 of the talk on patrolling and make notes.

Check your notes with your partner; then check with the class.

T6 | Listening: Listen and Make Notes 2

Listen to Part 2 of the talk on patrolling and make notes.

Check your notes with your partner; then check with the class.

T7 | Vocabulary: Explain These Terms

1. bypass
2. inhibited
3. inherent
4. thorough reconnaissance
5. realistic rehearsal
6. positive control
7. all-round security
8. close reconnaissance
9. prearranged
10. SALUTE

T8 | Transcript Tasks: Complete the transcript extracts, then listen to check

T9 | Grammar: Verb Forms

Complete the sentences with the correct verb forms. Use the verbs given.

1. If a reconnaissance in person _____ (not possible) then the work of patrol scouts _____ (become) even more important.

2. Information about the enemy should include: strength; armament and equipment; actions; location and direction of movement; unit destination, if _____ (know); time enemy was observed; and the patrol's location when the observation was made.

3. If in danger of capture, the messenger _____ (immediately destroy) the message.

4. If the patrol _____ (provide) with a radio, a definite radio schedule for checking in _____ (arrange) before departure of the patrol.

5. If a close reconnaissance of enemy lines _____ (require), the radio _____ (be) left in a concealed location at a safe distance from the enemy.

T10 | Consolidation Tasks

Transcript Tasks

Listening 1

There are 5 keys to successful patrolling. These [1] _____: detailed planning, realistic rehearsals, thorough reconnaissance, positive control and all-around security. One. Detailed planning. Every portion of the patrol [2] _____ be planned and all possible contingencies must be considered. Two. Productive, realistic rehearsals. Each phase of the patrol [3] _____ be rehearsed, beginning with actions in the objective area. Similar terrain and environmental conditions are used when conducting rehearsals. Three. Thorough reconnaissance. Ideally, the patrol leader [4] _____ physically conduct a reconnaissance of the route and objective. Photographs and/or maps [5] _____ be used to supplement the reconnaissance. If a reconnaissance in person **is** not possible then the work of patrol scouts becomes even more important. Four. Positive control. The patrol leader [6] _____ maintain positive control of all aspects of the execution of the patrol, and this includes supervision during patrol preparations. Five. All-around security. Security [7] _____ be maintained at all times, particularly near the end of the patrol where there is a natural tendency to relax.

Listening 2

Now let's look at reporting. The commander dispatching the patrol [1] _____ instruct the patrol leader on whether and when messages [2] _____ to be sent back during the patrol and what communication means to use. Messages [3] _____ be oral or written. They [4] _____ be sent through a messenger or through radio or other signals. They [5] _____ be accurate, clear, and complete. Every message [6] _____ answer the questions: what, where, and when. The patrol leader [7] _____ be careful to distinguish between fact and opinion. Information about the enemy [8] _____ include: strength; armament and equipment; actions; location and direction of movement; unit destination, if known; time enemy [9] _____ observed; and the patrol's location when the observation [10] _____ made.

Unit 155 Patrols 3

T1 | Speaking: Talk and Report

Look at P155.1 and P155.2. What can you see?

T2 | Vocabulary: Match the words and the definition

1. passage of lines   to patrol to find out intelligence about the activities, positions and resources of an enemy, or about the geographic characteristics of a particular area.

2. rally point   measures like overwatch, setting sentries etc. to protect your force

3. front lines   own or allied combat positions

4. halt   an operation to move through another friendly force's combat positions

5. objective area   meeting the enemy

6. friendly lines   place to meet after an action

7. passive security   target area

8. contact   chasing

9. in pursuit   stop

10. reconnoiter   forward combat positions

Agree on the correct translation with your partner.

T3 | Listening: Listen and Make Notes 1

Listen to Part 1 of the talk on patrolling and make notes.
Check your notes with your partner; then check with the class.

T4 | Listening: Do Transcript Task 1 on the next page

T5 | Listening: Listen and Make Notes 2

Listen to Part 2 of the talk on patrolling and make notes.
Check your notes with your partner; then check with the class.

T6 | Listening: Do the Collocation Task for Listening Part 2 on the next page

T7 | Vocabulary: Explain These Terms

- patrol assembly area
- passage point
- challenge
- en route

T8 | Consolidation Tasks

Transcript Tasks

Part 1: Complete the text with the words given: Listen to check

assembly	challenge	concealed	contact	coordinated	forward
forward	friendly	passage x 3	positions	reconnoiters	route x 2

At the start and end of the patrol the patrol will need to make a [1] _____ of lines. This is an operation in which a force moves [2] _____ or rearward through another force's combat [3] _____ with the intention of moving into or out of [4] _____ with the enemy.

During the initial preparation for the patrol, the patrol leader selects a patrol [5] _____ and reconnoiters the area of [6] _____ designated by the commander.

The patrol leader also checks the [7] _____ from the patrol assembly area to the [8] _____ point or contact point where the patrol will depart [9] _____ lines. If possible, both the route to the passage point and the [10] _____ through the frontlines should be [11] _____ from the enemy's view.

The patrol leader also [12] _____ the area for return passage of lines and coordinates with the unit commander responsible for the area of passage for passage points and lanes as necessary. The patrol leader provides the [13] _____ unit with information about the size of the patrol, general route, and expected time of return. The manner of [14] _____ and recognition of the returning patrol should be [15] _____ in detail.

Part 2: Complete the collocations, then listen to check

1. exercising _____
2. providing _____
3. rally _____
4. staying _____
5. patrol _____
6. arm-and-hand _____
7. patrol _____
8. main _____
9. areas of _____
10. the eyes and _____
11. maintain _____
12. terrain _____
13. predetermined _____
14. a registration _____
15. fire _____
16. patrol _____
17. parent _____
18. assembly _____
19. forward unit _____
20. objective rally _____

Unit 156 Movement

T1 | Speaking: Talk and Report 1

Look at P156.1 - 3

What can you see?

What are the weather conditions?

What are the soldiers doing?

T2 | Speaking: Talk and Report 2

What is the difference between movement and manoeuvre?

T3 | Reading: Read And Check Your Answer

Tactical movement is the movement of a unit assigned a tactical mission under combat conditions when not in direct ground contact with the enemy. Tactical movement is based on the anticipation of early ground contact with the enemy, either en route or shortly after arrival at the destination. Movement ends when ground contact is made or the unit reaches its destination. Movement is not maneuver. Maneuver happens once a unit has made contact with the enemy.

T4 | Vocabulary: Check the meaning of these words

lead element	vulnerable	row	contact	flanks	oriented
trail element	subordinate unit	path	obstacles	security	control

Agree on a translation of the words.

T5 | Vocabulary: Matching

Match the formation name, diagram and description on the next page.

Check with your partner, then with the class.

T6 | Speaking: Talk and Report

What are the advantages and disadvantages of each formation?

T7 | Listening: Listen to check

Listen to the advantages and disadvantages of each formation.

Check your notes after each section. Do you agree?

Formation	Diagram	Description
1. Line	a. ■■ ■ ■	I One lead element. Majority of observation and direct fires oriented to the flanks; minimal to the front. One route means unit only influenced by obstacles on that one route.
2. Column/file	b. ■ ■ ■ ■	II Similar to the wedge formation. Fourth element follows the lead element.
3. Vee	c. ■ ■■ ■	III All elements arranged in a row. Majority of observation and direct fires oriented forward; minimal to the flanks. Each subordinate unit on the line must clear its own path forward.
4. Box	d. ■ ■ ■ ■	IV Two lead elements. Trail elements follow lead elements. All round security.
5. Wedge	e. ■■■■	V Two lead elements. Trail elements move between the two lead elements. Used when contact to the front is expected.
6. Diamond	f. ■ ■ ■ ■	VI Elements deployed diagonally left or right. Observation and fire to both the front and one flank. Each subordinate unit on the line clears its own path forward.
7. Echelon (right)	g. ■■ ■■	VII One lead element. Trail elements paired off abreast of each other on the flanks. Used when the situation is uncertain

Unit 157 Camouflage, Cover and Concealment

T1 | Speaking: Talk and Report 1

Look at P157.1 – 4. What can you see?

T2 | Vocabulary: Camouflage

Match the collocations and explain the terms.

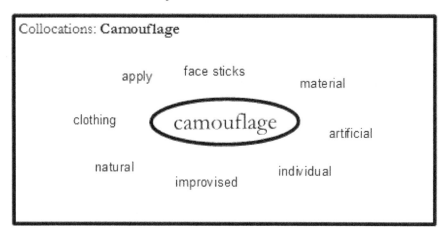

Collocations: **Camouflage**

apply   face sticks   material

clothing   camouflage   artificial

natural   improvised   individual

T3 | Speaking: Talk and Report 2

What is the difference between 'cover' and 'concealment'?

T4 | Reading: Cover and Concealment

Read the text below: Do you agree with it?

Cover is protection from the fire of hostile weapons. Concealment is protection from observation or surveillance from hostile air and ground observation, but not from hostile fire. Both cover and concealment are divided into two main categories: natural and artificial. Natural cover includes small hills, ditches, rocks or vegetation. Fighting holes, bunkers, and brick walls are examples of artificial cover. Some features, such as buildings, provide both cover and concealment. In deciding whether to seek cover or concealment, a scout must make the best choice to complete the mission.

[From: MCWP 3-11.3 Scouting and Patrolling U.S. Marine Corps 17 April 2000]

T5 | Vocabulary: Concealment and Concealed

Complete the sentences with 'concealed' or concealment'.

1. Scouts move from one _____ position to another. When not changing positions, they remain motionless.

2. Scouts move to the chosen observation post by a _____ route

3. If possible, both the route to the passage point and the route through the frontlines should be _____ from the enemy's view.

4. An ambush is a surprise attack from a _____ position.

5. Because the movement of the patrol must be _____ from the enemy, the patrol normally moves through terrain that provides _____ and takes up the best available _____ firing positions

6. The ambush patrol should have maximum cover and _____ , not only for the firing positions, but for the routes of withdrawal.

7. Cities provide cover and _____ for both friendly forces and enemy forces.

8. This position must provide the patrol _____ from enemy observation and, if possible, cover from enemy fires.

9. In selecting approach and return routes, the patrol leader chooses routes that best use _____ and avoid opposition and obstacles.

10. A scouting fire team takes advantage of available cover and _____ without delaying its advance.

11. Although total darkness provides _____ , scouts must observe the same principles of _____ during moonlight conditions as in the daytime.

12. Fog, smoke, or even light haze offer _____ for movement; however, the enemy may have thermoimagery and night vision devices.

T6 | Vocabulary: Cover 1

Look at the examples of 'cover' and answer the questions

1. What is the difference?

   seek/take/provide cover

2. Explain the meaning of the phrases:

   cover
   | the withdrawl
   | the patrol's movement
   | the far bank
   | larger areas, faster
   | the sounds of movement

T7 | Vocabulary: Cover 2: Explain the meaning of the phrases

use available cover	remain motionless under cover
take advantage of cover	vegetation/artificial cover
assess the cover	helmet cover

T8 | Vocabulary: Complete the text with the words given

camouflage x 11	camouflaged x 2	conceal	concealment x 4	cover x 2

[1] _____ is the use of [2] _____ and disguise to minimize the possibility of detection and/or identification of troops, material, equipment, and installations. The purpose of [3] _____ is to provide [4] _____ of military objects from enemy observation. [5] _____ is also used to [6] _____ an object by making it look like something else. A scout's mission usually requires

Individual and equipment [7] _____. If natural [8] _____ is not adequate, the position is [9] _____. In using [10] _____, remember that objects are identified by their form (outline), shadow, texture, and color. The principal purpose of [11] _____ in the field is to prevent direct observation and recognition.

Individual [12] _____: Successful individual [13] _____ involves the ability to recognize and take advantage of all forms of natural and artificial [14] _____ available (vegetation, soil, debris, etc.) and knowledge of the proper use of artificial [15] _____ materials.

Aids to Individual [16] _____: A scout must recognize the terrain's dominant color and pattern and must change the appearance of clothing and equipment accordingly in order to blend and not contrast with the terrain. The helmet is [17] _____ by breaking up its shape, smooth surface, and shadow. Use of a helmet cover works best. In the absence of a helmet [18] _____, mud can be irregularly blotched on the helmet to disguise its form and dull the surface. A helmet [19] _____ may be improvised from irregularly colored cloth or burlap to blend with the background. Any equipment that reflects light should be covered with a nonreflective material that aids in the [20] _____ of the weapon (for example, black electrical tape or mud). The straight line of the rifle or other infantry weapons may be very conspicuous to an enemy observer.

[From: MCWP 3-11.3 Scouting and Patrolling U.S. Marine Corps 17 April 2000]

T9 | Speaking: Talk and Report 3

Look at P157.5 – 18. What kind of terrain is shown in each photograph?

Discuss the cover available and the opportunities for concealment

Unit 158 Patrols: One Slide Briefings

Give Briefings On Patrol Skills and Ambushes

There are two Briefings to give.

Briefing 1: Patrol Skills

There are 23 one slide briefings.

See **Unit 158 Briefing 1 Patrol Skills**.

Each slide is on one aspect of patrolling.

Slides 18 -22 [Urban patrols] are linked.

There are briefer notes for each slide.

Each student should present one slide to the class.

Unit 158 Briefing 2: Ambushes

There are slides on 8 different kinds of ambush.

There are briefer notes for each slide.

T1 | Speaking: Briefing Preparation

Prepare your briefing and practice giving it to your partner.
Listen/watch their briefing and give him/her feedback.

T2 | Speaking: Briefing

Give your briefings to the class.
Be ready to answer questions.

T3 | Feedback: Give feedback on your colleagues' briefings

Did you understand everything?
If not, what did you not understand?

T4 | Feedback: Your teacher will give you feedback on your briefing

Unit 159 Going on Patrol: Patrol Orders

Learn To Give Patrol Orders Using A Form

T1 | Speaking: Talk and Report 1

Look at P159.1. What can you see?

T2 | Speaking: Talk and Report 2

You are going on patrol. What would you expect in patrol orders?

> **Note:** These patrol order units are adapted from British Army patrol orders. They might be different from the form of orders which your army uses. This is good as it will give you practice in understanding orders which are different to the ones you are used to. Later in the book we will look at US Army style WARNOs and OPORDS.

T3 | Vocabulary: Look at the Patrol Briefing Form on the next page

Check you understand everything.

T4 | Grammar: Verb Forms

What verb forms would you expect in the different parts of the patrol briefing? Why?

T5 | Listening: Listen to a patrol briefing

Look at Map M159.1 on page 288.

Listen to the patrol briefing and complete a Patrol Briefing Form with notes and a Route Card. Mark the route etc. on the map.

Use the blank forms from your Workbook.

Route Card Out / Back			Map Series		Sheet		Edition	Mag Variation	
	From		To		Bearing (Mag)				Ground Description
Leg	Location	Grid	Location	Grid	Grid	Mag	Distance	Time	
1									
2									

Check with your partner, then the class. [Check with M159.2 and T159.1]

Patrol Briefing Form

1 GROUND [General description of area/objective area in detail.]

2 SITUATION

[Enemy Forces: strength, weapons, patrols, tactics, routine, morale, dress sentries, minefields/ fortifications etc.]

[Friendly forces: positions/fire support/minefields etc.]

3 MISSION [Recce, OP, assault etc.]

4. EXECUTION

4.2 Preparatory Moves [Time of leaving base area/Method of move/Route to & Location of Drop Off Point(DOP)/Action at **DOP**/Time out from **DOP**]

4.3 Route Out [As per Route Card] [Order of March [OOM]/Action on *Enemy* preseen and *Ambushed*/Action on *Casualty*/Action if *Separated*/Action if *Lost*]

4.4 Action in FRV [Occupation of FRV:Move in/Secure/Formation/Position & Groups/signals for FRV]

4.5 Action on Objective

Recce

[Composition/Tasks/Position/Route/Formation/Signal to open fire/Action if located by the Enemy/Action if separated from the Patrol]

Cover/Fire Group

[Composition/Tasks/Position/Route/Formation/Signal to open fire/Action if located by the Enemy/Action if separated from the Patrol]

4.6 Withdraw [Signal to Withdraw/OOM/Action in FRV/Head check & Signal to Move Out/Action if in Contact/Action if a Group fails to return]

4.7 Route Back [Route Back as per Route Card/OOM/ RVs/Obstacles/Action on Enemy (Preseen & Ambush)/Signal to Open Fire/Action on Casualties/Action if lost/Action if Separated/ Action on Arrival at Base location/Time in]

4.8 Summary of Execution [Summarise all above]

5 SERVICE SUPPORT

Dress/ Equipment/ Weapons/ Ammo/ Rations/ Medical/ Transport:

6 COMMAND & SIGNALS

Chain of Command: I/C	2I/C	3I/C	
Signals: Frequency	Call signs		

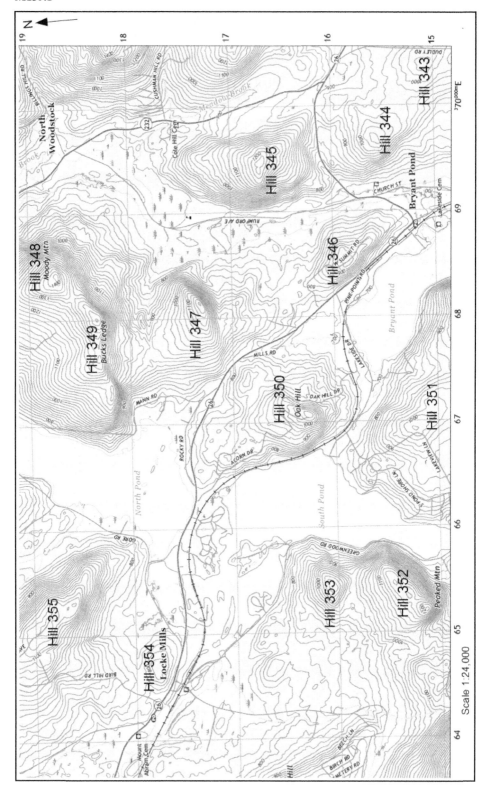

Unit 160 Going on Patrol: Patrol Briefing 1

Practice Giving Patrol Orders Using A Form

T1 | Speaking: Plan a Patrol

Work in pairs.

Use your maps.

Plan a patrol

Complete a detailed Patrol Briefing and Route Card for the patrol.

Use the **Patrol Order Content Evaluation Form** in the Workbook (p. 203) to help you prepare your order.

T2 | Speaking: The Briefing

Give your briefings to the class.

Be ready to answer questions.

Listen to the other briefings.

Complete a Patrol Briefing Form during each briefing and mark the route on the map and prepare a Route Card.

T3 | Evaluation: Evaluate one or more of the briefings

Use the the **Patrol Order Delivery Evaluation Form** from the Workbook (page 205) to prepare feedback for your colleagues.

T4 | Feedback: Give feedback on your colleagues' briefings

Did you understand everything?
If not, what did you not understand?

T5 | Self-Evaluation

When all the briefings have finished put your briefing notes and route card on display on the walls around the room.

Each student can go and read the notes and see if their own notes they made while listening are accurate (or not). Check you have **all** the information required and that it is **all** correct.

T6 | Feedback: Your teacher will give you feedback on your briefing

Unit 161 Talking about Attacks 1

T1 | Speaking: Talk and Report 1

Look at P161.1 - 3. What can you see?

T2 | Reading: Talk and Report 3

What are the differences between a deliberate and a hasty attack?

Check your ideas with the class.

T3 | Reading: Read to check your ideas from T3

> A hasty attack is an attack done quickly, with much less time for planning or recon than a deliberate attack. It is done with only the resources that are immediately available and it is used to exploit a tactical opportunity (e.g. to attack an open flank), to maintain the momentum, or to regain the initiative. The hasty attack is conducted using the principles of fire and movement. Suppressive fire is used on the enemy force. Then the maneuver element advances to make contact with the enemy.

T4 | Speaking: Talk and Report 4

What are these forms of attack? Why are they used?

ambush | raid | counter-attack | spoiling attack | feint | demonstration

Check your ideas with the class.

T5 | Listening: Listen and Make Notes

Listen to the talk about special attacks. Make notes about:

- Ambush
- Raid
- Counter-attack

- Spoiling attack
- Feint
- Demonstration

Check your notes with your partner, and the class. Check your notes with T129.1.

T6 | Transcript Task: Complete the transcript on the next page, then listen to check

actual	after	attack	change	concealed
deceive	deceive	decisive	defending	destroy
destroy	disrupt	fire	flank	ground
halted	impending	move	preparation	preparing
primary	success	swift	time	withdrawal

T7 | Consolidation Tasks

Transcript Task

There are a number of special forms of attack we need to consider. These are: ambush, raid, counterattack, spoiling attack, feint, and demonstration. As forms of the attack, they share many of the same planning, [1] _____ , and execution considerations of the offense. Let's look at them one by one. Number one. The ambush. An ambush is a form of attack by [2] _____ from [3] _____ positions. Ambushes are used on a moving or temporarily [4] _____ enemy. The ambush may be an assault to close with and [5] _____ the enemy, or be an attack by fire only. An ambush does not require [6] _____ to be seized or held. The [7] _____ reason for conducting an ambush is to destroy the enemy. Number two. The raid. A raid is a limited-objective form of an [8] _____. They are usually small-scale. They involve [9] _____ penetration of hostile territory to secure information, capture prisoners, confuse the enemy, or [10] _____ installations. A raid always ends with a planned [11] _____ to a friendly location upon completion of the mission. Number three. The counterattack. The counterattack is a form of attack by part or all of a friendly [12] _____ element against an enemy attacking force. The general objective of a counterattack is to deny the enemy his goal of attacking. The counterattack regains the initiative or denies the enemy [13] _____ with his attack. The platoon counterattacks [14] _____ the enemy begins his attack, reveals his main effort, or opens up his [15] _____ to attack. Number four. The spoiling attack. A spoiling attack is a form of attack that is launched while the enemy is in the process of planning or [16] _____ to attack. The purpose of a spoiling attack is to [17] _____ the enemy's offensive capabilities and timelines, destroy his personnel and equipment, and gain additional [18] _____ for the defending element to prepare positions. The purpose is not to secure terrain or other physical objectives. Number five. The feint. A feint is a form of attack used to [19] _____ the enemy as to the location and time of the actual operation. Feints attempt persuade the enemy to [20] _____ his dispositions. The enemy must be convinced that the feint is the [21] _____ attack. But a [22] _____ engagement must be avoided. Lastly, number six. The demonstration. A demonstration is a form of attack designed to [23] _____ the enemy as to the location or time of the actual operation by a display of force. Demonstrations attempt to deceive the enemy and induce him to [24] _____ reserves and shift his fire support to locations where they cannot immediately impact the actual operation. It must appear to be an actual [25] _____ attack.

Unit 162 Talking about Attacks 2

T1 | Speaking: Talk and Report 1

Look at P162.1 and P162.2. What can you see?

T2 | Speaking: Talk and Report 2

What can you remember about ambush, raid, counter-attack, spoiling attack, feint and demonstration?

T3 | Vocabulary: Complete the definitions

Complete the definitions 1 – 5 with the correct word.

envelopment	turning movement	infiltration	penetration	frontal attack

1. _____ is a form of maneuver in which an attacking element seeks to rupture enemy defenses on a narrow front to create both assailable flanks and access to the enemy's rear.

2. _____ is a form of maneuver in which an attacking element conducts undetected movement through or into an area occupied by enemy forces to gain a position of advantage in the enemy rear.

3. The _____ is a form of maneuver in which the attacking element seeks to avoid the enemy's principal defensive positions by seizing objectives to the enemy's rear.

4. _____ is a form of maneuver in which an attacking element seeks to avoid the principal enemy defenses by seizing objectives to the enemy flank or rear in order to destroy him in his current positions.

5. _____ is a form of maneuver in which an attacking element seeks to destroy a weaker enemy force or fix a larger enemy force along a broad front.

T4 | Reading: Study the diagrams in P162.3 – P162.7 about the attacks in T2

T5 | Speaking: Talk and Report

Using the diagrams in T4, discuss the attacks with a partner. Then change partners and take turns in explaining the attacks. Then, as a class, explain the attacks to your teacher.

T6 | Speaking: Talk and Report

These are important considerations when planning a deliberate attack. Why?

**assembly area | reconnaissance | movement to the line of departure |
maneuver | deployment | assault | consolidation and reorganization**

Check your ideas with the class.

Unit 163 Talking about Attacks 3

T1 | Speaking: Talk and Report 1

Look at P163.1 and P163.2. What can you see?

T2 | Speaking: Talk and Report 2

What do you remember about these terms from **Unit 162**?

> **assembly area** | **reconnaissance** | **movement to the line of departure** |
> **maneuver** | **deployment** | **assault** | **consolidation and reorganization**

T3 | Reading: Read to check your ideas from T2

A deliberate attack is a type of offensive action characterized by preplanned coordinated employment of firepower and maneuver to close with and destroy the enemy. The deliberate attack is a fully coordinated operation that is usually reserved for those situations in which the enemy defense cannot be overcome by a hasty attack.

The **assembly area** (AA) is the area a unit occupies to prepare for an operation. To prepare the platoon for the upcoming battle, the platoon leader plans, directs, and supervises mission preparations in the assembly area. This time allows the platoon to conduct precombat checks and inspections, rehearsals, and sustainment activities. All leaders should aggressively seek information about the terrain and the enemy. Before a deliberate attack, the platoon and company should gain enemy, terrain, and friendly information from the reconnaissance conducted by the battalion reconnaissance platoon. However, this may not always occur.

The platoon will typically **move** from the AA to the line of departure as part of the company movement plan. The point of departure is the point where the unit crosses the line of departure and begins moving along a direction of attack or axis of advance. The company commander will plan the approach of all platoons to the objective to ensure synchronization, security, speed, and flexibility. He will select the platoons' routes, movement techniques, formations, and methods of movement to best support his intent for actions on the objective. The platoon leader must recognize this portion of the battle as a fight, as **maneuver**, not as a movement. He must be prepared to make contact with the enemy.

As the platoon **deploys** and moves toward the assault position, it minimizes delay and confusion by beginning the final positioning of the squads as directed by the company commander. An assault position is the last covered and concealed position short of the objective from which final preparations are made to assault the objective. The probable line of deployment is a phase line the company commander designates as a location where he intends to completely deploy his unit into the assault formation before beginning the assault.

Actions on the objective, the **assault**, begin when the company or platoon begins placing direct and indirect fires on the objective. This may occur while the platoon is still moving toward the objective from the assault position or probable line of deployment. Supporting fire from the weapons squad will suppress the enemy. The objective will be breached by the breach element and a foothold seized. Then the assault element will move through the breach lane to assault the objective and exploit the penetration.

Once enemy resistance on the objective has ceased, the platoon quickly **consolidates** to defend against a possible counterattack and prepares for follow-on missions. Consolidation consists of actions taken to secure the objective and defend against an enemy counterattack. **Reorganization**, normally conducted concurrently with consolidation, consists of preparing for follow-on operations. Regardless of the situation, the platoon must posture itself and prepare for continued offensive operations.

[Adapted from FM 3-21.8]

T4 | Reading: Read the text again and answer these questions

1. What happens in the assembly area?
2. What is the point of departure?
3. Why is the approach to the objective manoeuvrer, not movement?
4. What is the assault position?
5. What is the probable line of deployment?
6. When does the assault begin?
7. What is the sequence of the assault?
8. Why are consolidation and reorganisation important?

Check with your partner, and the class.

T5 | Language Analysis: Analyse the Text

T6 | Listen and Read: Listen to a reading of the text

Which words do you need to practice saying? Which words do you need to learn?

T7 | Vocabulary: Collocations

Look at P163.3 and complete the collocations from the text.

T8 | Consolidation Tasks

Study Page: Patrols: Revision and Extension

Extend your knowledge about patrols in English

T1 | Vocabulary: Complete the definition with the correct words

detachment	larger	main	mission	semi-independently	specific

A patrol is a [1] _____ sent out by a [2] _____ unit to conduct a [3] _____ mission. Patrols operate [4] _____ and return to the [5] _____ body upon completion of their [6] _____.

T2 | Vocabulary: Complete the purposes of patrols with the correct words

deterring	engaging	gathering	preventing
protecting	providing	reassuring	regaining

[1] _____ information on the enemy, on the terrain, or on the populace.

[2] _____ contact with the enemy or with adjacent friendly forces

[3] _____ the enemy in combat to destroy him or inflict losses.

[4] _____ or gaining the trust of a local population.

[5] _____ public disorder.

[6] _____ and disrupting insurgent or criminal activity.

[7] _____ unit security.

[8] _____ key infrastructure or bases.

T3 | Listening: Listen and Make Notes

Listen to a talk about the purposes of different types of patrol

Raid Patrols:

Ambush Patrols:

Security Patrols:

Area Patrols:

Route Patrols:

Zone Patrols:

Point Patrols

Contact Patrols:

Tracking Patrols:

Presence Patrols:

Check with **Transcript: Study Page: Patrols Revision**.

Collocations: **Orders 1**

operation

mission   await

effective

patrol

review   order   oral   verbal

give

standing

specific

appropriate

Match the words with 'order' to make collocations

verb + order |

_____

_____   an order

_____

adjective + order | a/an

_____

_____

_____   order

_____

_____

_____

noun + order | a/an

_____

_____   order

_____

Unit 164 Orders 1

T1 | Speaking: Talk and Report

Look at P164.1 – 2. What is happening?

T2 | Vocabulary: Types of Order

Complete the text with these words and acronyms.

clarify	confirmation	FRAGO	OPORDs
role	tempo	WARNO	WARNOs

Leaders receive their missions in several ways—ideally through a series of warning orders ([1]_____), operation orders ([2] _____), and briefings from their leader/commander. However, the [3] _____ of operations often precludes this ideal sequence, particularly at the lower levels. This means that leaders may often receive only a [4] _____ or a fragmentary order ([5] _____), but the process is the same.

After receiving an order, leaders are normally required to give a [6] _____ briefing to their higher commander. This is done to [7] _____ their understanding of the commander's mission, intent, and concept of the operation, as well as their [8] _____ within the operation. The leader obtains clarification on any portions of the higher headquarters' plan as required.

[From US Army FM 3-21.8 (FM 7-8)]

T3 | Speaking: Talk and Report

What three things should a **mission order** contain?

T4 | Reading: Read to find out the answer to the question in T3

Mission orders address only the required information. They provide the framework of *what* the commander wants done—not *how* it is to be done. Such orders need only three important things. First, they must clearly state what the commander issuing the order wants accomplished. Second, they must point out limiting factors that must be observed for coordinating purposes. Third, they must state what resources are to be made available to the subordinate commander and what support he can expect outside his command.

[From FM 7-20]

T5 | Reading: Read and Order

Troop leading is the process a leader goes through to prepare his unit to accomplish a tactical mission. It begins when he is alerted for a mission. It starts again when he receives a change or a new mission.

What order should the 8 steps below (ideally) be in?

	Complete the plan.
	Issue a warning order.
	Issue the complete order.
	Make a tentative plan.
Step 1	Receive the mission.
	Reconnoiter.
	Start necessary movement.
	Supervise.

Check with the class. Do you all agree?

When might the order of steps need to change?

T6 | Speaking: Talk and Report

Discuss with your partner:

1. What will the initial assessment of the mission involve?
2. What kind of factors do you need to consider?
3. What will come out of the initial assessment?

T7 | Reading: Read and Answer

Read the text and answer the questions in **T6**. Do you agree with the text?

> Upon receiving the mission, leaders perform an initial assessment of the situation (mission, enemy, terrain, troops-time, civil conditions [METT-TC] analysis), focusing on the mission, the unit's role in the larger operation, and allocating time for planning and preparing. The two most important products from this initial assessment should be at least a partial restated mission, and a timeline. Leaders issue their initial WARNO on this first assessment and time allocation.
>
> [From FM 3-21.8 (FM 7-8)]

T8 | Vocabulary: Read and Complete

Complete the text below with these words.

allocate	detailed	estimate	extremely
fast-paced	SOPs	subordinates	tentative

Based on their knowledge, leaders [1] _____ the time available to plan and prepare for the mission. They issue a [2] _____ timeline that is as [3] _____ as possible. In the process they [4] _____ roughly one-third of available planning and preparation time to themselves, allowing their [5] _____ the remaining two-thirds. During [6] _____ operations, planning and preparation time might be [7] _____ limited. Knowing this in advance enables leaders to emplace [8] _____ to assist them in these situations.

[From FM 3-21.8 (FM 7-8)]

T9 | Vocabulary: Complete the collocations from the text

1. operation _____
2. required _____
3. subordinate _____
4. initial _____
5. preparation _____
6. time _____
7. coordinating _____
8. tactical _____
9. tentative _____
10. tempo of _____

T10 | Speaking: Talk and Report

What are the most important things to remember about orders and giving orders?

Report to the class on your discussion. Do you all agree?

Unit 165 Orders 2: WARNO/WARNORDs 1

Learn The Language Of Warning Orders

T1 | Speaking: Talk and Report 1

Warning Orders in the US Army follow a five paragraph format.

Is this the same as in your army?

What are the five paragraphs in the five paragraph model?

T2 | Reading: Matching

Match the paragraph headings (1-5) with the descriptions of the contents (A-G) One paragraph has three sections.

Para 1: Situation _____

Para 2: Mission _____

Para 3: Execution _____

Para 4: Service Support _____

Para 5: Command and Signals _____

A	Brief description of the enemy and friendly forces situations. Point out key locations on the ground, map or sketch. Attachments and detachments to the squad/platoon.
B	Brief statement of the tentative concept of the operation.
C	Concise statement of the task and purpose (who, what, when, where, and why) If not all information is known, state which parts of the mission statement are tentative.
D	Combat Service Support tasks to be accomplished that are different from the Tactical Standard Operating Procedures: Equipment and transportation.
E	Location of Command Post; succession of command (if not SOP); Standard Operating Instructions in effect.; Signals/code words.
F	Tasks to subordinate key personnel: Platoon sergeant; squad leaders; RATELO; aidman; attachments. Tasks to soldiers helping prepare OPORD. Tasks as needed to others.
G	Time schedule: earliest time of move; Time and place of OPORD; probable execution time. Inspection times and items to be inspected different from SOP. Rehearsal time, location, and actions to be rehearsed.
	[All Texts: Source: FM 7-8]

Read the paragraphs of the sample oral WARNO.

Write in the paragraph number (1-5).

Para 1: Situation   Para 4: Service Support

Para 2: Mission   Para 5: Command and Signals

Para 3: Execution

This is a warning order. Hold your questions until I finish.

No changes to platoon organization. The platoon CP will stay here.	Para:

It is the mission of Third Platoon to attack and seize Hill 876 GRID 123456 on 11 0200Zulu July 19 in order to provide fires on Hill 899 in support of the battalion's attack. We will be one of the two assault platoons along with Second Platoon. First Platoon will be the base of fire along with the company mortars and Javelins.	Para:

The scouts have identified a motorized rifle platoon with at least two BTRs defending Hill 876 vicinity GRID 123456. They are digging in and it looks like they plan to defend the road junction at GRID 126463. The rest of the enemy company is further to the west, around Hill 899.	Para:

Sergeant First Class Fowler talk to me about resupply after this warning order. I want you to plan for casualty evacuation and to give paragraph 4 of the OPORD. Staff Sergeant Crawford, you and your squad will be the lead squad. Make sure you recon the route from here to the Line of Departure. Sergeant Brown, as Forward Observer, I need you to get the fire-plan from the Fire Support Centre as soon as possible. Staff Sergeant Steele, send Sergeant White and his team up here in 20 minutes to begin making the terrain model of the objective.	Para:

Standard Operating Instructions, we have are still in effect.	Para:

Timeline is as follows: I want a platoon rehearsal for squad and fire team leaders, the aidman, the Forward Observer, and, of course, Sergeant First Class Fowler here at our Command Post at 1330. Platoon rehearsals will be for action at the objective. Squads rehearse breaching and react to contact drills on your own. We have a company rehearsal for platoon and squad leaders at 1600 at the company Command Post. We will meet here at 1530 and move together. I will do a full platoon rehearsal at 2100 so we can do at least one go of it in the dark. Line of Departure time is 0200. The earliest we will have to move is 2330. After 2330 we have to be ready to	Para:

move within 10 minutes of the order to do so. My final inspection will be here at the Command Post. My OPORD will be here at the platoon Command Post at 1030.	

Captain Williams just issued a warning order for the company to prepare for an attack at 11 0200Zulu July 19 to seize Hill 876 in order to provide suppressive fire for the Battalion's main attack on Hill 899. There are no attachments or detachments.	Para:

Each squad will carry four AT4s.	Para:

Time is now 0620. What are your questions?

T4 | Reading: Read and Answer

Read the order again and answer these questions:

1. Where are the platoon going to attack?
2. What is the objective?
3. When will the attack start?
4. Where will the main attack be?
5. Why does Hill 876 need to be taken?
6. Is the platoon being reinforced for the attack?
7. When is company rehearsal for team leaders?
8. What will happen at 1330?
9. What will the platoon rehearse at 2100?
10. Who will organise breaching and reacting to contact drills?
11. Who will plan for casualty evacuation?
12. Why is the fireplan important?
13. Who will make the terrain model?
14. Are there any changes to SOI?

T5 | Speaking: Discuss the WARNO

Re-read the WARNO and make sure you understand everything.

T6 | Speaking: Talk And Report 2

Evaluate the WARNO. Is it a good example of a WARNO? What would you change/add? What could be abbreviated? For example, could you say LD instead of Line of Departure?

T7 | Listen and Read: Listen to a reading of the text

Which words do you need to practice saying? Which words do you need to learn?

T8 | Consolidation Tasks

Unit 166 Orders 3: WARNO/WARNORDs 2

T1 | Speaking: What do you remember?

What are the five parts of a Warning Order in the US Army?

What information do you have in each part?

T2 | Grammar: Complete the WARNO with the words given

Complete the text with these words in the correct form.

You will have to use some words more than once.

are	attack	dig	have	hold	is	issue	need
meet	plan	recon	rehearse	send	talk	want	will

This is a warning order. [1] _____ your questions until I finish.

Situation

The scouts [2] _____ identified a motorized rifle platoon with at least two BTRs defending Hill 876 vicinity GRID 123456. They [3] _____ _____ in and it looks like they [4] _____ to defend the road junction at GRID 126463. The rest of the enemy company is further to the west, around Hill 899. Captain Williams just [5] _____ a warning order for the company to prepare for an attack at 11 0200Zulu July 19 to seize Hill 876 in order to provide suppressive fire for the Battalion's main attack on Hill 899. There [6] _____ no attachments or detachments.

Mission

It is the mission of Third Platoon to [7] _____ and seize Hill 876 GRID 123456 on 11 0200Zulu July 19 in order to provide fires on Hill 899 in support of the battalion's attack. We [8] _____ be one of the two assault platoons along with Second Platoon. First Platoon [9] _____ be the base of fire along with the company mortars and Javelins.

Execution

Coordinating Instructions

Timeline [10] _____ as follows: I [11] _____ a platoon rehearsal for squad and fire team leaders, the aidman, the Forward Observer, and, of course, Sergeant First Class Fowler here at our Command Post at 1330. Platoon rehearsals [12] _____ be for action at the objective. Squads [13] _____ breaching and react to contact drills on your own. We [14] _____ a company rehearsal for platoon and squad leaders at 1600 at the company Command Post. We will [15] _____ here at 1530 and move together. I [16] _____ do a full platoon rehearsal at 2100 so we can do at least one go of it in the dark

Line of Departure time is 0200. The earliest we [17] _____ have to move is 2330. After 2330 we [18] _____ to be ready to move within 10 minutes of the order to do so. My final inspection [19] _____ be here at the Command Post. My OPORD [20] _____ be here at the platoon Command Post at 1030.

Sergeant First Class Fowler [21] _____ to me about resupply after this warning order. I [22] _____ you to plan for casualty evacuation and to give paragraph 4 of the OPORD. Staff Sergeant Crawford, you and your squad [23] _____ be the lead squad. Make sure you [24] _____ the route from here to the Line of Departure. Sergeant Brown, as Forward Observer, I [25] _____ you to get the fireplan from the Fire Support Centre as soon as possible. Staff Sergeant Steele, [26] _____ Sergeant White and his team up here in 20 minutes to begin making the terrain model of the objective.

Service Support

Each squad [27] _____ carry four AT4s.

Command and Control

No changes to platoon organization. The platoon CP [28] _____ stay here.

Standard Operating Instructions, we [X] _____ are still in effect.

Time [29] _____ now 0620. What [30] _____ your questions?

T3 | Listening: Listen and Answer

Work in groups of five. You are **A**, **B**, **C**, **D** and **E**.

A: you are SFC Kapenda   **B:** you are SSG Nampala   **C:** you are SGT Kapweya

D: you are SSG Lilonga   **E:** you are SGT Angula

Listen to another WARNO and answer the questions.

1.   Where are the platoon going to attack?
2.   What is the objective?
3.   When will the attack start?
4.   Where will the main attack be?
5.   Is the platoon being reinforced for the attack?
6.   When is the rehearsal?
7.   Who will organise breaching and reacting to contact drills?
8.   Who will plan for casualty evacuation?
9.   Who will make the terrain model?
10.   Are there any changes to SOI?
11.   Who is going to be lead squad?
12.   Who will get the fireplan?

Check as a class.

Unit 167 Orders 4: WARNO/WARNORDs 3

T1 | Speaking: What do you remember?

What are the five parts of a Warning Order in the US Army?

What information do you have in each part?

T2 | Speaking: Give a WARNO

Work in groups.

Use your maps.

Decide on your positions and the enemy dispositions.

Decide on an attack.

Prepare a WARNO.

One of your group will give the order to the class.

The other students in the other groups will listen to the WARNO and make notes.

T3 | Feedback: Give feedback on your colleagues' briefings

Did you understand everything?

If not, what did you not understand?

T4 | Self-Evaluation

When all the briefings have finished put your WARNO notes on display on the walls around the room.

Each student can go and read the WARNO notes and see if their own notes they made while listening are accurate (or not). Check you have **all** the information required and that it is **all** correct.

T5 | Feedback: Your teacher will give you feedback on your briefing

Collocations: **Orders 2**

wait for

warning

convey   initial

special

unit   written   order   deployment

new   issue

tasking   conflicting

Match the words with 'order' to make collocations

verb + order |

_____

_____   an order

_____

adjective + order | a/an

_____

_____

_____   order

_____

noun + order | a/an

_____

_____   order

_____

_____

Unit 168 Orders 5: OPORDs 1

T1 | Speaking: Talk and Report 1

Operation Orders in the US Army follow the same five paragraph format as WARNO.

Is this the same as in your army?

What are the five paragraphs in the 'five paragraph model'?

T2 | Reading: Matching

Match the paragraph headings (**1 - 5**) with the descriptions of the contents (**A - F**) Task Organisation has been done for you.

Task Organisation	D
Para 1: Situation	_____
Para 2: Mission	_____
Para 3: Execution	_____
Para 4: Service Support	_____
Para 5: Command and Signals	_____

A	_____
	a. _____.
	1. location of higher unit command and CP.
	2. Location of the platoon leader or CP.
	3. Location of the PSG or alternate CP.
	4. Succession of command (if different from SOP)
	b. _____
	1. SOI index in effect.
	2. Listening silence, if applicable
	3. Methods of communication in priority
	4. Emergency signals, visual signals
	5. Code words.
B	_____
	Intent. Give the stated vision that defines the purpose of the operation and the relationship among the force, the enemy and the terrain.
	a. Concept of the operation: refer to the operation overlay and concept sketch. Explain, in general terms, how the platoon, as a whole, will accomplish the mission. Identify the most important task for the platoon (mission essential task) and any other essential tasks. If applicable, designate the decisive points, form of maneuver of defensive techniques, and any other significant factors or

principles. Limit this paragraph to 6 sentences.

      1.   Maneuver: address all the squads and attachments by name, giving them an essential task. Designate the platoon's main effort; that is who will accomplish the most important task. All other tasks must relate to the main effort. Give missions statements for each subordinate element.

      2.   Fires. Refer to the fire support overlay and target list. Describe the concept of the fire support to synchronize and complement the scheme of maneuver. If applicable address priority fires (include changes), priority targets (who controls fires on them) and any restrictive control measures on the use of fires.

      3.   Additional combat assets (engineer, ADA). State the concept of employment of any combat support attachments or who gets priority of their use, how they are to be used (priority of effort), and how they will be controlled and by whom.

b. Tasks to Maneuver units. Specify tasks other than those listed in 3a(1.), and the purpose of each for squads and attachments. List each in separate number sub-paragraphs. Address the reserve last. State any priority or sequence.

c. Tasks to Combat support units. List tasks to CS units in sub-paragraphs in the order they appear in the task organisation. List only those specific tasks that must be accomplished by those units not specified elsewhere.

d. Co-ordinating instructions. List the details of co-ordination and control applicable to two or more units in the platoon. Incl. ROE and order of march.

C   _____

Provide information essential to the subordinate leader's understanding of the situation.

a. enemy forces: refer to the overlay or sketch. Include pertinent intelligence provided by higher HQ and other facts and assumptions about the enemy. This analysis is stated as conclusions and addresses:

      1.   Disposition, composition and strength.

      2.   Capabilities. A listing of what the enemy is able to do and how well.

      3.   Most probable course of action.

b. friendly forces. Provide information that subordinates need to accomplish their tasks.

      1.   Higher unit. A verbatim statement of the higher units commander's mission statement from paragraph 2 and concept of the operation statement from paragraph 3a.

      2.   Left unit's mission.

      3.   Right unit's mission.

      4.   Forward unit's mission.

      5.   Mission of the unit in reserve or following.

	6. Units in support or reinforcing the higher unit. c. attachments and detachments
D	**Task Organisation** Explain how the unit is organised for the operation. If there is no change to the previous task organisation indicate: "no change".
E	_____ Provide a clear, concise statement of the task to be accomplished and the purpose for doing it (WHO, WHAT, WHEN, WHERE, AND WHY). The leader derives the mission from his mission analysis.

F	_____ include CSS instructions and arrangements supporting the operation that are of primary interest to the platoon. Include changes to established SOPs or a previously issued order. Paragraph 4 is often prepared and issued by the PSG.
	    a) General. Reference the SOPs that govern the sustainment operations of the unit.
	    b) Materials and services: supply, transportation, services, maintenance of weapons and equipment, medical evacuation.
	    c) Personnel: Identify the EPW collection point and any additional instructions on EPW handling not covered in SOP.
	    d) Miscellaneous

	[FM 7-8]

Check you understand everything about OPORDs.

T3 | Speaking: Talk and Report 1

Evaluate the OPORD instructions. What would you change/add?

Look at the abbreviations: which would you use? Which would you say in full?

Notes

Unit 169 Orders 6: OPORDs 2

T1 | Speaking: What do you remember?

What are the five parts of an OPORD in the US Army?

What information do you have in each part?

T2 | Reading: Read and Match

Read the paragraphs of the example oral OPORD. Write in the paragraphs (**A - S**).

Task Organisation	**K** _____
Para 1: Situation	_____
Para 2: Mission	_____
Para 3: Execution	_____
Para 4: Service Support	_____
Para 5: Command and Signals	_____

A	3rd Platoon attacks 14 0200Zulu Jun 19 to seize western edge of Hill 652 OBJ CAT, vicinity of GRID 170834 to prevent disruption of battalion main attack.
B	Purpose of mortar fires is to screen observation of the breaching operation. First Squad has priority of 60 mm mortar fire. During consolidation, Third Squad will have priority of fires. Battalion will fire a three-minute preparatory fire on OBJECTIVE COW to disrupt enemy command and control.
C	Order of march for Company C is First Platoon, Command Post, Second Platoon, Mortars, Third Platoon. Order of march for the platoon is First Squad, HQ, Second Squad, Third Squad. Movement formation is platoon file, travelling overwatch.
D	Company casualty collection points are located here at GRID 162824 and GRID 165827. Platoon Casualty Collection Point after seizure of OBJECTIVE CAT will be directly behind this Infantry Fighting Vehicle position here at GRID 171835.
E	Signals: Radio: Tactical frequency is 65 Khz; the TACEVAC frequency is 37 Khz. Challenge is: Arrow; Password is Maize; Running Password is Apache; the number combination password is seven.
F	Mortars will occupy firing positions, vicinity of GRID 167828 not later than 14 0425Zulu Jun 19.
G	First Squad, shift fires to contact point 1, allowing Second Squad a clear ap-

	proach into the trench line. Second Squad, prepare satchel charges for bunkers. Third Squad, be prepared to assault IFVs.
H	Concept of the operation is to penetrate OBJECTIVE CAT from the northeast. First Squad will suppress the trench line allowing the main attack by Third Squad to maneuver and enter the trench. Once the foothold is established, Second Squad enters and clears the trench line from east to west. Key to this mission is speed in establishing the foothold (the decisive point) and providing suppressive fires to allow main attack access to the trench line. This should keep them busy and keep them from disrupting the battalion main attack.
I	Friendly forces: Charlie Company seizes OBJECTIVE FOX, vicinity of GRID 162827 to prevent enemy from concentrating combat power against the battalion main effort. Alpha Company on OBJECTIVE COW. The CO's intent is to isolate the northern portion of the OBJECTIVE preventing the enemy main effort from concentrating against our breach in the south. He wants to execute the main attack as quickly as possible. This will prevent the enemy from affecting the battalion attack. On our left First Platoon fix the enemy on OBJECTIVE FOX to allow Second Platoon to establish a breach. On our right, Second Platoon establish a breach, vicinity of GRID 163826 to allow main attack to clear OBJECTIVE FOX. To our rear, company mortars suppress enemy on OBJECTIVE FOX to screen breaching effort. Attachments and detachments: Second squad has three Dragons attached, which will remain under platoon control until seizure of OBJECTIVE CAT.
J	Enemy forces: the scouts have confirmed a full strength motorized rifle platoon with Infantry Fighting Vehicles on our portion of the company objective. They are dug in and expected to fight hard to retain this terrain. Their approximate positions and orientation are as reflected on the terrain model.
K	Task organization is First Squad with two of the platoon's machine guns, Third Squad, Second Squad with three Dragons.
L	First Squad suppresses trench line to allow Second Squad to enter the trench line. Second Squad, the main effort, clears the trench line preventing disruption of battalion attack. 3rd Squad establishes foothold in trench line allowing Second Squad to enter trench line.
M	Line of departure time 14 0300Zulu Jun 19. MOPP1 in effect. Platoon rehearsal for key leaders: 1300. Company rehearsal 1400. Consolidation is in accordance with terrain model. Timing: 1300 Platoon rehearsal; 1400 Company rehearsal; 1700 inspection; 1730 chow; 1830 rest; 2100 night rehearsals; 0045 stand-to;

		0115 final inspection; 0200 Line of Departure time; 0515 Assault time.
N		Company expects to receive some replacements late 15 June. We should receive two infantrymen.
O		The time is now 1007. What are your questions?
P		Company Commander will follow us. He will set up Company Command Post in the vicinity of the trench line. I will follow First Squad during movement and will assault with Second Squad. Platoon Sergeant will follow Second Squad, then move to the support-by-fire position with First Squad. No changes to platoon organization.
Q		Enemy Prisoner of War collection point will be behind First Squad objective.
R		Company trains will be located at this trail intersection, vicinity of GRID 161823 after seizure of OBJECTIVE FOX.

T3 | Reading: Read and Answer

You are 3rd Platoon. Read the order again and answer these questions:

1. Where is the attack going to take place?
2. What are the objectives?
3. When will the attack start?
4. Where will the main attack be?
5. What is the order of march?
6. What does each squad in the platoon have to do?
7. What is the time schedule?
8. Where are the casualty evacuation points?
9. Where will the commanders be during the attack?
10. What are the signals?

T4 | Speaking: Discuss the OPORD

Re-read the OPORD and make sure you understand everything.

T5 | Speaking: Talk And Report

Evaluate the OPORD.

Is it a good example of an OPORD?

What would you change/add?

T6 | Listen and Read: Listen to a reading of the text

Which words do you need to practice saying? Which words do you need to learn?

T7 | Consolidation Tasks

Unit 170 Orders 7: OPORDs 3

T1 | Speaking: Test Your Partner

Ask your partner: What information do you have in the first/second/third/fourth/ fifth part of a OPORD in the US Army?

T2 | Grammar: Complete the OPORD with the words given

Complete the text of the OPORD with these words in the correct form. e.g. *will assault* You will have to use some words more than once.

assault	attach	be	breach	clear
confirm	control	disrupting	enter	fire
fix	have	isolate	locate	observation
penetrate	position	prepared	rehearsal	retain
seize	should	suppress	suppressive	terrain
want	will			

Task organization is First Squad with two of the platoon's machine guns, Third Squad, Second Squad with three Dragons.

Situation

Enemy forces: the scouts [1] _____ _____ a full strength motorized rifle platoon with Infantry Fighting Vehicles on our portion of the company objective. They are dug in and expected to fight hard to [2] _____ this terrain. Their approximate [3] _____ and orientation are as reflected on the [4] _____ model.

Friendly forces: Charlie Company [5] _____ OBJECTIVE FOX, vicinity of GRID 162827 to prevent enemy from concentrating combat power against the battalion main effort: Alpha Company on OBJECTIVE COW. The CO's intent is to [6] _____ the northern portion of the OBJECTIVE preventing the enemy main effort from concentrating against our breach in the south. He [7] _____ to execute the main attack as quickly as possible. This will prevent the enemy from affecting the battalion attack.

On our left First Platoon [8] _____ the enemy on OBJECTIVE FOX to allow Second Platoon to establish a [9] _____. On our right, Second Platoon establish a breach, vicinity of GRID 163826 to allow main attack to clear OBJECTIVE FOX. To our rear, company mortars suppress enemy on OBJECTIVE FOX to screen breaching effort.

Attachments and detachments: Second squad has three Dragons

---

[10] _____, which will remain under platoon [11] _____ until seizure of OBJECTIVE CAT.

Mission

3rd Platoon attacks 14 0200Zulu Jun 19 to seize western edge of Hill 652 OBJECTIVE CAT, vicinity of GRID 170834 to prevent disruption of battalion main attack.

Execution

Concept of the operation is to [12] _____ OBJECTIVE CAT from the northeast. First Squad [13] _____ _____ the trench line allowing the main attack by Third Squad to maneuver and enter the trench. Once the foothold is established, Second Squad [14] _____ and clears the trench line from east to west. Key to this mission [15] _____ speed in establishing the foothold (the decisive point) and providing [16] _____ fires to allow main attack access to the trench line. This should keep them busy and keep them from [17] _____ the battalion main attack.

Maneuver

First Squad suppresses trench line to allow Second Squad to enter the trench line. Second Squad, the main effort, [18] _____ the trench line preventing disruption of battalion attack. 3rd Squad establishes foothold in trench line allowing Second Squad to enter trench line.

Fires

Purpose of mortar fires is to screen [19] _____ of the breaching operation. First Squad has priority of 60 mm mortar fire. During consolidation, Third Squad [20] _____ _____ priority of fires. Battalion [21] _____ _____ a three-minute preparatory fire on OBJECTIVE COW to disrupt enemy command and control.

Tasks to maneuver units

First Squad, shift fires to contact point 1, allowing Second Squad a clear approach into the trench line. Second Squad, prepare satchel charges for bunkers. Third Squad, [22] _____ _____ to assault IFVs.

Tasks to combat support units

Mortars will occupy firing positions, vicinity of GRID 167828 not later than 14 0425Zulu Jun 19.

Co-ordinating instructions

Order of march for Company C [23] _____ First Platoon, Command Post, Second Platoon, Mortars, Third Platoon. Order of march for the platoon is First Squad, HQ, Second Squad, Third Squad. Movement formation is platoon file, travelling overwatch.

Line of departure time 14 0300Zulu Jun 19. MOPP1 in effect. Platoon rehearsal for key leaders: 1300. Company rehearsal 1400. Consolidation is in accordance with terrain model.

Timing: 1300 Platoon [24] _____; 1400 Company rehearsal; 1700 inspection; 1730 chow; 1830 rest; 2100 night rehearsals; 0045 stand-to; 0115 final inspection; 0200 Line of Departure time; 0515 [25] _____ time.

Service and Support

Company trains [26] _____ _____ _____ at this trail intersection, vicinity of GRID 161823 after seizure of OBJECTIVE FOX.

Company casualty collection points [27] _____ _____ here at GRID 162824 and GRID 165827.

Platoon Casualty Collection Point after seizure of OBJECTIVE CAT will be directly behind this Infantry Fighting Vehicle position here at GRID 171835.

Company expects to receive some replacements late 15 June. We [28] _____ receive two infantrymen.

Enemy Prisoner of War collection point [29] _____ _____ behind First Squad objective.

Command and Control

Company Commander will follow us. He will set up Company Command Post in the vicinity of the trench line. I will follow First Squad during movement and [30] _____ _____ with Second Squad. Platoon Sergeant will follow Second Squad, then move to the support-by-fire position with First Squad. No changes to platoon organization.

Signals: Radio: Tactical frequency is 65 Khz; the TACEVAC frequency is 37 Khz. Challenge is: Arrow; Password is Maize; Running Password is Apache; the number combination password is seven.

The time is now 1007. What are your questions?

[Adapted from: FM 7-8]

Listen to check.

T3 | Reading: Read the OPORD again and draw a sketch map of the situation

Unit 171 Orders 8: OPORDs 4

T1 | Speaking: Test Your Partner

Ask your partner: What information do you have in the first/second/third/fourth/fifth part of a OPORD in the US Army?

T2 | Listening: Listen and Answer

Work in 3 groups.

Your teacher will group you into groups: A, B, and C.

Group A, you are 1st Squad | Group B: 2nd Squad | Group C: 3rd Squad.

Listen to an OPORD and answer the questions.

1.   Where is the attack going to take place?
2.   What is the objective?
3.   When will the attack start?
4.   Where will the main attack be?
5.   What is the order of march?
6.   What do you have to do?
7.   What are the other squads doing?
8.   What is the time schedule?
9.   Where are the casualty evacuation points?
10. Where will the company commander be during the attack?
11. What are the signals?

Check as a class. [and T171.1]

T3 | Transcript Task: Complete the transcript on the next page, then listen to check

T4 | Listening: Listen and Answer

Work in 2 groups.

Your teacher will group you into groups: A and B.

Group A, you are 1st Squad | Group B: 2nd Squad

Listen to the OPORD and make notes. Use the Map on page 318. Mark the route etc.

Check with M171.1 and Transcript T171.2.

Transcript Task

attached	attack	breach	concentrating	disruption
fix	intent	main x 2	mission	objective
positions	screen	seizure	strength	suppress
task	terrain	vicinity x 2		

Gentlemen this is an [1]_____ OPORD. Squad leaders, pen and paper. Prepare to copy.

[2] _____ organization is First Squad with two of the platoon's machine guns, Second Squad, Third Squad.

Situation

Enemy forces: the scouts have confirmed a full [3] _____ motorized rifle platoon with one, I repeat one, MBT on our portion of the company [4] _____ . They are dug in and expected to fight hard to retain this [5] _____ . Their approximate [6] _____ and orientation are as reflected on the terrain model.

Friendly forces: Charlie Company seizes OBJECTIVE GOLF, which is this crossroads here and this small hill, [7] _____ of GRID 232894 to prevent enemy from [8] _____ combat power against the battalion [9] _____ effort which is Alpha Company at OBJECTIVE CROW. Battalion's CO's [10] _____ is to isolate the west-ern portion of the objective preventing the enemy main effort from concentrating against our [11] _____ in the west. He wants to execute the [12] _____ attack as quickly as possible. This will prevent the enemy from affecting the battalion attack. On our left First Platoon will [13] _____ the enemy on OBJECTIVE GOLF to allow Second Platoon to establish a breach. On our right, Second Platoon establish a breach, [14] _____ of GRID 236895 to allow main attack to clear OBJECTIVE GOLF. To our rear, company mortars [15] _____ enemy on OBJECTIVE GOLF to [16] _____ breaching effort.

Attachments and detachments

The platoon has four Javelins [17] _____ , which will remain under platoon control until [18] _____ of objective.

Mission

It is the [19] _____ of Third Platoon to attack 20 0415Zulu Aug 19 to seize northern edges of Hill 926 OBJECTIVE LION, vicinity of GRID 226896 in order to prevent the [20] _____ of battalion main attack.

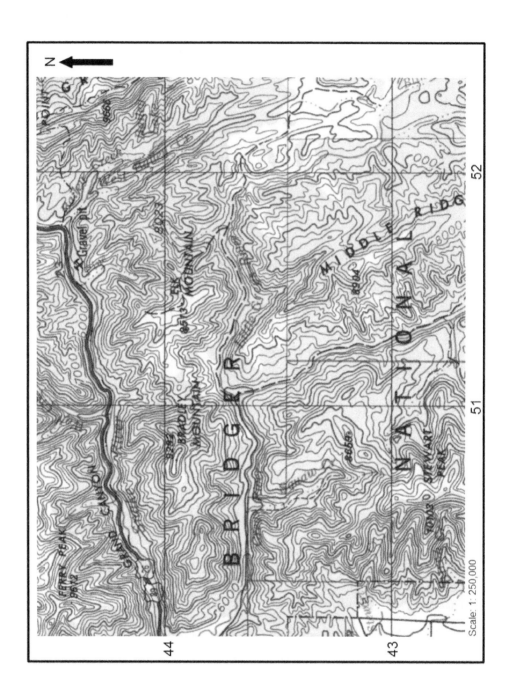

Scale: 1: 250,000

Unit 172 Orders 9: OPORDs 5

T1 | Speaking: Prepare an OPORD

Work in groups.

Use your maps.

Decide on your positions and the enemy dispositions.

Decide on an attack.

Prepare a OPORD.

T2 | Speaking: The Order

One of your group will give the order to the class.

Be ready to answer questions.

The other students will listen to the OPORD and make notes.

T3 | Feedback: Give feedback on your colleagues' briefings

Did you understand everything?
If not, what did you not understand?

T4 | Self-Evaluation

When all the briefings have finished put your OPORD notes on display on the walls around the room.

Each student can go and read the OPORD notes and see if their own notes they made while listening are accurate (or not). Check you have **all** the information required and that it is **all** correct.

T5 | Feedback: Your teacher will give you feedback on your briefing

Collocations: **Orders 3**

transmit

unambiguous

duty

obey

follow

legal

order

illegal

lawful

general   clear   concise   convoy

Match the words with 'order' to make collocations

verb + order
_____
_____   an order
_____

adjective + order | a/an
_____
_____
_____   order
_____
_____
_____
_____

noun + order | a/an
_____   order
_____

Unit 173 Orders 10: WARNO and OPORD Simulation

Practice The Language Of WARNO And Operation Orders

T1 | Speaking: Preparation and Execution

You will need three rooms for this simulation. Your teacher will decide on the groups and the timing for this simulation. Use your maps. Agree on the friendly and enemy troop dispositions for the simulation. Then split into three groups.

> **Group 1:** The Company Commander and Second in Command (2 persons)
>
> **Group 2:** Platoon Commanders (4 platoons = 4 persons)
>
> **Group 3:** Squad leaders (the rest of the class – divided into squad leaders)

Make sure everyone knows who is who and what rank they are.

Start: In Room One

The CO and 2IC will decide on an operation in **Room One** and then issue an OPORD to the Platoon Commanders (**Group 2**) in **Room Two**. Platoon Commanders do a confirmation briefing to the CO on the OPORD.

Meanwhile in Room Three

Group 3 will **not** hear this order. They should be waiting in **Room Three**.

Next in Room Three

Group 2 Platoon Commanders go to **Room Three** and will issue WARNOs to their Group 3 squad leaders in **Room Three.**

Next in Room Two

Group 2 Platoon Commanders return to **Room Two** and develop individual OPORDs for their platoons.

Then in Room One

Platoon Commanders return to **Room One** and give a backbrief to the CO and 2IC on their platoon OPORDS.

Then in Room Three

Group 2 Platoon Commanders go back to **Room Three** and issue their OPORDs. The CO and 2IC observe this and make notes but do not intervene. After the OPORDs have been issued orally the Squad leaders will answer the questions below about the orders. The Company Commander and 2IC will check the answers.

Checking Questions:

1. What is the mission?
2. What does each squad have to do?
3. What is the timeline?

Each Squad Leader should get **100%** of the information correct. If a Squad Leader fails this test then the entire group has to redo the simulation with new orders.

Unit 174 Debriefing

T1 | Speaking: Talk and Report 1

Why should soldiers be debriefed after an operation?

Discuss the question with your partner and then with the class.

T2 | Speaking: Talk and Report 2

1. What kind of questions do debriefers ask after a patrol?
2. What kind of information are they looking for?

T3 | Grammar: Reorder the Words

Look at the sentences on below. Reorder the words to make questions.

[Notes: PL = Platoon Leader | ORP = Objective Rally Point | frag = fragmentary order]

1. Did PL use area proper formation a in crossing the the danger?

2. Were contact checkpoints made on enemy and reports at?

3. Did PL the ORP a select suitable?

4. Did the adequately PL secure site the?

5. Did during control ORP the the the the patrol PL occupation of maintain of?

6. Did maintain the PL or patrol communications ensure with the?

7. If was PL made, did action the contact take appropriate?

8. Was leader's maintained recon during the security?

9. Did the objective action issue a order for PL at the frag?

10. Did the best terrain the employ advantage the at PL objective to the?

11. Did use the objective make of supporting PL at the arms?

12. Was objective action at the successful the?

13. Was objective orderly from the quickly withdrawal accomplished and?

14. Did the ORP quietly from the patrol quickly and withdraw?

T4 | Speaking: Prepare

Work in small groups.

Use your large-scale maps and plan a patrol.

The patrol can be mounted or a foot patrol.

What is the purpose of the patrol?

Decide on the composition of the patrol and the equipment and weapons to be taken.

Plan the route on a route card.

Decide the departure/arrival time.

Decide on the number of patrol personnel.

Decide on the reporting points on your route.

The patrol has returned

What happened during the patrol?

Agree in your group what happened and when it happened. For example: Were you attacked? Did you observe something important?

You decide and make notes. Include all relevant information.

Make sure everyone has a copy of the notes and has read them. Then give all the notes to your teacher. You now have to remember what happened on the patrol.

T5 | Speaking: Debrief

Work in pairs. Debrief a soldier from one of the other groups.

Find out exactly what happened on the patrol, when it happened, and what intel they learned about the enemy/belligerents/warring factions/situation etc.

Make notes.

When you have finished debriefing the soldiers compare your notes with other de-briefers. Do you have the same information? Compare your notes with the original notes from **T3**.

T6 | Speaking: Radio Calls

Script and demonstrate radio calls based on the patrols. Use the Radio Call Forms in your Workbook.

1. PATROL REPORT [PATROLREP] (Workbook: p. 194)
2. CASUALTY REPORT [CASREP] (Workbook: p. 195)
3. INTELLIGENCE REPORT [INTREP] (Workbook: p. 196)

Unit 175 Phase 2 Test: Adventure Training Briefings

T1 | Speaking: Briefing Preparation

Work in groups of five.

There are four 5-slide Briefings to prepare and give on Adventure Training Programmes.

1. Desert Adventure
2. Mountain Adventure
3. Jungle Adventure
4. Temperate Forest Adventure

For each briefing you will have to brief about:

- Location of Training, Terrain and Purpose.
- Expected Weather
- Possible Dangers
- Equipment Required
- Programme

Prepare one slide each but work as a team to prepare and practice your briefing. Some slides have notes; for other slides you will have to decide on what information to give. Use **Unit 175 Phase 2 Speaking Test Briefing Slides 1 - 4.**

T2 | Speaking: Briefing

Brief the class on your Adventure Training Programme.
Be ready to answer questions.

T3 | Listening: Make Notes

You should make notes of your colleagues' briefings.

T4 | Speaking: Questions

Ask questions about your colleagues' briefings.

T5 | Feedback: Give feedback on your colleagues' briefings

Did you understand everything?
If not, what did you not understand?

T6 | Feedback: Your teacher will give you feedback on your briefing

T7 | Speaking: Talk and Report

After all the briefings discuss these questions:

1. Which was the most exciting Adventure Training Programme?
2. Which was the most dangerous Programme?
3. Which would you most like to do? Why?

Phase 3

Unit 176 Prelude to Phase 3: A Case Study

T1 | Reading: The Case Study

Read through the first part of the case study and look at the map on the next page. Make notes on what the situation was and what happened. Make sure you are clear on the sequence of events.

Day 1	
1800 hrs	Lead elements of Alpha Company 1st Battalion mechanized infantry reach the outskirts of town X and move through the suburbs south of the river to the 1st bridge over the river Y.
1825 hrs	On the southern approach to the bridge, Alpha Company's lead IFV is hit by an RPG; there is sustained MG fire, mortars, RPGs from across the river. Column halts. Nightfall. Captain Garcia orders Alpha Company to to take cover and return fire. The city is held by unknown numbers of regular enemy forces from the 5th Infantry Division and irregular civil defence forces.
1900 hrs	Colonel Jones sets up Battalion HQ 10 kms to south of 1st bridge. Alpha Company is reinforced by B Company and two platoons of Charlie Company mechanized infantry.
2130 hrs	The 12 Main Battle Tanks of Delta Company and one platoon of Charlie Company mechanized infantry are pushed to the east towards the lake and salt marshes. They halt at 2305.
	The plan for Day 2 is for the tanks of Delta Company to bypass the city and take the second bridge from the NE. Meanwhile the mechanized infantry will push through the city to secure the first bridge from the south and link up with Delta company. With both bridges and the main road through the city secured, the Battalion will hold for the 2nd Division to pass through the town on their way to the capital city in the north.
Day 2	
0430 hrs	Alpha Company launches an assault across the river and establishes a bridgehead on the other bank. Light casualties.
0630 hrs	Bravo Company crosses the river and pushes into the city along the main road. At the next junction (Grid 583201) the column of IFVs comes under attack. The two lead IFVs are destroyed. Two soldiers are killed and 4 wounded. The firefight lasts over an hour. Radio Net is flooded with traffic.

Check your notes with your partner.

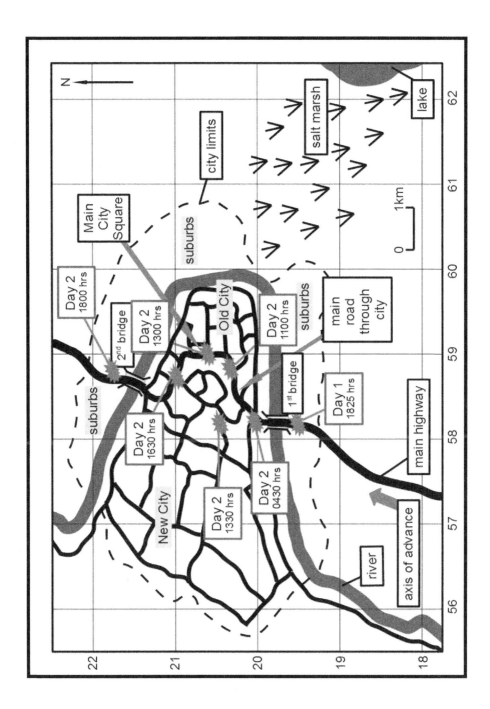

The map contains the following labels:

N

city limits

Main City Square

salt marsh

lake

Day 2 1800 hrs

suburbs

2ⁿᵈ bridge

Day 2 1300 hrs

Old City

Day 2 1100 hrs

suburbs

main road through city

1ˢᵗ bridge

Day 1 1825 hrs

main highway

Day 2 1630 hrs

suburbs

New City

Day 2 1330 hrs

Day 2 0430 hrs

river

axis of advance

0   1km

T2 | Speaking: Prediction

Look at the map. What do you think happened next in the operation?

Agree some predictions with the class.

Listen to the second part of the case study and note what happened.

Make sure you are clear on the sequence of events.

Check your notes with your partner.

Were your predictions from T2 correct?

T4 | Speaking: Talk and Report: Lessons Learned

Discuss these question with your partner.

1.   What went wrong? Why?

2.   What should the commanders have done?

3.   What training should the commanders give their officers and men?

4.   What should the commanders make sure happens next time?

5.   Who was responsible for the blue on blue casualties?

Discuss your answers with the group/class.

Language Reminder

Talking about a specific past time event: C Company **attacked** at 0430 hours..

Evaluation: This was **well done/ poorly executed/ a (complete) disaster**.

Saying what **should have happened**:

should + have + done:

The Commander **should have waited**.

should not have done:

The Commander **shouldn't have attacked** then.

Methodology Note: E2D2PEF

In this part of the course there are five **Tactical Problems,** and, after **some** more units on Peacekeeping and natural disasters, five **Peacekeeping Problems** to solve.

Work in small groups, study and solve these problems and then present your solution to the class. You should use this procedure: E2D2PEF

E	**Examine** the situation. Read the situation first, then check your understanding with your colleagues.
2D	**Discuss** and **Decide** on a course of action with your group colleagues.
2P	**Prepare** to present. Script your presentation; practice; improve. **Present** your solution to the class.
E	Listen to the **Evaluation** of the presentation by the audience.
F	Receive **Feedback** from the teacher.

Remember this is a language practice exercise. There are no right or wrong solutions to the problems. There are different courses of action; some might be better than others but there is no key to check your solution against.

In the **evaluation** and **feedback** stage, you should use the following criteria:

The Evaluation Criteria for the Audience

1. Was the solution to the problem a good/reasonable solution?

2. Was the briefing clear and logically structured?

3. Did you understand everything? If not, what did you not understand?

Unit 177 Tactical Problem 1

T1 | Speaking: Talk and Report

Look at P177.1. What can you see?

T2 | Reading: Read the Tactical Problem

It is 0630 hours. You are the company commander of Charlie Company. You have 120 soldiers in 3 platoons. Your company has been driven by convoy to a remote abandoned airfield near the Bree mountains in Sordor (see the sketch map on the next page). The convoy has just returned to base. Your mission is to defend the airfield so that additional forces may be introduced to the area for the region's defense and insurgent suppression operations. You have been assigned one squad each of heavy machine guns (M2 .50 caliber machine guns) and AT Missiles from Weapons Company. You have no indirect fire support. With you are a team of 50 workers whose job it is is to repair the airfield so that it will be operational. They have one bulldozer and hand tools. The repair work is expected to take a month.

The mountains are the home base of the Chui Liberation Front rebels who have been terrorising the area for 15 years. The local villagers are expected to be friendly but are wary of interacting with government forces. Insurgents will be living in the villages and you expect a rapid response to your deployment. Because of the distances involved and the difficult road conditions you do not expect further forces to arrive for 48 hours.

Weather Forecast:

Today: Thunderstorms likely. High 32 °C. Winds SW at 10 to 15 km/h. Chance of rain 100%: 10 mm.

Tonight: Partly to mostly cloudy. Low 24 °C. Winds light and variable. 20% chance of precipitation: 1 mm.

Tomorrow: Partly cloudy early with thunderstorms becoming likely during the afternoon. High 33 °C. Winds SW at 10 to 15 km/h. Chance of rain 90%: 12 mm

Tomorrow night: Cloudy skies early, followed by partial clearing. Low 23 °C. Winds light and variable. 20 % chance of precipitation: 1 mm.

Requirement: Decide how you will deploy your platoons to defend the airfield. Include an overlay sketch and provide a brief discussion of the rationale behind your actions.

T3 | Speaking: Work in groups: use the E2D2PEF procedure

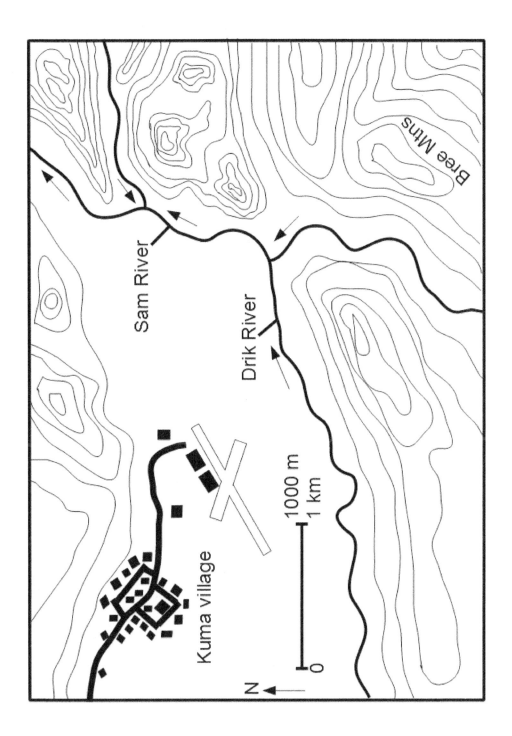

Unit 178 Tactical Problem 2

Solve The Problem Using Speaking Skills, Grammar And Military Vocabulary

T1 | Speaking: Talk and Report

Look at P178.1. What can you see?

T2 | Reading: Read the Tactical Problem

It is 0830 hours. You are the lieutenant in charge of Alpha platoon. You have 38 soldiers in your platoon. The platoon has been convoyed to a crossroads 87 km east of the capital Fretoun (see the sketch map on the next page). The convoy has just returned to the capital. The terrain is slightly hilly and covered in dense jungle. There is secondary jungle along the roads and primary forest further away from the roads. You have one 4 x 4 Hilux and a full tank of fuel. You have rations for four days. Your mission is to defend the crossroads so that forces defending the capital have time to prepare against an expected rebel attack. Each soldier has their individual weapon (~250 rounds each) and each squad has 1 FN Minimi 5.56mm light machine gun (3000 rounds total). You have 15 claymore mines. You have no indirect fire support. You expect to be reinforced within 48 hours. There is a small settlement at the crossroads and approximately 50 civilians living there: 15 adult men, 10 women, 5 youths about 18 years old, 20 children under 16. There is a well in the village and a petrol station. Approximately two thousand rebels are expected to advance on the main east-west road towards the capital. They are armed with AK 47s, machetes and spears. Intelligence reports put the advance guard of the rebel formation approximately 20 miles to your east. They are on advancing on foot and have no vehicles.

Weather Forecast:

Today: Partly cloudy. High 29 °C. Winds E at 10 to 15 km/h. Chance of rain 0 %

Tonight: Mainly clear. A stray shower or thunderstorm is possible. Low 16 °C. Winds light and variable. 10 % chance of precipitation: 1 mm.

Tomorrow: Partly cloudy in the morning followed by scattered thunderstorms in the afternoon. High 27 °C. Winds ESE at 10 to 15 km/h. Chance of rain 40%: 1 mm.

Tomorrow night:: Variable clouds with a slight chance of thunderstorms overnight. Low 17 °C. Winds light and variable. Chance of rain 30%: 1 mm.

Requirement: Decide how you will deploy your platoon to defend the crossroads. Also devise a plan of retreat in the event that your position is overwhelmed. Include an overlay sketch and the rationale behind your actions.

T3 | Speaking: Work in groups: use the E2D2PEF procedure

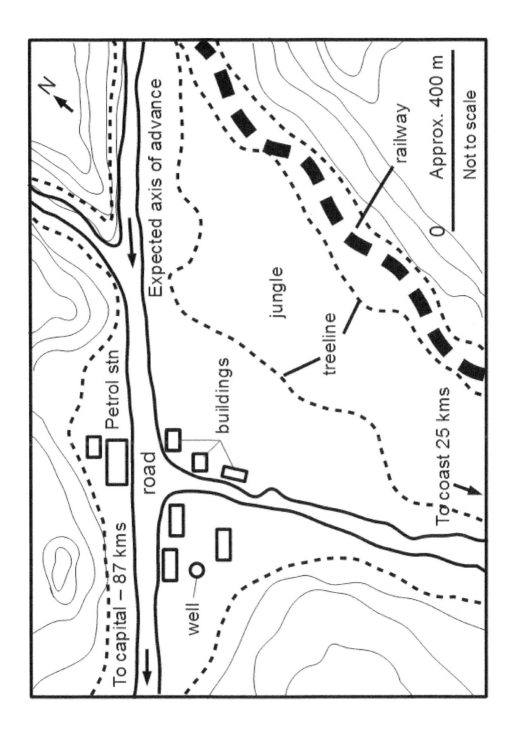

Unit 179 Tactical Problem 3

T1 | Speaking: Talk and Report

Look at P179.1. What can you see?

T2 | Reading: Read the Tactical Problem

It is 0830 hours. You are the sergeant in charge of a squad of soldiers from Red Platoon. You have 2 fireteams of 4 soldiers armed with their personal weapons; each fireteam has one light machine gun. You are on the front-line of your sector in the city of Eborakum. The rest of Red Platoon is in the corner building next to yours and Blue Platoon is to their left; Yellow platoon is on your right (see the sketch map on the next page). Your assault on the area around the Town Hall was stopped yesterday as you ran low on ammunition and the enemy forces' resistance increased. You did not capture the Town Hall, which was your primary objective. There was sporadic small arms and mortar fire during the night. Most of the buildings are damaged and the roads in your area are practically impassable to vehicles due to fallen masonry and other debris. You have two tanks in support but these are in position to the rear of Yellow Platoon. You have just been resupplied with ammunition and two replacement soldiers. The Company CO is meeting with platoon leaders to plan the attack on the Town Hall.

You survey the scene in front of you across the Town Square and see four enemy tanks enter the Town Square from the NW and NE entrances to the square, supported by a large body of infantry.

Weather Forecast:

Today: Fog. High 2 °C. No wind. 0 % Precipitation.

Tonight: Fog. Low -5 °C. No wind. 0 % Precipitation.

Tomorrow: Sunny. High 1 °C. Winds W at 15 to 25 km/h. 0 % Precipitation.

Tomorrow night:: A few clouds from time to time. Low -1 °C. Winds N at 15 to 35 km/h. 0 % Precipitation.

Requirement: Decide on your course of action. Include an overlay sketch of your dispositions and provide a brief discussion of the rationale behind your actions.

T3 | Speaking: Work in groups: use the E2D2PEF procedure

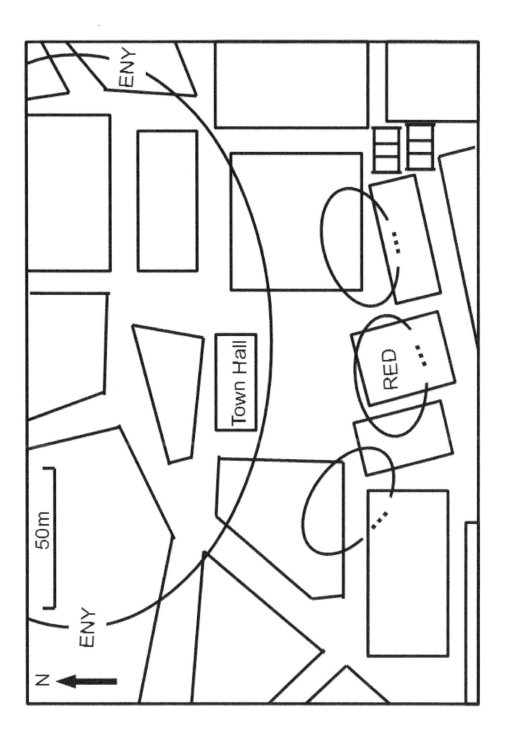

Unit 180 Tactical Problem 4

T1 | Speaking: Talk and Report

Look at P180.1. What can you see?

T2 | Reading: Read the Tactical Problem

It is 1630 hours. Sunset is at 1736. It is very hot and humid (38 °C), there are large thunder clouds overhead and it has just started to rain. You are the commander of convoy E2D. You have been on the road since 0630 and are behind schedule due to breakdowns on the rough roads. Your destination is 55 kms to the north on the main supply route into the region. Your next radio check is at the Zambek river . Your helicopter gunship escort has just left to return to base because it was running low on fuel – you have been told there is no more air cover available.

The convoy route goes through hilly jungle terrain with secondary jungle growing right to the road edge. The last friendly outpost is 5 kms to your rear. The next friendly outpost – a FOB – is 10 kms ahead. Your convoy consists of 105 soldiers and 8 civilian truck drivers arranged like this:

Advance guard: 1 x Ratel.

Convoy Commander in Ratel.

Main body of convoy: 1 x Ratel / 2 x 5T truck / 1 x tanker /1 x Ratel / 2 x 5T trucks.

Rear Guard/Reserve: 1 x 5T truck/ 1 x Medical Vehicle/1 x Maintenance truck / 2 x Ratels.

Your advance guard has just crossed the ford on the Zambek river and has been ambushed (see the sketch on the next page). You have had a radio call from the advance guard reporting the ambush is in strength, and you can now hear sporadic firing to your rear.

Requirement:

Decide how you will react to the ambush.

Include an overlay sketch and provide a brief discussion of the rationale behind your actions.

T3 | Speaking: Work in groups: use the E2D2PEF procedure

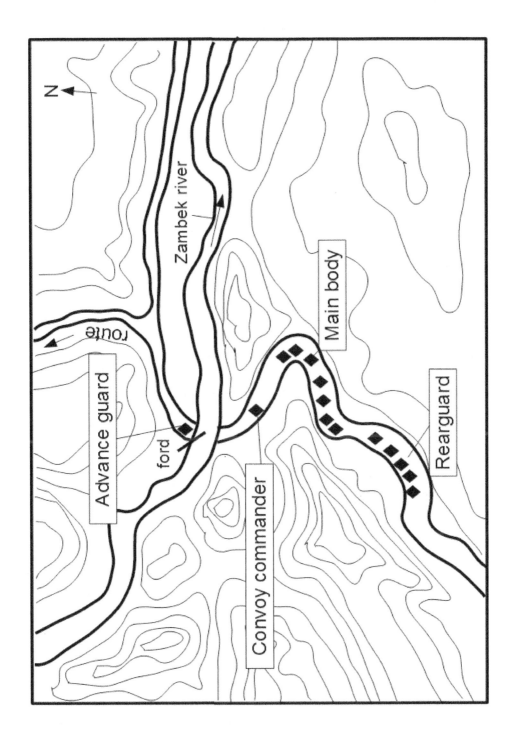

N

Zambek river

route

Advance guard

ford

Main body

Convoy commander

Rearguard

Unit 181 Tactical Problem 5

T1 | Speaking: Talk and Report

Look at P181.1. What can you see?

T2 | Reading: Read the Tactical Problem

It is 1430 hours. You are the company commander of Bravo Company of an African Union force. You have 100 soldiers in 3 platoons. You have just been airlifted into a small combat outpost in the remote mountains of Woolonga. Each soldier has their individual weapon (~250 rounds each) and each squad has 1 FN Minimi 5.56 mm light machine gun (3000 rounds total). You have 50 claymore mines and you have brought three 81 mm mortars with you with 500 HE mortar bombs. You are reinforcing the garrison of the outpost as intelligence suggests that insurgents will attack the outpost in the next few days. You have completed your inspection of the position (see the sketch map on the next page). The garrison consists of 50 local soldiers, 10 police officers and two training advisors from a third country. You have a bulldozer and three IFVs at the base. There is no indirect fire support of the base. Air support in the region is limited to three helicopter gunships, but they do have other missions to fly. There is a village near the outpost and approximately 150 civilians of all ages living there. The inhabitants sympathise with the insurgents. There is a battalion sized force of insurgents operating in the mountains to the north-west and you expect any attack to come from that direction. You do not expect a full battalion sized attack as other units of the African Union force are engaging them in other areas to the north and north-east.

Weather Forecast:

Today: Sunny. High 32 °C. Winds WSW at 10 to 15 km/h. 0 % Precipitation.

Tonight: Clear skies. Low 12 °C. Winds NNE at 15 to 25 km/h. 0 % Precipitation.

Tomorrow: Sunny. High 33 °C. Winds W at 15 to 25 km/h. 0 % Precipitation.

Tomorrow night: A few clouds from time to time. Low 13 °C. Winds N at 15 to 25 km/h. 0 % Precipitation.

Requirement: Decide how you will deploy your platoons and improve the defences of the outpost. What patrols will you organise? What is your base defence plan? What support do you require to make the defence of the position possible? Include an overlay sketch of your dispositions and provide a brief discussion of the rationale behind your actions.

T3 | Speaking: Work in groups: use the E2D2PEF procedure

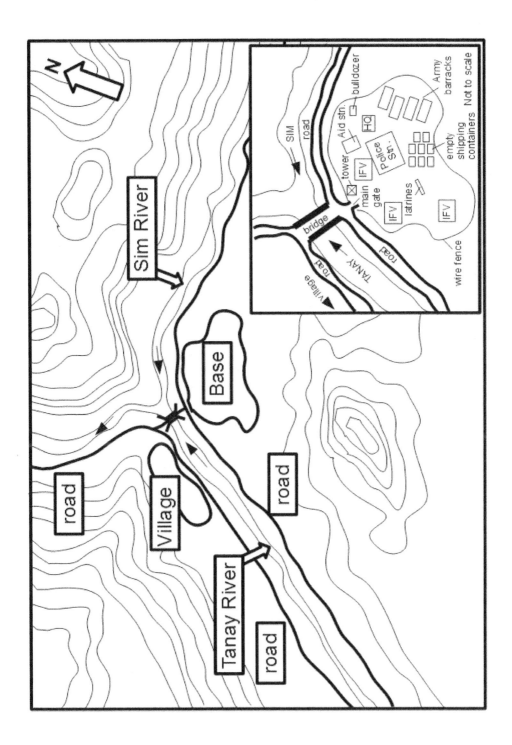

Unit 182 Peacekeeping Missions

T1 | Speaking: Talk and Report

1. When might your country send you on a peacekeeping mission?
2. What are the differences between wartime and peacekeeping missions?

T2 | Vocabulary: Check the meaning of these words

consent	impartiality	violation	credibility	legitimacy
mandate	demobilization	volatile	enforcement	imminent

What might these words have to do with peacekeeping?

T3 | Listening: Listen and Make Notes 1

Listen to Part 1 of a talk on peacekeeping missions and make notes. Check your notes with your partner; then check with the class. What will be in Part 2 of the talk?

T4 | Listening: Listen and Make Notes 2

Listen to Part 2 of the talk on peacekeeping missions and make notes. Check your notes with your partner; then check with the class. What will be in Part 3 of the talk?

T5 | Listening: Listen and Make Notes 3

Listen to Part 3 of the talk on peacekeeping missions and make notes. Check your notes with your partner; then check with the class. What will be in Part 4 of the talk?

T6 | Listening: Listen and Make Notes 4

Listen to Part 4 of the talk on peacekeeping missions and make notes.
The speaker makes a mistake – what is it?
Check your notes with your partner; then check with the class.

T7 | Listening: Transcript Tasks

Do the transcript tasks on the next page and then listen to check.

T8 | Vocabulary: Complete these collocations from Part 4 Listening [T6]

1. conflict _____
2. good _____
3. stable _____
4. outbreak of _____
5. rule of _____
6. de-mining _____
7. local _____
8. legal _____
9. resolve conflict _____
10. range of _____
11. human _____
12. lasting peace _____

T9 | Speaking: Discuss and Agree

Decide on the five most important differences between peacekeeping missions and wartime ops. Agree with the class.

Transcript Tasks

Complete the extracts with the words given; then listen to check.

Part 1

basis	consent x 3	enforcement	party	withdraw

So, let's talk more about [1] _____ , impartiality, and the use of use of force. The [2] _____ of consent is that all, or at least the main parties agree – they [3] _____ to the presence of UN PKO forces. If they don't [4] _____ or if they [5] _____ consent then the operation is at risk. What we don't want is to become a [6] _____ to the conflict. We don't want to be drawn towards [7] _____ action.

Part 2

image	impartial	patrol	process	relations	violations

Now, let's look at impartiality. The only way the mission will succeed is if the UN PKO forces are seen by all sides as being [1] _____ . We're like a referee and we will observe and point out [2] _____ of the undertakings of the peace [3] _____ . That's our job. To [4] _____ . To observe. To report on what all sides are doing. While we need to establish and maintain good [5] _____ with all the parties, a peacekeeping operation must avoid any activities that might compromise its [6] _____ of impartiality.

Part 3

consent	deter	disrupt	enforcement	force
force	imminent	necessary	order	

...But [1] _____ can be used on PKOs. In certain volatile situations, the Security Council has given UN peacekeeping operations "robust" mandates. These robust mandates authorize PKO forces them to "use all [2] _____ means" to [3] _____ forceful attempts to [4] _____ the political process, protect civilians under [5] _____ threat of physical attack, and/or assist the national authorities in maintaining law and [6] _____. Now robust peacekeeping should not be confused with peace [7] _____. Peace enforcement is where you are trying to make the parties come to the table. Robust peacekeeping involves the use of [8] _____ at the tactical level with the authorization of the Security Council and the [9] _____ of the host nation and/or the main parties to the conflict.

Unit 183 Peacekeeping ROE

T1 | Speaking: Talk and Report

1.   What do you remember about ROE?
2.   What are the differences between wartime and peacekeeping ROE?

T2 | Vocabulary: Check the meaning of these words

adhere	authorization	conditioned	consent	deterrence
disengage	escalation	ethos	guidance	impartiality

What might these words have to do with peacekeeping?

T3 | Listening: Listen and Make Notes 1

Listen to Part 1 of a talk on peacekeeping ROE and make notes. Check your notes with your partner; then check with the class. What will be in Part 2 of the talk?

T4 | Listening: Listen and Make Notes 2

Listen to Part 2 of the talk on peacekeeping ROE and make notes. Check your notes with your partner; then check with the class.. What will be in Part 3 of the talk?

T5 | Listening: Listen and Make Notes 3

Listen to Part 3 of the talk on peacekeeping ROE and make notes. Check your notes with your partner; then check with the class. What will be in Part 4 of the talk?

T6 | Listening: Listen and Make Notes 4

Listen to Part 4 of the talk on peacekeeping ROE and make notes. Check your notes with your partner; then check with the class.

T7 | Reading: Read and Answer

Read through the Sample ROE below and answer the questions.

1.   Can you defend yourself against a threat?
2.   Can you use maximum firepower?
3.   Can you seize property [e.g. a car or a house] to accomplish your mission?
4.   When can you detain civilians?
5.   When should you be ready to defend yourself?

> **Sample ROE**
> Nothing in these rules of engagement limits your rights to take appropriate action to defend yourself and your unit.
> - You have the right to use force to defend yourself against attacks or threats of attack.

- Hostile fire may be returned effectively and promptly to stop hostile acts.
- When [your] forces are attacked by hostile elements, mobs, and/or rioters, [your] forces should use the minimum force necessary under the circumstances
- and proportional to the threat.
- You may not seize the property of others to accomplish your mission.
- Detention of civilians is authorized for security reasons or in self-defense.

Remember:
- [Your country] is not at war.
- Treat all persons with dignity and respect.
- Respect local customs and traditions of the host nation.
- Use minimum force to carry out the mission.
- Always be prepared to act in self-defense.

T8 | Vocabulary: Complete the sample ROE

Check you know the words below. Then complete the ROE below.

aimed	aims	ammunition	challenge	consolidate
deadly	deliberately	engagement	humanely	incendiary
intentionally	minimum	minimum	open	possession
property	property	protection	rounds	soon
surrender	violations	warning	will	wounded

Commander's Guidance on Use of Force

1. Mission

Your mission is to stabilize and [1] _____ the peace in [X]

2. Self Defense

a. You have the right to use force (including authorized weapons as necessary) in self-defense.

b. Use only the [2] _____ force necessary to defend yourself.

3. General Rules

a. Use the [3] _____ force necessary to accomplish your mission.

b. Do not harm hostile forces/belligerents who want to [4] _____ . Disarm them and turn them over to your superiors.

c. Treat everyone, including civilians and detained hostile forces/belligerents, [5] _____ .

d. Collect and care for the [6] _____ , whether friend or foe.

e. Respect private [7] _____ . Do not steal. Do not take "war trophies."

f. Prevent and report all suspected [8] _____ of the Law of Armed Conflict to superiors.

4. Challenging and Warning Shots

a. If the situation permits, issue a [9] _____ :

(1) English: "[Name of Mission]! STOP OR I [10] _____ FIRE!"

(2) [In local language: with pronunciation guide]

b. If the person fails to halt, the on-scene commander may authorize standing orders to fire a [11] _____ shot.

5. Opening Fire

a. You may open fire only if you, friendly forces, or persons or property under your protection is threatened with [12] _____ force. This means—

(1) You may open fire against an individual who fires or [13] _____ his weapon at you, friendly forces, or per sons with designated special status under your [14] _____ .

(2) You may open fire against an individual who plants, throws, or prepares to throw an explosive or [15] _____ device at you, friendly forces, or persons with designated special status or [16] _____ with designated special status under your protection.

(3) You may open fire against an individual who [17] _____ drives a vehicle at you, friendly forces, and persons with a designated special status or property with designated special status under your protection.

b. You may also fire against an individual who attempts to take [18] _____ of friendly force weapons, [19] _____ , or property with designated special status, and there is no other way of avoiding this.

6. Minimum Force

a. If you have to [20] _____ fire, you must—

(1) Fire only [21] _____ shots

(2) Fire no more [22] _____ than necessary,

(3) Take all reasonable efforts not to unnecessarily destroy property, and - stop firing as [23] _____ as the situation permits.

b. You may not [24] _____ attack civilians or property that is exclusively civilian or religious in character, except if the property is being used for military purpose and your commander authorizes [25] _____

[Source: FM 3-07.31]

T9 | Speaking: Discuss and Agree

Decide on the five most important differences between peacekeeping and wartime ROE. Agree with the class.

Unit 184 Peacekeeping OPs

T1 | Speaking: Talk and Report

1. What do you remember about observation posts?
2. What are the differences between wartime and peacekeeping OPs?

T2 | Vocabulary: Check the meaning of these words

Make sure you know the meaning of these words.

biased	cornerstone	credibility	entanglements	presence
redundant	status	violation	visible	zigzagged

What might these words have to do with peacekeeping OPs?

T3 | Listening: Listen and Make Notes 1

Listen to Part 1 of a talk on peacekeeping OPs and make notes. Check your notes with your partner; then check with the class. What will be in Part 2 of the talk?

T4 | Listening: Listen and Make Notes 2

Listen to Part 2 of the talk on peacekeeping OPs and make notes. Check your notes with your partner; then check with the class. What will be in Part 3 of the talk?

T5 | Listening: Listen and Make Notes 3

Listen to Part 3 of the talk on peacekeeping OPs and make notes. Check your notes with your partner; then check with the class.

T6 | Listening: Transcript Tasks

Complete the transcripts for Part 1 and 3 with the words given below and then listen to check.

agreements	biased	be x 4	confidence	cornerstones
could / be	credibility	must / be	need	operational
platform	presence	report	should x 4	should / be x 5
should / fly	should / paint	violations		

T7 | Speaking: Discuss and Agree

Decide on the five most important pieces of advice about peacekeeping OPs.

Agree with the class.

Transcript Tasks

Part 1

Now, I'm going to talk about Observation Posts on peacekeeping operations. As we all know an OP is the basic working [1] _____ for military observance. And observing and reporting are the [2] _____ of Peacekeeping Operations. Observers, remember they can be both military and civilian, observe and [3] _____ information on activities within their [4] _____ areas. OPs demonstrate the [5] _____ of the peace force to all parties and to the population, enhance [6] _____ building in the peace process, monitor, record, and report actions in support of the stipulations of the peace [7] _____ , and prevent [8] _____ of the peace agreements..........Reports should be accurate and factual. Reporting which is inaccurate and [9] _____ reporting can adversely affect the operational situation. This can damage the image and [10] _____ of the peacekeeping force.

Part 3

All Positions and OPs [1] _____ _____ distinctively marked and provide protection for the occupants. They [2] _____ _____s urrounded by a protective wall. This [3] _____ _____ an earth mound wall, rock construction wall, gabions, T-walls, etc. Outside the perimeter wall there [4] _____ _____ extensive wire entanglements and the entrance gate should be zigzagged. Inside the perimeter there [5] _____ _____ a shelter capable of withstanding the type of fire which is likely in the area. All OPs [6] _____ line and radio communications to next higher HQ and specific written orders and a specified minimum strength. The OP [7] _____ maintain constant, reliable, redundant, and secure communications with the next superior authority and other OPs as the situation dictates. Timely reporting of activities [8] _____ the key to success. You [9] _____ carefully consider communication security, especially if the belligerent parties [10] _____ intent on taking advantage of the situation. It [11] _____ very important to keep sufficient supplies on hand to sustain the OP for a period if cut off from support. This [12] _____ include food, fuel, construction materials and ammo. All Positions and OPs [13] _____ _____ _____ white with UN markings in black or blue. The Position/OP number [14] _____ also be prominently displayed. These markings [15] _____ _____ visible from the air. The UN flag [16] _____ _____ _____ at all times – this includes at night. In fact, the Position/ OPs itself and the flag [17] _____ _____ well lit at night, which will take some getting used to. Remember, a key part of peacekeeping [18] _____ to be a visible presence.

Unit 185 Peacekeeping Patrols

Learn How To Talk About Peacekeeping Patrolling

T1 | Speaking: Talk and Report

Look at P185.1. What can you see?

T2 | Speaking: Talk and Report

1. What do you remember about patrolling?
2. What are the differences between wartime and peacekeeping patrolling?

T3 | Vocabulary: Check the meaning of these words

Make sure you know the meaning of these words.

curfew	frank	intentionally	outlying	overt
permissive	pilgrim	reassure	stabilized	thorough

What might these words have to do with peacekeeping patrols?

T4 | Listening: Listen and Make Notes 1

Listen to Part 1 of a talk on peacekeeping patrolling and make notes. Check your notes with your partner; then check with the class. What will be in Part 2 of the talk?

T5 | Listening: Listen and Make Notes 2

Listen to Part 2 of the talk on peacekeeping patrolling and make notes. Check your notes with your partner; then check with the class. What will be in Part 3 of the talk?

T6 | Listening: Listen and Make Notes 3

Listen to Part 3 of the talk on peacekeeping patrolling and make notes. Check your notes with your partner; then check with the class.

T7 | Listening: Transcript and Vocabulary Tasks

Do the tasks on the next page and then listen to check.

T8 | Speaking: Discuss and Agree

Decide on the five most important pieces of advice about peacekeeping patrolling. Agree with the class.

T9 | Speaking: Peacekeeping Patrol

Work in groups.

Use your maps.

Plan a patrol during a PKO.

Brief the class on your patrol. Include ROE.

Transcript Tasks

Part 1

acquiring	alert	apprehending	danger	frank	hasty
identifying	neutralizing	outlying	permissive	reassurance	stabilized

Right then, today we are going to consider patrolling. Patrolling is the basis of peace support operations in a hostile area. It is aimed at [1] _____ information, [2] _____ and [3] _____ persons, and [4] _____ hostile groups. …..Peacekeeping Operations forces use presence patrols when the situation in the area is [5] _____ and there is no direct [6] _____ for the forces….. The intention is to show the local people that forces are in the area and [7] _____ . The patrol is armed, but is acting in a friendly and [8] _____ way. These patrols are only conducted during daylight hours and depend on the situation being [9] _____ enough to allow them………… Recon patrols will need to visit all [10] _____ communities in order to both acquire information and provide the [11] _____ of a security force presence. These patrols may have to search areas and they may also need to set up [12] _____ roadblocks.

Part 2: Complete the phrases and listen to check or listen and complete these phrases.

1. confirm or supervise a _____.
2. gain information for intel _____
3. indicate a UN _____ to parties
4. to keep a _____
5. It can keep them _____
6. out of sight, out of _____
7. an element of _____ to ops
8. a sign of possible _____
9. to insert ambush parties along _____ lanes.
10. Patrols can provide _____ for parties
11. at different times of _____
12. a period of _____

Part 3: Complete the collocations and listen to check or listen and complete them.

1. minimum _____
2. special _____
3. specialist _____
4. clearly _____
5. minimum _____
6. overt _____
7. a vital _____
8. thorough _____
9. security _____
10. tactical _____
11. no go _____
12. written _____

Unit 186 Peacekeeping Checkpoints

T1 | Speaking: Talk and Report

Look at P186.1. What can you see?

T2 | Speaking: Talk and Report

1. What do you remember about checkpoints?
2. What are the differences between wartime and peacekeeping checkpoints?

T3 | Vocabulary: Check the meaning of these words

assurance	co-located	curtailing	designated	incursions
infiltration	installation	latrine	network	synergy

What might these words have to do with peacekeeping checkpoints?

T4 | Listening: Listen and Make Notes 1

Listen to Part 1 of a talk on peacekeeping checkpoints and make notes. Check your notes with your partner; then check with the class. What will be in Part 2 of the talk?

T5 | Listening: Listen and Make Notes 2

Listen to Part 2 of the talk on peacekeeping checkpoints and make notes. Check your notes with your partner; then check with the class. What will be in Part 3 of the talk?

T6 | Listening: Listen and Make Notes 3

Listen to Part 3 of the talk on peacekeeping checkpoints and make notes. Check your notes with your partner; then check with the class.

T7 | Listening: Transcript Tasks

Do the transcript tasks on the next page and then listen to check.

T8 | Speaking: Discuss and Agree

Decide on the five most important pieces of advice about peacekeeping checkpoints. Agree with the class.

T9 | Speaking: Peacekeeping Checkpoint

Work in groups.
Use your maps.
Plan a checkpoint.
Brief the class on your checkpoint. Include ROE.

Transcript Tasks

Part 1: Complete the collocations and listen to check <u>or</u> listen and complete them.

1. manned _____
2. blocking _____
3. controlling _____
4. powers of _____
5. increase _____
6. communication _____
7. checking _____
8. routine _____
9. enforce control _____
10. concept of _____
11. gather _____
12. status of forces _____
13. specific _____
14. deter _____

Part 2: Which preposition? Complete the text, then listen to check.

There are basically two kinds [1] _____ checkpoints. They can be static or mobile. Static checkpoints are deployed permanently [2] _____ fixed locations. These are also known [3] _____ deliberate checkpoints. Normally a position adjoins the checkpoint installation. Troops who man the checkpoint will live [4] _____ the position. Checkpoint are usually deployed [5] _____ a road or major track, normally [6] _____ a crossroads or junction or [7] _____ the entrance to a controlled area. Often, static CPs are established or positioned [8] _____ or near existing national borders, [9] _____ cease fire lines, on known infiltration routes, in or [10] _____ towns and villages or [11] _____ vital ground to show that it is occupied [12] _____ the UN.

Part 3

How is the text structured? Complete the text with the words given. Listen to check.

all	also x 2	but	now	often	sometimes	the	this x 2

[1] _____ let's consider checkpoint operation. [2] _____ checkpoints will have a method of slowing traffic. [3] _____ can be ramps and/or a zigzag device............ A static checkpoint should normally be manned on a 7-day week/24-hour day basis. [4] _____ a checkpoint can be closed and converted to a road-block where movement is forbidden during given hours. [5] _____ blocking of the road/track does not relieve the position of its normal security/observation mission. CHPs [6] _____ vary in the degree of search they are required to carry out e.g. military vehicles only or all vehicles. .... If searching women, forces must have women searchers, and provide special accommodation. [7] _____ , the frequency of checks and checkpoint location are part of the cease fire agreement. Alternating the CP routine of checking is [8] _____ important. There are two kinds of checks - individual personal checks or vehicle checks. There are [9] _____ total checks and spot checks. Total check occurs when everyone passing the CP is searched. [10] _____ form of checking is hard on resources.

Unit 187 Peacekeeping Convoys

T1 | Speaking: Talk and Report

Look at P187.1. What can you see?

T2 | Speaking: Talk and Report

1. What do you remember about convoys?
2. What are the differences between wartime and peacekeeping convoys?

T3 | Vocabulary: Check the meaning of these words

Make sure you know the meaning of these words.

compromise	confusion	divulge	hijack	infiltration
intersperse	patterns	predictable	predominantly	scrambled

What might these words have to do with peacekeeping?

T4 | Listening: Listen and Make Notes 1

Listen to Part 1 of a talk on peacekeeping convoys and make notes. Check your notes with your partner; then check with the class. What will be in Part 2 of the talk?

T5 | Listening: Listen and Make Notes 2

Listen to Part 2 of the talk on peacekeeping convoys and make notes. Check your notes with your partner; then check with the class. What will be in Part 3 of the talk?

T6 | Listening: Listen and Make Notes 3

Listen to Part 3 of the talk on peacekeeping convoys and make notes. Check your notes with your partner; then check with the class.

T7 | Listening: Transcript Tasks

Do the transcript tasks on the next page and then listen to check.

T8| Speaking: Discuss and Agree

Decide on the five most important pieces of advice about peacekeeping convoys. Agree with the class.

T9 | Speaking: Peacekeeping Convoy

Work in groups.
Use your maps.
Plan a convoy.
Brief the class on your convoy.

Transcript Tasks

Part 1: Which modal verb? Complete the sentences and then listen to check.

1. Now, depending on the threat in their area of operations, they _____ be at special risk when travelling.

2. If there is any threat to their security, SOPs _____ probably require you to travel in two vehicle convoys with reliable communications.

3. The mission _____ consider supplying you with arms and/or an armed escort.

4. But studies of this question in the past have almost invariably led to the conclusion that arming the observer _____ compromise their ability to carry out their duties and would create a potentially dangerous confusion between armed troops and unarmed military observers.

5. A United Nations Force _____ be in a low-risk situation.

6. In high risk situations, a UN Force _____ employ the convoy system with at least two vehicles in each convoy.

7. There _____ be four armed personnel in each convoy.

8. Standard convoy procedures _____ be employed.

Part 2: Complete the collocations. Listen to check.

1. standard _____
2. small _____
3. advance _____
4. monitor _____
5. main _____
6. passenger-carrying _____
7. rear _____
8. order of _____
9. advance _____
10. column _____
11. point _____
12. medical _____
13. security _____
14. security _____

Part 3: Articles? Complete the text with **a, an** or **the**. Then listen to check.

There's always [1] _____ danger of hijacking. SOPs will include [2] _____ anti-hijack drills and you should be familiar with these. This drill should include [3] _____ initial hijack message from [4] _____ vehicle under threat or from [5] _____ OP or vehicle observing the incident. This report should include [6] _____ position for example, 1 Km N of Position 10. .... And other details like [71] _____ direction of travel, for example, going North. This should be followed by [8] _____ hijack alert to all stations. This should trigger [9] _____ resulting actions: one, checkpoints should be closed to create road-blocks. Two, [10] _____ mobile reserves - unit and force – should be alerted. Three – [11] _____ mobile patrol from [12] _____ nearest unit to [13] _____ location of incident should be dispatched immediately. If there are helicopters on standby these should be scrambled as part of [14] _____ search. Local authorities and others in [15] _____ position to help should be contacted immediately.

Unit 188 Using Interpreters

T1 | Speaking: Talk and Report 1

1. When might a peacekeeper need to use an interpreter
2. What should you remember when using an interpreter?

T2 | Vocabulary: Check the meaning of these words

Make sure you know the meaning of these words.

dialect	expertise	gestures	jargon	loyalty
mannerisms	paraphrase	prejudices	punctuality	status

What might these words have to do with using interpreters??

T3 | Speaking: Talk and Report 2

1. Why do you need to be careful when selecting an interpreter?
2. What kind of skills/qualities does a good interpreter need?

T4 | Reading: Read the text on the next page to check your ideas

T5 | Reading: Read the text again and answer these questions

1. Why is an 'insider' necessary?
2. Why is the interpreter's nationality important?
3. How might gender, age and race affect an interpreter's ability to do the job?
4. Why should you consider the interpreter as 'part of the team'?
5. What are the benefits of having two interpreters?

T6 | Speaking: Talk and Report 3

Discuss with your partner:

1. How should you use interpreters?
2. What advice would you give to someone who has never used one?

T7 | Listening: Listen and Make Notes

Listen to a talk on using interpreters and make notes. Check your notes with your partner; then check with the class.

T8 | Listening: Transcript Tasks

Do the transcript tasks on page 355 and then listen to check.

T9 | Speaking: Discuss and Agree

Decide on the five most important pieces of advice about selecting or using interpreters. Agree with the class.

Selecting an Interpreter

There are ten considerations for selecting an interpreter.

Firstly, find an interpreter who is a native speaker of the local dialect. The interpreter's speech, background, and mannerisms should be completely acceptable to the target audience so that attention is given only to what is said. They shouldn't be thought of as an outsider.

Secondly, social status. In some situations and cultures, if an interpreter is considered in lower social standing (e.g. in military rank or membership in an ethnic or religious group) than the audience, that interpreter is ineffective. You will need to accept local prejudices as facts which you cannot change.

Thirdly, English fluency is a key area. As a rule, if the interpreter understands the peacekeeper and the peacekeeper understands the interpreter, then the interpreter's command of English is satisfactory. Check the interpreter's "understanding" by asking him to paraphrase a statement in English.

The fourth point is intellectual intelligence. Find interpreters who are quick, alert, and responsive to changing conditions and situations.

Fifthly, there is technical ability. Try to find out your interpreter's areas of expertise and educate him in other areas as required.

Sixthly, it's very important that your interpreter is reliable. If you are interviewing candidate for an interpreter position, note who arrives late for the interview. Make sure that the interpreter understands the military's concern with punctuality.

Consideration seven is loyalty. If the interpreter is a local national, it is safe to assume that the interpreter's first loyalty is to the host nation, or local sub-group, not the you or the UN. The security implications of this are clear. Be very cautious in explaining concepts to give the interpreter "a greater depth of understanding." Operate on a need to know basis.

Included in point 8 are gender, age, and race. These all have the potential to seriously affect the mission.

Point 9 is compatibility. You and the interpreter will be working as a team. You need to be compatible and have a harmonious working relationship.

The last point is a safeguard: Choose more than one interpreter. If several qualified interpreters are available, select at least two. Interpreting is an exhausting job; four hours is about the maximum active interpreting time for an interpreter's peak efficiency. Also one interpreter can be used in an active role and the other can pay attention to the body language and side conversations of others present.

[Adapted from: FM 3-07.31 Peace Ops]

Transcript Tasks

Task 1. Underline the words which are stressed most, as in the first three sentences.

<u>Right</u>, <u>now</u> let's look at using an <u>interpreter</u>. There are <u>two</u> sides to this. The <u>first</u> <u>one</u> is <u>you</u>. You need to polish your personal English language skills. The clearer your English is the easier it is for the interpreter to translate. Use simple, direct English – don't use profanity, slang, or military jargon. In many cases, such expressions cannot be translated. Even those that can be translated do not always retain the desired meaning. Swearing – profanity – curse words should be avoided. It is unprofessional and may be offensive and will be counter-productive.

Task 2. Complete the collocations

1. technical _____
2. a rule of _____
3. proper _____
4. word for _____

5. target _____
6. simple _____
7. simple _____
8. cultural _____

Task 3. Which verb? Why?

This is how to work with an interpreter. You [1] _____ stand next to the interpreter or have them stand slightly back. The focus [2] _____ be on you. You [3] _____ always look at and talk directly to the subject or audience.

Task 4. Which word? Complete the text, then listen to check.

Don't talk **to** the interpreter. Remember [1] _____ speak slowly and clearly. Repeat as often [2] _____ necessary. Speak directly [3] _____ the audience or the person you are talking [4] _____. Do not address the subject or audience [5] _____ the third person through the interpreter. Speak [6] _____ the individual or group as if they understand English. .... Don't speak [7] _____ them as if they were children. Only say what you want [8] _____ be translated. While the interpreter is translating and the subject or audience is listening, avoid doing anything distracting. .... This shows respect. From time [9] _____ time you should check the interpreter's accuracy, consistency, and clarity. .... Finally, when you have an effective interpreter, make them feel like a valuable member [10] _____ the team. Praise them and treat them as a member of the team.

Unit 189 Peacekeeping: Civil Disturbances

T1 | Speaking: Talk and Report

1. What kind of civil disturbances might happen during a peacekeeping mission?
2. What might cause disturbances?

T2 | Vocabulary: Check the meaning of these words

cordon	curfew	dominate	escalate	instigators
isolate	likelihood	multidimensional	overwhelming	snatch

What might these words have to do with civil disturbances?

T3 | Listening: Listen and Make Notes 1

Listen to Part 1 of a talk on civil disturbances and make notes. Check your notes with your partner; then check with the class. What will be in Part 2 of the talk?

T4 | Listening: Transcript Task Part 1 Extract 1: Which word?

civil	control	decisive	incidents	incidents
likelihood	negative	professionalism	seriously	situation

> OK, now we're going to look at civil disturbances. The [1] _____ of civil disturbances during a PSO is high. And how you handle these [2] _____ can have a [3]_____ effect on mission accomplishment. Handled poorly, the reaction to a [4] _____ disturbance can quickly escalate out of [5] _____ . This can have potential long-term [6] _____ effects for the mission. If you do well on the other hand, and cope with the incident well, the [7] _____ can help the PSO force's discipline and [8] _____ . And potentially it can result in fewer such [9] _____ in the future. If you demonstrate professionalism, all sides will take you more [10] _____ .

T5 | Listening: Part 1: Extract 2: Complete the Collocations: Listen to check

1. trouble _____
2. situation _____
3. peaceful _____
4. violent _____
5. ground _____
6. tactical _____
7. decisive _____

8. lethal _____
9. non-lethal _____
10. hostile _____
11. aviation _____
12. organized _____
13. disruptive _____
14. lethal _____

T6 | Listening: Listen and Make Notes 2

Listen to Part 2 of the talk on civil disturbances and make notes. Check your notes with your partner; then check with the class.

T7 | Listening: Transcript Task Part 2

Which modal verb? Complete the text, then listen to check.

> As part of control operations Commanders [1] _____ impose a general curfew over a wide, but clearly defined, area. This [2] _____ be a whole city, district, or region. Or it [3] _____ be restricted it to a small area such as a town center, a housing estate, or a particular series of streets. The size of the area and the duration of time for which a curfew is imposed [4] _____ depend on the situation. Curfews [5] _____ be used to assist the security forces in re-establishing control after rioting and serious disturbances have taken place, by restricting civil movement and allowing tempers to cool. They [6] _____ be used to prevent civil movement in a selected area while a search or incident investigation is carried out. A curfew [7] _____ disrupt hostile groups by making movement of individuals difficult and they [8] _____ allow the security forces greater freedom of operation. Remember though: do not impose a curfew for punitive reasons or as a threat to impress on the civil population the inconvenience and hardship that [9] _____ arise [10] _____ hostile activities take place. The population [11] _____ usually obey a curfew, but boredom, shortage of food, or even the feeling that the curfew is being unfairly or ineffectively enforced [12] _____ lead to curfew breaking and consequential incidents. You [13] _____ clearly define the actions troops are allowed to take against curfew breakers.

T8 | Speaking: Discuss and Agree

Decide on the five most important pieces of advice about dealing with civil disturbances. Agree with the class.

T9 | Speaking: Civil Disturbance Challenge

Work in groups. Use the town plan in M189.1 or in **Unit 189 Briefing Slides**. Prepare a SITREP on a civil disturbance. Then report the SITREP to another group. They can ask ten questions to clarify the situation. Then they have to decide on a course of action. Evaluate their course of action.

Give them a mark 1 -10. 1 = Poor; 10 = Excellent.

Unit 190 Natural and Man-made Disasters

Learn How To Talk About Natural And Man-Made Disasters

T1 | Speaking: Talk and Report

Look at P190.1 and P190.2. What can you see?

T2 | Vocabulary: Check the meaning of these words

Make sure you know the meaning of these words.

civil disturbance	earthquake	famine	typhoon	chemical spill
volcanic eruption	hurricane	flood	tornado	drought
forest/bush fire	tsunami	landslide	oil spill	avalanche

1. Rank them in order of seriousness [1= most serious]
2. Discuss your rankings with the class and agree on a final ranking.

T3 | Reading: Read and answer the questions

Read the text about disasters on the next page and answer the questions.

1. Can you predict volcanic eruptions and earthquakes?
2. Where do typhoons and hurricanes occur?
3. What dangers do floods increase?
4. What might happen after a natural disaster?
5. Why are famines man-made?
6. What are the causes of forest fires?
7. What caused the nuclear accident at Fukushima?

Check your answers with your partner; then check with the class.

T4 | Language Analysis: Analyse the Text

T5 | Listen and Read: Listen to a reading of the text

Which words do you need to practice saying? Which words do you need to learn?

T6 | Speaking: Discuss and Agree 1

Look at the diagram in P190.3. Rank the humanitarian services in order of importance. 1 = most important; 7 = least important.

e.g. *Food and water are the most important because ......*

T7 | Speaking: Discuss and Agree 2

Which kinds of disasters are you most likely to meet on missions?

Disasters

Natural disasters include earth processes such as volcanic eruptions and earthquakes. These are unpredictable and happen in geologically unstable areas of the world. Earthquakes can lead to tsunamis like we saw in Indonesia in 2004 and Japan in 2011. Over 200,000 people died in the Indonesian tsunami. Other natural disasters can be caused by storms such as hurricanes here in the Atlantic and typhoons in the Pacific.

On a smaller scale, tornadoes in the US can devastate whole towns. Landslides can destroy towns and villages as well; avalanches of snow in winter in mountain areas can kill many people. There was a recent case in Italy when a hotel was hit by an avalanche.

Floods of rivers due to high rainfall can affect large areas and have high death tolls. Floods increase the spread of waterborne diseases. Areas hit by natural disasters can be even more affected by disease and civil strife after the event. Thousands of people in Haiti contracted cholera after the 2010 earthquake.

Man-made disasters include famine where there is not enough food. I'm including famine under man-made disasters because it is caused by the breakdown in food production and distribution systems for whatever reason.

Civil disturbances, civil wars, and riots can all cause enormous suffering. Chemical and oil spills can damage the natural environment and human health.

Forest and bush fires might be natural but they can also be caused by humans, deliberately or accidentally. These can burn for days and destroy huge areas of forest and grassland, as well as towns and villages.

Nuclear accidents are another possibility. Nuclear power stations are vulnerable to terrorist attack and to natural disasters such as we saw at the Fukushima Daiichi Nuclear Power Plant after the 2011 Japanese earthquake and tsunami.

Unit 191 Disaster Listening Tasks

T1 | Speaking: Talk and Report

What disasters do you remember from Unit 190?

What do you remember about each?

T2 | Listening: Listen and Make Notes 1

Listen to this talk about the types of disaster and make notes.

Are the points made the same as in the text in Unit 160?

T3 | Listening: Listen and Make Notes 2

Now listen to a talk about Foreign Disaster Relief

Look at the Figure below and make detailed notes about what the speaker says.

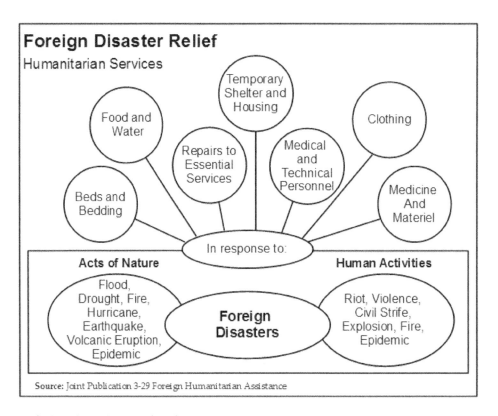

Foreign Disaster Relief
Humanitarian Services

- Food and Water
- Temporary Shelter and Housing
- Clothing
- Repairs to Essential Services
- Medical and Technical Personnel
- Beds and Bedding
- Medicine And Materiel

In response to:

Acts of Nature

Flood, Drought, Fire, Hurricane, Earthquake, Volcanic Eruption, Epidemic

Foreign Disasters

Human Activities

Riot, Violence, Civil Strife, Explosion, Fire, Epidemic

Source: Joint Publication 3-29 Foreign Humanitarian Assistance

T4 | Listening: Listen and Make Notes 3

Now listen to a talk about the conditions you'll find in disaster areas..

What do you think would be the most difficult to deal with?

Unit 192 Disaster Case Studies / Country Briefings

Practice Giving A Briefing On Disasters and Countries

There are two Briefings to deliver.

Briefing One
Unit 192 Briefing Slides Disaster Case Studies

Each slide is a case study of a disaster.

There are briefer notes for each slide.

Each student should present one slide to the class or group.

Briefing Two
Unit 192 Briefing Slides Country Briefings

Each slide is a country briefing.

There are briefer notes for each slide.

Each student should present one slide to the class or group.

T1 | Speaking: Briefing Preparation

Prepare your briefing and practice giving it to your partner.

Listen/watch his briefing and give him feedback.

T2 | Speaking: Briefing

Give your briefing to the class.

Be ready to answer questions

Your teacher will give you feedback on how well you briefed the class.

Listen to your colleague's briefings.

Make notes, ready for T3.

Be ready to ask questions and give feedback.

T3 | Speaking/Listening: Quiz

After the briefings your teacher will ask you questions about the briefings.

Use your notes from the briefings to answer the questions.

Unit 193 Dealing with the Media

T1 | Speaking: Talk and Report 1

Look at P193.1. What can you see?

T2 | Speaking: Talk and Report 2

1. When might you meet the media?
2. Why is it important to have good relations with the media?

T3 | Vocabulary: Check the meaning of these words

Agree on translations for these words.

journalist	documentary	anonymous	gossip
authorised	flattering	comment	rumour

What might these words have to do with peacekeeping?

T4 | Listening: Listen and Make Notes 1

Listen to Part 1 of a talk on media relations and make notes. Check your notes with your partner; then check with the class. What will be in Part 2 of the talk?

T5 | Listening: Listen and Make Notes 2

Listen to Part 2 of the talk on media relations and make notes. Check your notes with your partner; then check with the class.

T6 | Listening: Transcript Tasks

Do the Part 1 and Part 2 transcript tasks on the next page and then listen to check.

T7 | Speaking: The Media Scrum Role Play

One of you plays a soldier returning from an aid convoy which was attacked by in-surgents. You were the only survivor. You return to base. The media is waiting for you. You don't want to talk to the media. The rest of the class plays the media. You want answers to your questions. First prepare your questions. All you know is that an aid convoy has been attacked. The soldier has to walk through the media to enter the base.

T8 | Speaking: The Press Conference Role Play

Work in two groups.

Group 1: [five students]: You are media relations officers. Each of you has a role card: see P193.2 - 6. Read your role card and prepare to talk to the press.

Group 2: [the rest of the class]:You will play the media. You want answers to your questions about what happened last night and today. Listen to the Media Relations Officers and then ask your questions.

Press Conference: Group 1 students will take it in turns to hold a press conference .

Transcript Tasks

Part 1: Complete the text with the words below.

anonymous	authorised	background	careful	documentary
duty	flattering	interest	photographs	rumour

During your tour of [1] _____ you might be approached by the media as peacekeeping operations are of [2] _____ to the media. This might be a journalist writing for a newspaper, or a photojournalist taking [3] _____ and writing stories for a newspaper or website, or a radio or TV news crew, or even a [4] _____ filmmaker. It is [5] _____ to be asked for your opinion and talking to the media will make you feel important but you should be [6] _____. Don't give out information as an [7] _____ source. Don't give [8] _____ information, or a quote. Don't talk about things you aren't sure about – don't repeat gossip or [9] _____. The best rule of thumb is: If you are not [10] _____ to speak to the media, then don't.

Part 2: Complete the text with the words below.

answer x2	appointment	check	comment	duties	professional	trained

It is normal that a staff officer [1] _____ in media Relations will fill an [2] _____ as Military Press Information Officer (MPIO), or the officer concerned may have to cover press relations in addition to other [3] _____. Let them deal with the media. Or ask them to be present when you talk to the media. Then you can [4] _____ if you can answer the question asked. Useful phrases to learn are: "I'm sorry but I am not allowed to [5] _____ on that." or "Sorry, but I can't [6] _____ that question.", or "You'll have to as the MPIO about that." or more directly: "No comment." Be polite. Be [7] _____. But be firm. If you can't talk, then don't talk. If you are allowed to talk to the media but don't know the [8] _____ then say you will find out: say "I don't know the answer to that question but I'll try to find out for you."

Unit 194 Peacekeeping Problem 1

Solve The Problem Using Speaking Skills, Grammar And Military Vocabulary

T1 | Speaking: Talk and Report

Look at P194.1. What can you see?

T2 | Reading: Read the Peacekeeping Problem

It is 1518 hours. You are the commander of convoy D4R. You are in convoy from the port city of Porto Libre to the capital Mwane with a convoy of food and ammunition supplies for the PKO forces in the capital and neighbouring region. You left the port at 0630 and your ETA at the capital is 1700. Mwane is 54 kms away. Porto Libre is 135 kms to your rear. Sunset is at 1734 hours.

You are travelling through forested and hilly highland country crossed by large ravines. Your next radio check is at the San river bridge, which is just over the next ridge (see the sketch on the next page). Your convoy consists of 101 soldiers and a number of civilian truck drivers arranged like this:

Advance guard: 2 x Ratels

Convoy Commander in Ratel

Main body of convoy: 1 x Ratel / 3 x 5T truck / 1 x tanker /1 x Ratel / 3 x 5T trucks / 1 x Ratel / 3 x 5T truck / 1 x tanker /1 x Ratel / 3 x 5T trucks/ 1 x Ratel.

Rear Guard/Reserve: 1 x 5T truck/ 1 x Medical Vehicle/1 x Maintenance truck / 2 x Ratels

There was torrential rain last night and rain continued today, and heavy rain is forecast for this evening. Your advance guard crests the ridge and stops. It reports to you on the radio: the bridge is barricaded at each end and there are armed men on the bridge. The water level is very high, almost at the level of the bridge road surface. It is unclear what the men are doing. There might be some vehicles hidden in a copse of trees on the other side of the bridge.

There have been incidents on this road of former warring parties setting up roadblocks and extorting bribes to let convoys through. One month ago five aid workers were kidnapped and killed driving to Mwane on this same road.

There is another bridge crossing 15 kms downstream of this bridge but the road to the bridge is not as good as the main highway you are on. The turn off to the other bridge is 3 kms to your rear.

Requirement: Decide on your course of action. Include an overlay sketch and provide a brief discussion of the rationale behind your actions.

T3 | Speaking: Work in groups: use the E2D2PEF procedure

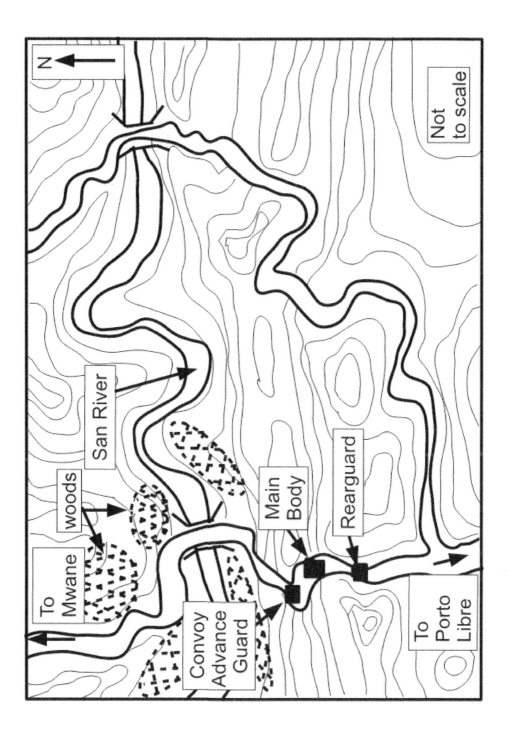

Unit 195 Peacekeeping Problem 2

T1 | Speaking: Talk and Report

Look at P195.1. What can you see?

T2 | Reading: Read the Peacekeeping Problem

It is 0430 hours. You are a sergeant on duty at an OP overlooking a wide wooded valley on the DMZ near the border of two countries which have just signed a peace agreement after a long war. In your OP you have two squads of soldiers. Each soldier is armed with his personal weapons and 100 rounds of ammunition. One squad is on duty, the other squad is sleeping. Everything has been quiet in your sector for months now. You are in radio contact with the main base and are due for a radio check at 0600.

It is twilight. Sunrise is in 18 minutes. It is 2 °C. The forecast is for a sunny day, 10 °C.

The border is just of 2 kms away, up the river and past the lake. Border crossings in your sector are limited to the main road crossing 10 kms to your NW. Your nearest base is near this border crossing. The valley you are in was one of the main invasion routes in the recent war (see the sketch map on the next page) and there is a dirt track leading to the border.

Looking across and up the valley you notice sudden movement through the trees on the west side of the lake and see columns of soldiers moving down the valley towards your position. The soldiers are heavily armed. Then you see columns of trucks and IFVs on the other side of the lake.

The lead soldiers in the infantry column start to spread out into a line formation and start moving uphill directly towards your position.

Requirement

Decide on your course of action.

Include an overlay sketch and provide a brief discussion of the rationale behind your actions.

T3 | Speaking: Work in groups: use the E2D2PEF procedure

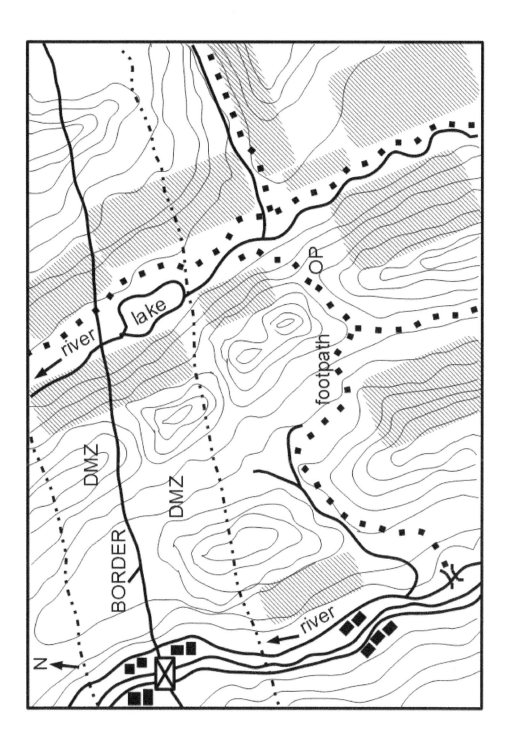

Unit 196 Peacekeeping Problem 3

Solve The Problem Using Speaking Skills, Grammar And Military Vocabulary

T1 | Speaking: Talk and Report

Look at P196.1. What can you see?

T2 | Reading: Read the Peacekeeping Problem

It is 2005 hours; 10 minutes to sunset. You are the commander of a company of peacekeepers based in a small provincial town called Milosis near the DMZ and frontier, 658 kms from the capital. This town was a rebel stronghold in the recent civil war. The summer heat has been intense and there has been no rain for several months now and the water shortage in the region is becoming critical. Food supplies are also short and the population relies of food aid convoys. The last two convoys had to turn back to the capital because of attempted hold-ups by armed gangs on the main convoy route. The next convoy is due in two days time; there are some food reserves at the food distribution centre but the World Food Programme logistics officer currently in charge in the town is refusing to release this food at this time. His chief is away in the capital and he feels he cannot make a decision. This morning there was an incident in the main market square when a sergeant in a peacekeeping 4x4 hit a small child and seriously injured him. The child was taken to the local hospital by the sergeant and his men and is being cared for there. The child's family are demanding compensation. The market has been closed all day and there is a large crowd in the square chanting and banging drums (see the map on the next page). They are demanding 'justice' and for the sergeant to be handed over to them. Isolated shots have been fired into the air from the crowd and one person has been taken to hospital from an injury for a falling bullet.

One of your platoons is on patrol to the north of the city along the line of the DMZ. The other two platoons are available for patrolling in the city and base security. The city police chief is a good officer but the local police are few in number, badly trained and sympathise with the local people rather than the central government in the remote capital. The provincial governor, appointed by the central government is not in residence at the moment but is on holiday. His deputy cannot be found. You have a squad monitoring the main square from a concealed position on a rooftop overlooking the square. You are in radio contact with this team. The police chief is with you and you are discussing the situation. You receive a radio call from your rooftop OP. One part of the crowd has started to move towards your position and a second, larger, group is moving towards the Food Distribution Centre.

Requirement: Decide on your course of action. Include an overlay sketch and provide a brief discussion of the rationale behind your actions.

T3 | Speaking: Work in groups: use the E2D2PEF procedure

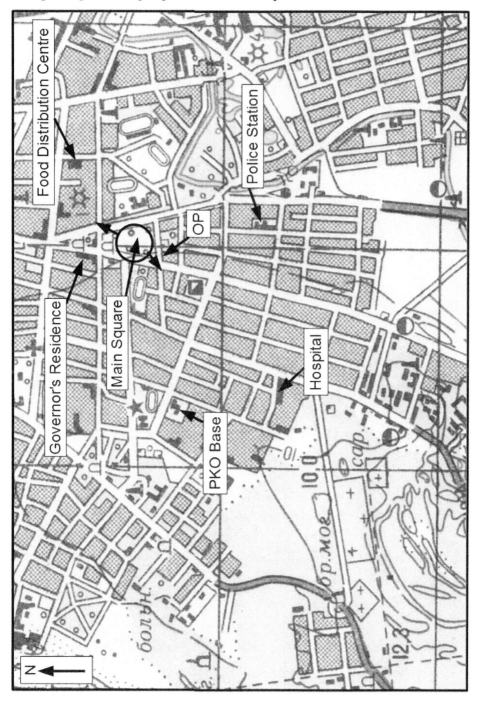

Unit 197 Peacekeeping Problem 4

T1 | Speaking: Talk and Report

Look at P197.1. What can you see?

T2 | Reading: Read the Peacekeeping Problem

It is 1145 hours. You are the sergeant in charge of two squads on a visibility/presence foot patrol through the old city of the capital Mwane. You are part of a PKO with a mandate to support the post-civil war transition to a stable government. Elections are being held next week to elect a new representative government of all parties. Your soldiers are carrying their personal weapons and have 40 rounds each but their weapons are not loaded. The magazine in each of the weapons is empty; loaded magazines are in pouches. Last week there were riots when a peacekeeper shot and wounded a youth who threw stones at a foot patrol on the outskirts of the city. All soldiers have been reminded of the ROE: only fire in self-defence. You are all wearing body armour, but instead of helmets you are all wearing your blue berets as your commander feels that this is less threatening to the local population. It is 39 °C, sunny and very humid. Thunderstorms are forecast for the afternoon. Your patrol started at 0945 and you are due back at your base at 1300. You are in a warren of narrow streets (see the sketch map on the next page). Your radios do not work very well in this terrain. The buildings are three stories high, with flat roofs. During the civil war there were massacres and ambushes in these streets as the two main warring factions fought for control of the city. Usually the streets are crowded with shoppers shopping at market stalls and small shops. Today, the streets are much quieter and most stalls are closed; some shops are open. You call a halt for a drink and a map check.

As you check your route with your corporals you hear two burst of automatic rifle fire both ahead and behind you. Then there is silence. After a minute there is another burst of automatic fire from a single AK47 into the street approximately 20m in front of you from a position on a roof.

Requirement

Decide on your course of action.

Include an overlay sketch and provide a brief discussion of the rationale behind your actions.

T3 | Speaking: Work in groups: use the E2D2PEF procedure

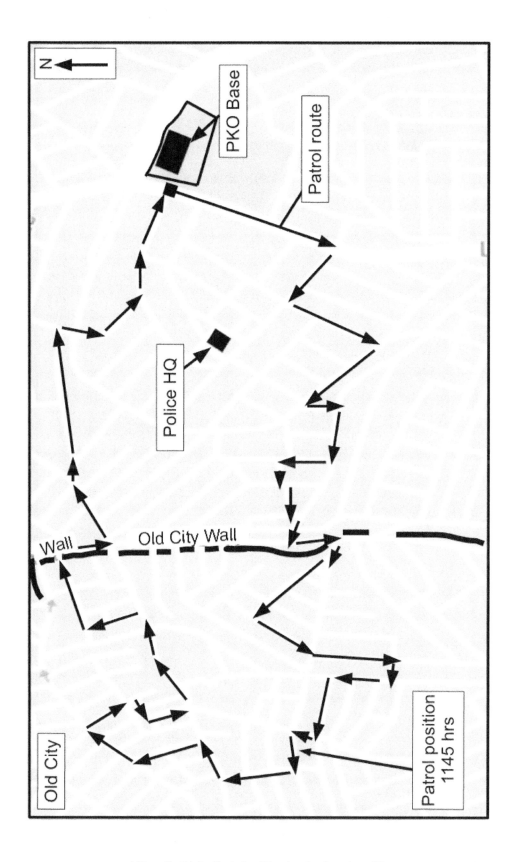

N

PKO Base

Patrol route

Police HQ

Old City Wall

Wall

Old City

Patrol position
1145 hrs

Unit 198 Peacekeeping Problem 5

T1 | Speaking: Talk and Report

Look at P198.1. What can you see?

T2 | Reading: Read the Peacekeeping Problem

It is 0618 hours. You are the the leader of a platoon of peacekeepers and you have just been helicoptered in to the small port city of Looville as the first wave of a deployment of two companies of peacekeepers. The other troops were to be deployed later today but you have just been told that the weather is making this impossible. You are on your own for the time being. There are massive thunderstorms throughout the region and torrential rain has made the roads impassible and flights impossible. It is 33 °C and very hot and humid. Each man is armed with his personal weapon and 100 rounds of ammunition, and carries 20 kg loads of personal equipment and food and water. You were expecting to be met by local security forces and to be transported to the port in trucks but there was no-one to meet you and you cannot contact anyone on the radio.

Your immediate task is to secure the port as a cargo ship containing food supplies for the starving city is arriving in two hours and the food needs to be off-loaded and distribution organised. Because of the condition of the port and the tidal conditions, the food will be offloaded onto small boats and then ferried to the inner harbour. The harbour cranes are out of action and the ship cannot be moored alongside the key. The outer harbour is blocked with sunken ships and the beaches are mined from the recent civil war.

You have been in contact with a representative of the World Food Programme in the city and you are supposed to rendezvous with her at 0700 to co-ordinate the operation. You know she has only five staff with her and needs your help to se-cure both the off-loading and distribution of the food supplies.

As you make your way on foot to the port from the LZ (see map on the next page) you see large crowds gathering. The people look tired, hungry and desper-ate. You see that some groups of young men are armed with AK-47s and have belts with ammunition pouches. You also notice a few men carrying RPGs here and there. As you cross the bridge over the river Shangawi the crowds are bigger and more excited: everyone notices you and your men.

Requirement: Decide on your course of action. Include an overlay sketch and provide a brief discussion of the rationale behind your actions.

T3 | Speaking: Work in groups: use the E2D2PEF procedurE

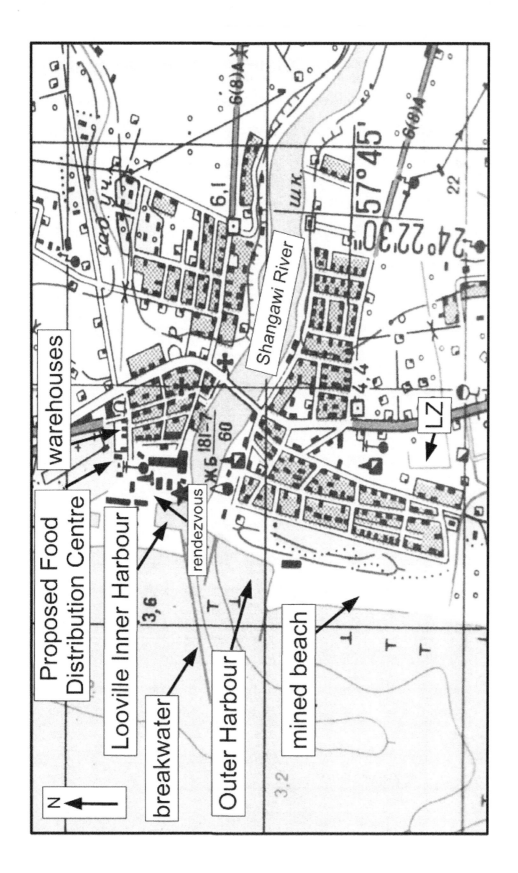

warehouses

Proposed Food
Distribution Centre

Looville Inner Harbour

breakwater

Outer Harbour

mined beach

rendezvous

N

Shangawi River

LZ

57° 45'

24° 22' 30"

6(8)A

22

6,1

6(8)A

шк.

4,4

181-7

60

3,6

3,2

Unit 199 At the Airport

T1 | Speaking: Talk and Report 1

Do you like travelling?

Have you travelled abroad by plane?

Which countries have you visited?

Tell your partner and then report to the class what your partner said.

T2 | Vocabulary: What can you see?

Look at P199.1. What can you see? Check with P199.2.

T3 | Vocabulary: Check you know the meaning of these words

Look at P199.3 to help you.

terminal	air traffic control tower	taxiway
runway	boarding bridge	apron

T4 | Vocabulary: Order the events

	Board the plane	
1	Book a flight	
	Buy something in the duty free shops	
	Check-in on-line	
	Collect luggage/baggage from Baggage Reclaim	
	Disembark from the plane	
	Fasten your seat belt	
	Go through Customs	
	Go through passport control	
	Go through passport control	
	Go through security checks	
	Go to Check-in/Baggage Drop	
	Go to the Gate	
	Land	
	Unfasten your seatbelt	
	Leave the airport	
	Listen to the safety instructions	
	Prepare for landing	

	Print boarding card
	Put your hand luggage under your seat or in the overhead bins
	Reach cruising speed and altitude
	Show boarding card
	Take a taxi to the airport
	Take off
	Wait in the departure lounge
	Take your hand luggage from under the seat or from the overhead bin

T5 | Vocabulary: Who said what?

Who would say what? *Traveller* or *airport/airline employee*?

I don't like making my own **travel arrangements** on the Internet, I go to a **travel agent** and get them to do all the work.	*Traveller*
I have to go on a **business trip** to Paris next week.	
Have a **safe journey!**	
It was a really **tiring journey**. I had to wait **for ages** for a bus to come.	
It's an **international flight** so the **check-in time** is two hours before the **departure time**.	
The **check-in desk** is over there – number 18 – with the big queue. Once we get our **boarding cards** then we can go through **passport control** and do some shopping!	
Did you pack all your **baggage/luggage** yourself?	
I have two bags to **check-in** and one bag as **hand-luggage**.	
I have checked you in on your **connecting flight**.	
Would you like a **window seat** or an **aisle seat**?	
Boarding time is usually half an hour before the plane leaves – check your **boarding card.**	
We've done our shopping, let's go to the **departure lounge** and sit and wait for the flight.	
The **in-flight entertainment** will be a selection of recent film releases.	
They will be waiting for us in **arrivals** at the airport.	

Check you know all the words in **bold**.

T6 | Reading: Read and answer the questions

> I went on a business trip to London last month. I had to get an international flight from Riga to Frankfurt and then a connecting flight to London. Check-in was two hours before departure time – at 4 am. I got to the desk to find out that the flight was delayed. I had to wait for five hours in the departure lounge. Of course I had missed my connection and had to wait in Frankfurt for another two hours for the next flight. I arrived in London 10 hours later than planned. I had managed to cancel my meetings when I was waiting in Frankfurt but they weren't happy.

1. Why was the writer going to London?
2. What time was the first plane supposed to leave?
3. What was the writer's route to London?
4. How long did the writer have to wait for planes?

T7 | Listening: Listen and answer the questions

Listen to the speaker talking about a journey he made.

Answer the questions below.

1. Where was the speaker travelling from/to?
2. When did he leave home?
3. Where did he travel to first?
4. What was his first flight?
5. How long did he have to wait for his second flight?
6. What was his second flight?
7. Who did he meet on the plane?
8. What was their story?
9. When was his third flight?
10. When did he reach his hotel?
11. What was his return journey like?
12. Where did he fly to?
13. Where did he stay?
14. How long was the total return journey?
15. What went wrong on the journey?

T8 | Speaking: Talk and Report

What is the longest journey you've ever made?
Tell your partner about it and then tell the class what your partner said.

Unit 200 Phase 3 Speaking Tests

Test 1: Deployment Briefing: Group Test

Work in small groups. There are four deployment briefings.

See **Phase 3 Speaking Test Briefing Slides 1 - 4**.

There are briefing notes for each briefing.

You will have to make up some information to complete the briefing.

Each student should present one slide of the briefing to the class.

1. **Briefing 1: Earthquake Relief Operation**
2. **Briefing 2: Civil War Ceasefire Operation**
3. **Briefing 3: Drought and Famine Relief Operation**
4. **Briefing 4: Civilian Non-Combatant Evacuation Operation**

T1 | Speaking: Briefing Preparation

Prepare your briefing and practice giving it to your group.

Listen/watch your colleagues briefings and give them feedback.

Language Reminder

Looking back: *There **has been** an earthquake in* _____.

*Fifty percent of the buildings in the region **have been destroyed**.*

Specific past time: *The earthquake **happened** at 0645 hrs local time on Thursday.*

The situation now: *Most of the population **is** homeless, without access to food or water.*

Looking forward: *We **have to ensure** relief supplies reach those in need.*

*We **will deploy** to _____ at _____.*

*You **will need** _____*

T2 | Speaking: Briefing

Give your briefing to the class.

Be ready to answer questions.

Make notes on your colleague's briefings.

Be ready to ask questions.

T3 | Speaking: Feedback

Your teacher will give you feedback on how well you briefed the class.

Give feedback to your colleagues on their briefings.

T4 | Speaking/Listening: Quiz

After the briefings your teacher will ask you questions about the briefings.

Use your notes from the briefings to answer the questions.

Test 2: A Two Minute Mini-Presentation on a Military Topic: Individual Test

You will be given a topic to present on. You will have one minute to prepare your presentation. Then you will talk for two minutes about the topic.

Use the **Mini Presentation Frame** below.

Presentation Frame

Introduction (15 seconds)

'Good morning/afternoon. I am _____ [Rank + Name].

Today I will talk about _____ [topic].

I will consider two points. The first is _____.

The second is _____.

I will take/answer questions at the end of my presentation.'

Point 1 (45 seconds)

'Let's consider first of all _____.'

Point 2 (45 seconds)

'The second point is _____.'

Conclusion (15 seconds)

'The most important point to remember is _____.

Thank you; that concludes my presentation.

Do you have any questions?'

List of Topics

A good soldier	Your country's contribution to peacekeeping
Conscription	The importance of the chain of command
A volunteer army	Training for army personnel
Army recruitment	The role of the army in society
Convoys	The importance of ROE
Patrolling	Marksmanship
Observation Posts	IFVs
MBTs	Individual weapons
Artillery	Air support
TCCC	Military bases

Sources and Acknowledgements

Sources

Many of the texts included in this book are from, or adapted from US Army Field Manuals, which are in the public domain, as they are published by the United States Government and its agencies. These sources are indicated under the texts. Some forms are kindly provided courtesy of the Montenegrin Armed Forces.

The patrol orders and route cards were sourced from https://www.arrse.co.uk/wiki/E-nirex, under the GNU Free Documentation License 1.2 cited on the site [https://www.gnu.org/copyleft/fdl.html].

Other texts use public domain information from sources like the CIA Factbook, and are specially written for this book.

The downloadable photographs and presentations include photographs sourced the US Department of Defense (and so are in the public domain), and the Ministry Of Defence (subject to Crown Copyright), and from Wikipedia, used according to the various Creative Common's licenses cited on Wikipedia. All the other photographs are my own, except for one, which is courtesy of Hamish McIlwraith. The whole set of photographs and presentations are therefore published under the same Creative Common's licenses and can be shared and used freely, as per the original license noted on the Wikipedia images. Maps are sourced from The US Geological Survey, or the Soviet Union.

Acknowledgements

Trialling in Latvia

Thanks to Aigars Saulīte, Inese Kinēna, Karīna Suruda, Andris Vasiļjevs, Ainārs Goldmanis and Jānis Tomašūns.

Trialling in Namibia

Many thanks to Beuhla Beukes of the British Council in Windhoek, and the University of Namibia, and the Namibian Armed Forces for organizing the trialling. Many thanks to Wing Commander Luther Kaunda Moongo, Lt. Col. Erick Nakanyala Toivo, Lt. Col. Laimi Pauvaneko Hawala, Col. Natanael Nangolo Ngolo, Capt. (N) Wilbard A Kapweya, Maj. Epafras Shaanika, Capt. Albin Kashuku, Maj. Titus H Iipinge, Maj. Emilia Nakambunda, Capt. Porisee Emsy Katjivena, Lt. Col. Wakaa Tjiveze, Maj. Martin David, Chief Curator Nikanor Chisengo, Lt. Col. Dawid Ashipala, Maj Rauna Shikongo, Capt. Martin Awala, Maj. Vaino M Kamelo, Capt. Elia Iileka, Capt. Vean Shigneg, Lt. Col. Martha Namufohamba, Capt. Onesmus S Aiyambo, Sqn. Ldr. Sebedeus N. Kanunga, Lt. Col. Simeon Nahole. and Senior Private Secretary Lea LK Pohamba for taking part in the trialling.

Military Advice

Particular thanks are due to SFC Ilgars Ciprus (Latvian Army), Mcpl/Cplc Aaron Hawthorn (Canadian Armed Forces), Lt. Naphtali Rivkin (U.S. Army, Retired), Lt. Col. Ugis Roamnvos (Latvian Army, Retired) for some advice on military matters. All remaining errors are mine.

Audio Recordings

Featuring the **Voice Talents** of (in alphabetical order) Alister McCarty, Cezars Torres, Christine Maxwell, Craig Rose, Dan Valahu, Daniel Puzzo, David Harris, Donald Maxwell, Graham Jones, Ilgars Ciprus, James Egerton, Michael Hudson, Michael Orr, Penny Roux, Phil Edwards, Ruth Waters, Tom Linton, and Vik Singh. Thanks guys.

And finally

Special thanks are due to my co-trainer in Namibia, Nick Fletcher, especially for the idea of using weapon specifications for speaking tasks. And also Hamish McIlwraith and Claire Whittaker, my colleagues at McIlwraith Education, a great team to work with.

And of course, my long suffering family – thank you for your support and patience.